The LMS Turbomotive

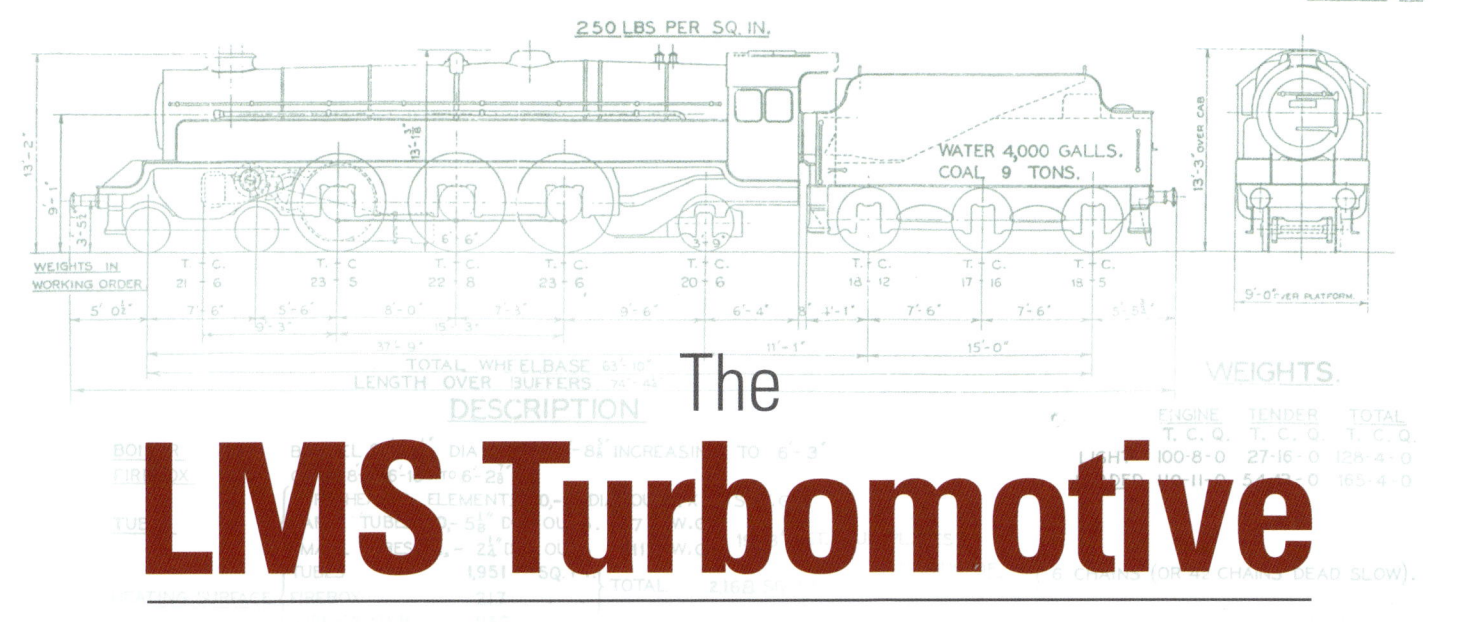

From Evolution to Legacy

Jeremy Clements and Kevin Robertson

First published in 2016 by Crécy Publishing

All rights reserved. No part of this book may be reproduced or transmitted in any form or by any means electronic or mechanical, including photocopying, recording or by any information storage without permission from the Publisher in writing. All enquiries should be directed to the Publisher.

© Jeremy Clements & Kevin Robertson 2016

A CIP record for this book is available from the British Library

Design: (cover): Rob Taylor, GDI Studios
(inside pages): Mark Nelson

Printed in Slovenia by GPS Print

ISBN 978-1-9093-2852-5

Crécy Publishing Limited
1a Ringway Trading Estate,
Shadowmoss Road, Manchester M22 5LH

www.crecy.co.uk

Note: Illustrations are credited where known. If no annotation is shown this is because there was nothing quoted on the rear of the print. We apologise to any photographer should this result in a missing or incorrect interpretation.

Front cover: The Turbomotive on arrival at Euston.

Back cover clockwise from top:
No 6202 known to all as the 'Turbomotive' but never officially named. From a painting by George Heiron
All three Swedish turbine engines survive and are presently stored at the Grängesberg Locomotive Museum.

A side view of the steam valves, gear train and transmission for the forward turbine.

The third generation of Union Pacific gas-turbine-electric locomotives (Nos 1-50) were nicknamed 'big blows'. Image within the public domain

Title page from top:
Weight diagrams for the locomotive as built with the domeless boiler.

A three-quarter official photograph of the completed locomotive.

Contents page:
6202 at Camden on 30 July 1935. W. Hermiston

Contents

Introduction		5
Bibliography		6
Chapter 1	**THE INNOVATION CHALLENGE**	7
Chapter 2	**TURBINE LOCOMOTIVE DEVELOPMENT**	16
Chapter 3	**THE LJUNGSTRÖM TURBINE**	31
Chapter 4	**STANIER AT THE LMS**	45
Chapter 5	**THE TURBOMOTIVE: CONCEPTION AND DESIGN**	62
Chapter 6	**MAINTENANCE AND MODIFICATIONS**	83
Chapter 7	**OPERATING PERFORMANCE**	95
Chapter 8	**REBUILD AND TRAGEDY**	109
Chapter 9	**THE PHILADELPHIA CONNECTION**	118
Chapter 10	**METAMORPHOSIS**	129
Chapter 11	**CONCLUDING ASSESSMENT**	140

Appendices

A	Motive power units using turbine drive	145
B	Weight, hammer blow and factor of adhesion	149
C	Large engine fleet comparison – LMS v. LNER	150
D-1	Maintenance history	150
D-2	Special instructions to drivers	151
D-3	Special instructions to fitters	152
D-4	Commentary on the slow-speed gear flexible drive failure	152
E	Assessment of GWR design features imported by Stanier to LMS	152
F	Digest of views expressed by other engineers	153
G	Executive connections	157
Index		158

A press photograph of No 6202 when new, passing beneath a fine LNWR signal gantry at Camden. *Hulton Getty Picture Library*

Introduction

RECOGNITION of the chronic energy loss between firebox and driving axle with the traditional steam locomotive stimulated several attempts at revolutionary solutions. For the most part, these inventive exercises during the first half of the 20th century progressed little, if at all, beyond the trials stage, with technical advantage unproven and financial justification no more than a mirage.

The conventional steam engine's inherent advantages presented immense obstacles to radical innovation. A century of development and refinement had placed it in a commanding position to withstand challenges from alternative traction. Despite its inefficiencies, its modest construction and maintenance costs linked with cheap locally sourced fuel yielded a reliable machine capable of hauling acceptable loads at acceptable speeds. Labour-intensive operating and service processes were often dirty and unpleasant, but such working conditions were accepted within contemporary social and economic standards.

Among the various British initiatives to promote an alternative mode of steam-generated motive power, the London Midland & Scottish Railway's turbine 'Pacific' locomotive No 6202 – the Turbomotive – was a remarkable venture for several reasons. It had been preceded by three decades of failed efforts to exploit turbine technology. It was the first collaboration between cutting-edge technology and the 'lo-tech' steam-manufacturing sector to produce a viable next-generation locomotive. It was the child of international cooperation on a scale unusual within the parochial railway mechanical engineering sector. Its working longevity far exceeded other machines that had sought to harness outside technology, and its daily performances were on a par with its reciprocating cousins.

The concept won a measure of international recognition unusual for a British design. SNCF planned a French version in the late 1930s, although Chapelon's attitude towards turbine power appears to have been dismissive, perhaps resenting a challenge to his seminal work with compounding. More tangibly, Baldwin produced a massive 6-8-6 turbine locomotive for the Pennsylvania Railroad in 1942, which drew heavily upon the Turbomotive format. Sadly this American manifestation suffered a severely shortened career in face of the railroad's heavy investment in an alternative form of large, rigid-framed locomotives, but not before it had produced some impressive feats of speed and haulage.

The LMS locomotive was also notable for its place in the evolution of rail-borne turbine power, and in validating its technical and commercial potential. Circumstantial evidence suggests that Sir William Stanier was influential in the formulation of the GWR's gas turbine programme. Thereafter, the nexus with Stanier became more tenuous, but the steam turbine continued to form part of a chain of endeavour that remarkably as late as 1963 included a coal-fired gas-turbine-electric locomotive. These late American initiatives resuscitated the 'power-station-on-wheels' concept (an idea tried and discarded in Britain in the 1920s) and demonstrated the enduring enthusiasm to see steam remain part of the motive power scene.

* * *

In the presence of the driver, Stanier is explaining a feature of the brand-new Turbomotive to a gentleman who, judging by his attire, must be a director of the LMS.

Sir William A. Stanier FRS. *Elliot & Fry Ltd*

Research for this work needed reference to a variety of sources beyond those normally consulted in the preparation of a railway history. There were too many to list here but certain deserve particular acknowledgement.

The story of the Swedish Ljungström locomotives that played such a pivotal role in the development of non-condensing turbine power was greatly helped by information kindly provided by Messrs Sten Holm-Janeslätt and also Dan Thunberg. In this respect, a visit by the authors to Grängesberg to inspect the famous trio in preservation was very worthwhile, and an experience that can be recommended to other enthusiasts. The assistance of staff at the Swedish Railway Museum at Gävle is also appreciated.

In the United Kingdom, the files of the Stephenson Locomotive Society provided an essential information base, and an important means of cross-checking the veracity of other authorities. The assistance and generosity of the officers of the Society is gratefully acknowledged, especially the Librarian Gerry Nichols.

Other prime sources include the National Railway Museum, where Tim Procter was invaluable in tracking down numerous documents. We would also like to thank David Hunt, whose pioneer article in the *LMS Journal* was a source of inspiration.

Individuals who have assisted (in alphabetical order) are Prof A. G. Atkins – who took time out from his own studies into the GWR to advise the authors on turbine operation – Jeremy English and Leonard de Jong. We feel certain human frailty will have led to others who have assisted being omitted and for this we humbly apologise.

Thanks are also due to our publisher and especially Jeremy and Gill, both for encouragement and also tolerance.

Nomenclature
Uniquely among the 'Big Four', the LMS never adopted formal designations for its locomotive classes, in contrast to the logical alphanumeric system of the LNER (and to a lesser extent of the Southern) and the unusual but easily understood 'xx' discipline of the GWR.

As a result, classes tended to be delineated in rather clumsy terms that relied on wheelbase and power classification, with potential for confusion. For example, Hughes's 'Mogul' and Stanier's first design for the LMS were both known as the 2-6-0 Class 4, later 5P4F, then 5P5F, and later still 5F. Visually and structurally the types were quite different and distinction was drawn by widespread use of the 'Crab' nickname for the Hughes machine. This lack of universal classification system led to nicknames being more widely used than on other railways.

In this tradition, Stanier's turbine 'Pacific' No 6202 quickly became known as 'The Turbomotive', an appellation initially frowned upon in official circles but one that soon gained acceptance as a sensible and descriptive identity for an unusual design. Another nickname, evidently mainly confined to crews, was 'Gracie Fields' because 'she sang as she ran'. (Gracie Fields, 1898-1979, singer, actress, comedienne and philanthropist, was a leading British film and music hall personality in the 1930s, and a 'darling' of forces overseas during the Second World War.)

Titles for other types in this work are adopted for convenience and to reflect the dignity of the locomotives they represented. 'Lizzie' was the common means of referring to Stanier's first class of reciprocating 'Pacifics', but 'Princess Royal' seems more appropriate in this context. 'Duchess' has been preferred over 'Princess Coronation' for the second 'Pacific' class – although 'Semi' lives on in our collective trainspotter memories.

Jeremy Clements, County Meath
Kevin Robertson, Hampshire
December 2015

Bibliography
Bond, R. C. 'Ten Years' Experience with the LMS Non-Condensing Locomotive No 6202' (Institution of Locomotive Engineers, Paper, 1948)
Bradley, D. L. *The Locomotive History of the South Eastern & Chatham Railway* (Railway Correspondence & Travel Society 1980)
Carleton, Paul *Pennsy Steam: A to T* (D. Carleton Railbooks, 1989)
Carney, Ian *Fowler's Fury: The Story of a Unique British Steam Locomotive* (Noodle Books, 2012)
Chapelon, André *La Locomotive a Vapeur* (Camden Miniature Steam Services, 2000)
Clements, Jeremy *The GWR Exposed* (Oxford Publishing Co, 2015)
Cook, A. F. *LMS Locomotive Design and Construction* (Railway Correspondence & Travel Society, 1990)
Dixon, Thomas W. Jnr *Norfolk & Western Steam: The Last 30 Years* (TLC Publishing Inc, 2013)
Durrant, A. E. *The Mallet Locomotive* (David & Charles, 1974)
Holland, Frank *Steam Locomotives of the South African Railways, Volume2: 1910-1955* (Purnell & Sons (SA) (Pty) Ltd, 1972)
Hunt David, Essery Bob and James, Fred *LMS Locomotive Profiles No 4 - The Princess Royal Pacifics* (Wild Swan Publications, 2003)
Johnson, Ralph O. *The Steam Locomotive* (Simmons-Boardmann Publishing Corporation, 1942)
Kitson Clark, Edwin *Kitsons of Leeds* (The Locomotive Publishing Co, c1938)
Robertson, Kevin *The GWR Gas Turbines - A myth exposed* (Alan Sutton, 1989)
The Leader Project: Fiasco or Triumph? (Ian Allan, 2009)
Rolt, L. T. C. *Red for Danger* (Pan Books, 1966)
Solomon, Brian *Baldwin Locomotives* (Voyageur Press. 2010)

Periodicals
Engineering
Engineering Progress
Glasgow Herald
LMS Journal
Model Engineer
Modern Transport
New York Times
Nottingham Evening News
The Beyer-Peacock Quarterly Review
The Engineer
The Railway Gazette
Wall Street Journal

CHAPTER ONE

The Innovation Challenge

THE key features of the robustly simple steam locomotive had been well established before 1900. The 20th century saw progressive increases in power, size and weight, but little further change in everyday machines beyond superheating, migration to piston valves, better lubrication systems, and improved bearings. The demands of heavier, faster express passenger trains stimulated these measures but many duties remained in the hands of smaller locomotives that in essence changed little.

Conservatism was economically attractive, as exemplified by the London & North Western Railway's reliance on the archetypal British 0-6-0, which greatly aided that company's focus on profit maximisation. The Class 'Dx', built up to 1872, totalled 943 examples, and the type was continued with the slightly enlarged '17-inch Coal Engine' until 1892. Crewe then graduated to eight-coupled freight power, but construction of 0-6-0s continued on other railways in vast numbers. The last of the genre, the Southern Railway's Class 'Q1' of 1942, had modern features and made innovative use of new materials, but conceptually was little different from the 'Dx' of eighty years earlier.

Heavier, faster trains needed larger locomotives, which led to questions of balance and weight distribution, and to unexpected challenges. The theoretically simple matter of enlarging the commonplace 4-4-0 into the 4-6-0 was fraught with difficulty, exacerbated by emerging recognition of the importance of hammer blow and the consequent desire to use more than two cylinders. By 1923 only the Great Western had successfully mastered multi-cylinder construction, but thereafter undertook no modifications of substance with its four-cylinder fleet beyond larger boilers and a higher degree of superheat, the latter more than 20 years later.

Locomotive performance was under continuing scrutiny with special focus upon express passenger machines, despite these forming only a small proportion of the motive power spectrum. The greater body of work and revenue related to mundane and unexciting duties where, provided there was sufficient adhesive power for the trainload, the type used was economically speaking of little consequence for a transport system that strove for punctuality but whose schedules were generally undemanding.

Nevertheless, modifications were introduced for marginal engineering or operational advance where the commercial justification was unconvincing. For example, the LNER acquired a large fleet of 2-8-0s originating from a Great Central design whose standardised advantages were partly negated through Gresley's antipathy towards Belpaire fireboxes. Under his regime (and that of his successor), four variants with round-topped boilers appeared, where the financial rationale for diversity was unclear. These were largely employed on slow-speed shuffles between passing loops in avoidance of faster traffic. Performance demands could be intense but only intermittently, and for short periods.

Equally, dogma fashioned practices that increased constructional cost for little economic gain. Churchward's seminal work on boilers was shown to impressive effect with express and heavy freight engines. It was questionable, though, whether the investment proposition stood up with the GWR's small 2-6-2Ts or 0-6-0s that usually worked secondary duties involving moderate loads, frequent station stops, and relaxed schedules.

With conservative attitudes abounding, challenges to tradition induced caution, particularly as supported by labour-intensive and primitive processes; the existing technology was reliable and, compared with other disciplines, low cost. The case for steam's ultimate replacement was partly based upon sharply improved utilisation that would yield a superior relationship between revenue and direct expenses, and practice over time proved this contention correct. However, the total conversion cost was not revealed since the new technology was truly feasible only following extensive infrastructural and operational reorganisation.

Revolutionary change in motive power thus had several hurdles to overcome. By the Grouping, the honing of essential design elements through a century of practice meant that fresh inventions had to be significantly superior, both theoretically and practically. Recognition that an innovative prototype was inevitably more expensive than a mass-produced item conforming with time-honoured methods meant that initial expenditure was not necessarily a preclusive factor. Nevertheless, uncontrolled cost could easily escalate and its limitation required imposition of deadlines. No project sponsor, be it a commercial manufacturer or a railway workshop, could write an open cheque, and a new idea had to prove viable within a finite period.

Sponsors of technological alternatives of the type reviewed in this work confronted three key criteria:

1. The initial capital cost of a prototype should not be significantly higher than that of a conventional machine it sought to replace. Technology change played a major role in this respect, as proven on the LMS. The Beyer-Ljungström locomotive cost more than six times a conventional counterpart, yet less than a decade later the build price of the Turbomotive exceeded that of No 6200 *Princess Royal* by only 61%.

2. Operating expenses should remain in line with traditional motive power, accepting always that a one-off machine lacks scale economies in spare parts and maintenance expertise. Further expense must be anticipated in longer periods out of service, i.e. opportunity cost of equipment standing idle.

3. Sustainable improved performance, measured by one or more of higher operating speeds, greater haulage capacity and better fuel consumption, was needed to justify the incremental capital and current expense.

The discipline of withholding volume production pending prototypical proving was doubly important with turbine drive experiments. Application of these principles to the initiatives described in this work allows judgement on how close each came to supporting a case for multiplication. Equally, it highlights the rashness of the Chesapeake & Ohio Railroad's adventure with its three Class 'M-1' steam turbine locomotives.

Experimental design exercises often relied on inter-company collaboration, as with high-pressure compound 4-6-0 No 6399 *Fury*, the result of a joint venture between the LMS and the North British Locomotive Co. The LMS, as owner of the chassis and tender, was able to recycle these components following termination of the exercise. The chassis was used in the creation of No 6170 *British Legion*, precursor to the 'Royal Scot' reboilering programme. On the other hand, North British was responsible for the novel boiler and thus the project's speculative features. *K. Robertson collection*

A notable aspect of revolutionary design experiments was the significance of commercial manufacturers. Railway companies regularly tried new ideas, e.g. variations in boiler and superheater dimensions, but these were on a modest scale with usually only marginal effect. With more imaginative ventures, they generally played a secondary role. For example, the LNER cooperated in the Kitson-Still project by making facilities available for road trials, supported by an indication of interest in acquiring the technology, subject to it being proven. In another case, the LMS entered a partnership to construct a high-pressure compound locomotive that took shape in the form of 4-6-0 No 6399 *Fury*. Cannily, the LMS's contribution comprised a chassis and tender over which it retained ownership, while the special boiler, on which the project risk rested, was the partner's responsibility.

The costly implications of throwing caution to the winds were apparent in the three members of Chesapeake & Ohio Railroad 4-8-0+4-8-4 Class 'M-1' 6,000hp steam turbine electrics. These enormous, complex machines were built in 1947/48 for the 'Chessie', that railroad's prestige express passenger service. Pre-delivery testing seems to have been brief and inadequate as they quickly proved unreliable, and never operated near their full potential. The train for which they had been built was terminated in 1948 and their use on lesser duties was equally trouble-prone. They were withdrawn and scrapped in 1950 – a high-profile and costly failure. *Railroad Museum of Pennsylvania*

The Kitson-Still 2-6-2T No KS1, seen here with indicator shelter fitted, had four pairs of horizontally opposed cylinders mounted above the frame, which drove a longitudinally placed crankshaft. This connected through double helical gears with the jackshaft set between the leading and centre driving axles. The cylinders were double-ended, the inner end being actuated by steam and the outer by a diesel injector. Steam was used to maximise low-speed torque on starting but, on reaching a speed of about 5mph, the diesel injectors took over and steam was shut off. Thereafter, heat from the cylinder jackets and diesel exhaust maintained steam pressure, which was needed for auxiliary purposes such as train heating and braking The limited space above the cylinders and driving wheels allowed only a modestly proportioned (diameter about 4ft 3in) oil-fired steam boiler, although this did not inhibit efficiency. Diesel power was cheaper to operate once in motion, but steam was essential at low speeds to avoid the need for a gearbox. Technically this was a reasonably successful experiment, but a costly commercial failure that contributed to closure of the Kitson business.

Although not directly relevant to turbine power, the Kitson-Still saga graphically illustrated the constraints facing commercial builders in the interwar years. Kitson was a Leeds-based company with its origins in the supply of locomotives to the Liverpool & Manchester Railway, but the Grouping had seen contraction of its traditional domestic market. The company therefore responded by investigating diesel power using three different transmission systems. Electric motors and associated equipment were found to be too cumbersome and heavy. A diesel-mechanical configuration with a change-speed gearbox was discarded because hydraulic or mechanical clutches lacked the structural durability needed to absorb the power output. The third option was direct drive combined with coupling rods in a system where starting of the diesel engine, and hence the train, was aided by compressed air.

The latter's hybrid concept led to appraisal of the Still engine where adequate low-speed torque could be generated without the need for a clutch. This led to Kitson-Still No KS1, a 2-6-2 tank engine with four pairs of double-ended cylinders whose pistons were driven by steam up to about 5mph, and thereafter by diesel power, which was cheaper to operate. The engine was extensively tested on the LNER, proving effective at low speeds on heavy freight trains. Fuel consumption rates were good, but financial viability demanded significant price and consumption differentials in favour of oil, which remained unrealised after a decade of development. Also, the LNER claimed not to have adequate traffic demanding a locomotive of KS1's power and speed range, suggesting a desire to keep the venture at arm's length.

Edwin Kitson Clark, the last chief executive officer of Kitson, was remarkably frank about the project's failure, which contributed to calling in the Receiver in 1934. He attributed the cause to three factors, which illustrate the risks implicit with fresh technology:

1. Although the principles had been successful in marine and industrial applications, the Still patentees had failed to provide ample advance evidence that the system was really suitable for a railway locomotive.

2. Over-engineering of components to prevent fractures resulted in undue weight, to the detriment of performance.

3. Lack of experience with internal-combustion engines hampered progress, i.e. inability to optimise technology beyond that typical with steam locomotives.

With hindsight, this project might be regarded as imprudent, but at the time there must have been little illusion about the need for engaging fresh ideas. The firm had promoted the Kitson-Meyer articulated locomotive in the 1900s, a concept eventually proven to have limited marketable potential. In 1907 its commitment to that type contributed to rejection of an approach from Mr H. W. Garratt, whose ideas later received a warmer reception at Beyer Peacock.

Kitson's abortive efforts with diesel engines highlighted that this power source was still in its infancy, and had yet to establish its commercial viability. This situation encouraged the search for other ways of extracting more from steam power, sometimes in unexpected quarters. Notwithstanding its modernisation programme, the Southern Railway needed to retain steam to serve sidings and minor branch lines where electrification was impracticable or financially unjustifiable. On the other hand, having no sources of suitable indigenous coal within its territory the company paid proportionately more for shipment of fuel from elsewhere in the UK.

Maunsell was thus responsive to an approach in 1930 from a Mr A. P. H. Anderson, a Scottish marine engineer, to experiment with a steam heat conservation system. This system was based on the proposition that exhaust could be compressed and liquefied without excessive expenditure of power, effectively a compromise between the two extremes in steam recycling:

a. Where exhaust steam is conserved at atmospheric pressure by withdrawal of latent heat (approximately 970 British Thermal Units per lb of steam), the resultant hot water at close to boiling point being returned to the boiler with minimal power needed to drive the feed pump.

b. Alternatively, uncooled exhaust steam is fed back once it has been compressed to boiler pressure, but the amount of work needed to effect that compression is so great as to render the net power output of the complete cycle very close to nil.

Southern Railway Class 'N' 2-6-0 No A816 was fitted with the Anderson Steam Conservation System. This type was selected for the experiment because the combination of outside motion and 5ft 6in driving wheels yielded the maximum amount of room for the additional equipment. The system had been originally conceived for use in marine and stationary locations and compressing its components into the small amount of spare space was a challenge that also confronted condensing turbine locomotives. The cooling equipment has been mounted beside the boiler on the running plate; a similar layout was installed on the right-hand side.

Front view of No A816, showing the fan mounted on the smokebox door and required to assist draught.

With the Anderson system, steam was partially cooled so that after withdrawal of about 600 BTUs per lb, a significant amount of latent heat remained in a steam-water mixture. Anderson referred to this as 'emulsion', which could be fed back to the boiler by means of a feed pump that demanded little more energy than a conventional condenser. The concept generated considerable scepticism and disbelief in the engineering community. However, pragmatist Maunsell stated that he was more interested in practical demonstration of its possibility than in theoretical argument about its impossibility.

The system was tried in a stationary plant at Surbiton, then applied to ex-SECR 2-6-0 Class 'N' No A816. Early results were promising in improved fuel and water consumption, but there were numerous problems with the ancillary equipment, not least with the fan needed to induce draught. The Anderson system, the product of a remarkable piece of original thinking, probably deserved more study and development. In the event, No A816 does not appear to have worked any revenue-earning services. The project was abandoned in 1933 and the guinea-pig locomotive reverted to normal condition.

This episode illustrated another barrier to innovation – hidebound views. The stationary test plant was open for inspection by any visitor, and H. Holcroft, who was engaged in the project throughout, noted that only a minority were prepared to accept that the system actually worked. Despite the evidence of their own eyes, most engineer-observers stubbornly clung to the belief, supported by textbook orthodoxy, that the concept was in some undefined manner fallacious, or that its success was a fluke.

Steam and/or water conservation formed an important part of design planning with the objective of partially or completely enclosed water circulation. Various turbine configurations achieved reductions in water consumption, a marginal consideration in temperate climates or on routes liberally provided with water troughs such as the West Coast Main Line. However, the promise of a closed system that functioned with purified water offered significant reduction in boiler repair costs.

The benefits of good-quality water were emphasised with the Bulleid 'Pacifics' of the Southern Railway, which were fitted with TIA (Traitement Integral Armand) feedwater treatment equipment. A small tank in the tender discharged chemical fluid into the main tender tank at a rate proportionate to water consumption. Substances that normally formed scaling were reduced to soft, non-adhering mud that was expelled regularly by means of a manually operated blow-down valve. Intervals between boiler washouts were extended from seven to fifty-six days, which fortuitously coincided with scheduled inspections of firebox plates and stays.

Apart from this enhanced availability level, direct boiler repair costs greatly benefited. A survey conducted by British Railways in 1955 revealed that these costs per mile for the 'Merchant Navy' Class were the lowest of any within its peer group ('Duchess'/'Royal Scot'/'A1'/'King'/'Britannia'). Even more impressive, they were very substantially lower than those for the ex-GWR 'County' Class, whose boilers were of similar age, and pressed to the same unusually high level of 280lb per sq in. (Conversely, the all-up repair and maintenance costs of the 'Merchant Navies' in original form were the highest of its peer group, which was a prominent factor in the decision that they should be rebuilt.)

While there are references to boilers and steam generation, the main focus of this work is upon power transmission, an area where the traditional steam engine is at its most cumbersome. Considerable structural strength, and hence weight, is necessary to ensure smooth, safe passage for steam under high pressure through valves and cylinders. Concurrently, the fore-and-aft thrust of pistons within cylinders plus the connecting and coupling rods demands yet more robustness to absorb the stresses generated. Weight is necessary for adhesion but it is preferable that its disposition be discretionary rather than obligatory.

While the steam locomotive remained the most refined form of land transport, there was little incentive to explore profound change. However, emergence of viable internal-combustion engines invoked comparisons to the detriment of the older technology, encouraging investigation of ways to redress the energy loss beyond the firebox. This was achieved marginally through compounding and superheating, but the essential disadvantages remained until late in the steam story. From the 1930s André Chapelon's careful application of scientific methods led to impressive corrective measures. Later still, L. D. Porta's analyses of fuel combustion wrought significant changes that came too late to sustain the steam locomotive against the encroachment of 'modern' traction.

Earlier, experiments in the 1920s had addressed reciprocation in the actuation of valves, another source of inefficiency. Arturo Caprotti's study of internal combustion engines led to the valve gear

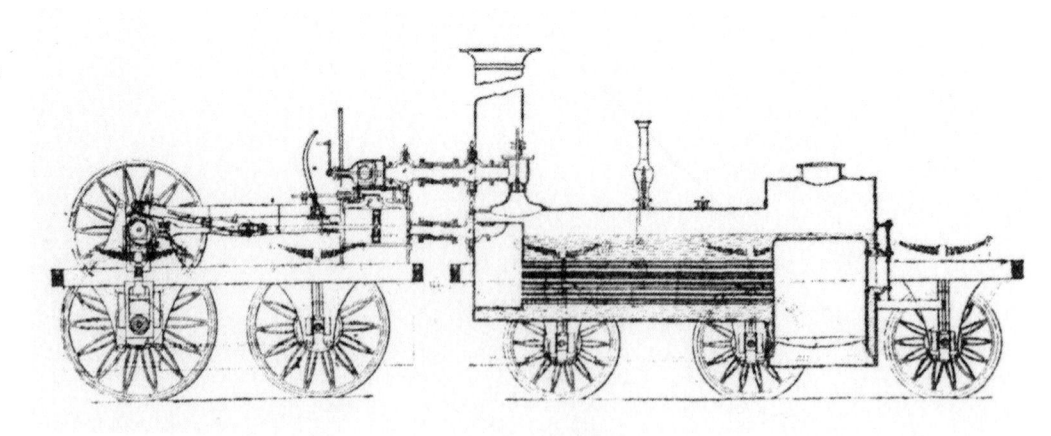

THE LMS TURBOMOTIVE

Thunderer, built by R. & W. Hawthorn 1838, employed an unusual boiler/chassis layout in an attempt to satisfy Brunel's demanding design criteria. *The Engineer*

In the Beyer-Ljungström turbine locomotive, separation of the boiler unit from the driving chassis was also necessary, resulting in a layout conceptually similar to that tried with the unsuccessful *Thunderer. Engineering*

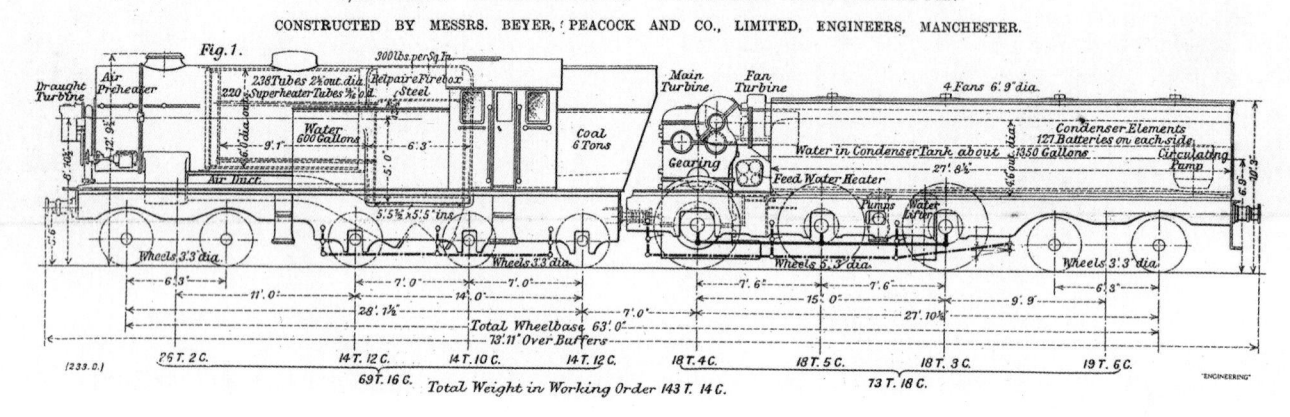

that bears his name whereby rotary cams actuated poppet valves to accommodate the differing volumes of inlet and exhaust steam. Dr Hugo Lentz made similar advances with a rotary cam valve system derived from stationary engines in mines and at industrial locations. This was an evolutionary reversion, as progress in early locomotive design had been helped by consciously moving away from stationary engine practice; now the future was perceived as paying increasing attention to alternative industrial experiences.

These and other types of valve systems could only partially reduce the embedded inefficiency of moving parts going back and forth to make wheels rotate. A combined engine and transmission assembly that relies solely on rotational movement between point of combustion and the driving axle enjoys advantages in optimised power-to-weight ratio and minimised internal friction that is not confined to locomotives. This was graphically demonstrated to one of the authors when comparing the performance of a (notionally) 600cc Wankel-engined Norton Commander motorcycle against conventional twin-cylinder British motorcycles (specifically the 750cc T140 Triumph Bonneville, 1000cc Vincent-HRD Black Shadow, and 850cc Norton Commando). The rotary-engined Commander was memorable for its extraordinary torque and lack of vibration, demanding a different riding style. Smooth running and absence of traditional engine noises made speed hard to judge – and the speedometer played an important role in the driving of certain turbine locomotives

The broad principles of the steam turbine have been recognised for about 2,000 years, but the modern version dates from 1887. Until then, the most practicable (by Gustaf de Laval) had been an impulse design that engaged substantial centrifugal forces and was limited in power output by the quality of material used in its construction. Charles Parsons, descendant of a prominent Anglo-Irish family of scientists and engineers, took turbine design further by allowing pressure to fall gradually through a number of turbine blades set in series, thus moderating the speed of steam movement and rotational velocity. Early applications were to generate electric power, but at the Diamond Jubilee Review at Portsmouth in June 1897 Parsons stole the show with his slender-hulled, steam turbine-mechanical yacht *Turbinia*. The Royal Navy's fastest ship could reach 27 knots, whereas *Turbinia* achieved 34. The lesson was not lost on the Admiralty; HMS *Dreadnought* entered service in 1906 as the first turbine-driven battleship, and the world's fastest.

Turbines in steamships and electricity generating stations enjoy minimal constraint upon their size. The volume of a ship's engine room places little inhibition on layout and accessibility and, indeed, a turbine is less demanding of space than a reciprocating engine of similar power. A boiler and turbine system in a power station enjoys even less constraint, whereas there are significant problems with locomotives. Despite its comparative inefficiency, the steam locomotive is a truly remarkable confederation of compromises within a restricted volume imposed by loading gauge and weight maxima. It is this confinement that made the turbine translation so difficult, and which resulted in some curious arrangements of boilers, powered chassis and tenders.

This dilemma was reminiscent of the challenge that contractors faced in trying to satisfy Brunel's requirements for the earliest GWR Broad Gauge locomotives. He stipulated that the rate of piston travel should not exceed 280 feet per minute at 30mph, with maximum boiler pressure restricted to 50lb per sq in, yielding a 'force of attraction' (presumably tractive effort) of 800lb on level track at that speed. Weight was to be limited to 10 tons 10 cwt (locomotive only in working order), but there had to be six wheels if the weight exceeded 8 tons. Circumvention of these seemingly mutually exclusive conditions necessitated some ingenious, albeit unsuccessful, solutions. The most extreme were found in two engines (*Thunderer* and *Hurricane*) built by R. & W. Hawthorn & Co. A comparison of the accompanying line drawing with the Beyer-Ljungström engine of 1926 shows certain layout similarities.

The awkward configuration of the Beyer-Ljungström machine demonstrated the problem of cramming in all the essentials. The condensing turbine drive system was greedy for space, necessitating divergences from the style and profile expected of a steam engine. Apart from its technical attributes, an aspect of the non-condensing LMS Turbomotive that set it apart from its British predecessors was its 'normal' appearance.

So far as can be determined, experiments in turbine transmission were conducted in about ten countries and summary details are provided in Appendix A. The technological challenges necessitated cooperation between railways and manufacturers, sometimes on an international level. This contrasted with the UK tradition of locomotive construction where the major railway companies built for their own needs, or where manufacturers such as North British produced for a variety of domestic and overseas operators.

As the pursuit of turbine efficiency migrated beyond steam, inter-industrial collaboration was even more crucial. The Great Western Railway, isolationist during the inter-war years and with a long history of doing things its own way, commenced its gas turbine project in 1946 as a joint venture with Metropolitan-Vickers. The GWR had no partnership experience in projects of this scale and intricacy, and progress was slowed by bureaucratic complexities in administering variations in specification, which must have been legion. The second project relied on a build-and-supply contract with Brown Boveri of Switzerland, which had previous experience with a gas turbine locomotive. Starting around six months after the GWR/Metropolitan-Vickers joint venture, this locomotive was finished first but also suffered from delays in construction.

A notable aspect of turbine drive was the extended period over which its possibilities were pursued. The earliest experiments would appear to have commenced in Britain in 1910. After the First World War, there were further attempts in common with other fresh ideas. The momentum reduced during the economically challenged 1930s but did not disappear. The United States was

The cause of British steam might have been more advanced by exploring foreign practice. A number of American-built locomotives were purchased for work in the UK but usually only because of a shortage of domestic manufacturing capacity. An exception was the trio of de Glehn 4-4-2 compounds acquired by the GWR. Chief Mechanical Engineer G. J. Churchward was not a noted inventor, but he was a great innovator with a refreshingly open mind that helped him make the most of other people's good ideas. The three 'Frenchmen' introduced new features to GWR practice, as well as being useful performers. Here is No 104 *Alliance*. Locomotive Publishing Co

quite a late entrant into the field, commencing with an experimental oil-fired steam electric turbine locomotive in 1938. This proved the start of a prolifically creative period including reversion to the 'power-station-on-wheels' configuration that echoed early British efforts. Concurrently, the steam lobby fought a rearguard action by using four or five driving axles in large, rigid-framed locomotives with reduced hammer blow achieved by the split-drive 'duplex' concept. These reciprocating machines were relevant to the story in highlighting difficulties with very large steam locomotives required to work at speeds up to 100mph.

Peripheral to this programme was the construction by Baldwin of a 6-8-6 non-condensing steam turbine locomotive that was significantly influenced by the LMS Turbomotive. This locomotive seemed to offer more technical and commercial potential than the duplex type, but the latter had by then gained more ascendancy than its operational capability possibly deserved. This solitary US non-condensing steam turbine thus had a regrettably short career. These American efforts are reviewed because they provide context for the possible role of turbines, not only in circumvention of hammer blow but also in overcoming size and weight constraints, were the steam locomotive to have a sustainable role in high-speed, heavy haulage.

These developments had no significant impact against the rapid post-war growth of diesel-electric power, but this period saw the most sustained manifestation of turbine power through the formidable gas turbine fleet of the Union Pacific Railroad, culminating in the most powerful single-unit locomotives ever built. However, in some ways more remarkable was Union Pacific's construction of a coal-fired gas-turbine-electric locomotive. That this ultimately unsuccessful project should have commenced in 1963, during an era of moderate oil prices, was a notable demonstration of continuing interest in the turbine drive principle.

Back in Britain, through hosting of the Beyer-Ljungström trials in the 1920s, and collaborating with North British in the *Fury* project, the London Midland & Scottish Railway was familiar with innovation. At the time, there was commercial imperative for the LMS to expand and improve its express passenger fleet, but it is intriguing that the Turbomotive project should have commenced so early in Stanier's tenure. There was much to do and playing safe with proven principles while leaving experimentation until later might have seemed more prudent. However, recall of the Beyer-Ljungström's positive aspects combined with later advances in Sweden greatly enhanced the technical and commercial prospects.

There were few truly radical efforts to reconfigure the modern steam locomotive in the era of the 'Big Four', and only three, two of them employing turbine drive, achieved the preliminary validation of entering revenue-earning service. Stanier's Turbomotive was unquestionably the most successful of that small group. Its progressive refinement in the preceding four years support the belief that by 1939 it provided a credible foundation for a second prototype less constrained by adoption of the 'Princess Royal' format in terms of chassis, wheels and boiler.

Unfortunately, the times were hostile towards imaginative ventures with steam. In 1947 H. G. Ivatt produced two conventional 'Pacifics' with several modern features (including roller bearings, as pioneered with the Turbomotive), allegedly for comparison against contemporary diesel-electric locomotives Nos 10000/1. Had these tests been conducted, there are grounds for believing that the steam turbine should have been included in an objective evaluation of future motive power policy. If nothing else, it would have been engrossing to monitor the performance of No 6256 *Sir William A. Stanier FRS* against Stanier's Turbomotive.

A good example of the comfort of convention was the first batch of LMS 'Royal Scot' 4-6-0s, needed to meet a motive power crisis. A letter of intent was agreed with the North British Locomotive Co in December 1926, the order was confirmed in February 1927, and all fifty locomotives were in service by the following November. Despite conception and construction under extreme pressure, they were a successful design although boiler problems emerged later. Perhaps the first shortcoming evident was drifting exhaust obscuring the driver's vision, for which several solutions were tried. No 6125 *Lancashire Witch*, the first of the twenty-five built by NBL at its Hyde Park Works, is fitted with a temporary, unsuccessful lifting device. *Real Photographs Co Ltd*

London & North Eastern Railway Class 'W1' 4-6-4 No 10000 is seen here in original condition. Regarded as Gresley's most unusual design, this experimental locomotive had three significant features: a marine-type Yarrow water tube boiler, a working pressure of 450lb per sq in, and four-cylinder compound working. This locomotive undertook revenue-earning duties during a six-year career that saw continuous development and modification, before it was rebuilt as a conventional 4-6-4. Mileage was substantially less than the Turbomotive covered in a similar period; probably the LNER engine embraced too many novel features at once.

CHAPTER TWO

Turbine Locomotive Development

PRIOR to the First World War there was a widespread belief that, within the usual space constraints, locomotive boilers had reached optimal efficiency through higher steam pressures and superheating, sometimes assisted by a tapered profile and Belpaire firebox. Long before it was revealed what was possible with gas producer combustion systems, it was natural to regard transmission as key to delivering greater power to the driving wheels. Requiring technology beyond the normal experience of railway workshops, commercial manufacturers led the exploration for appropriate solutions.

A turbine offered a possible way of reducing the energy loss that is embedded in reciprocating external-combustion engines. If that energy could be transmitted more efficiently with turbine drive, it followed that such a machine might generate the same level of work with less fuel consumption, or alternatively generate more power than could a conventional locomotive at similar operating cost.

The initial approach was based on a steam-driven turbine coupled to an electric generator that fed power to axle-hung electric motors. This arrangement pre-dated the diesel-electric locomotive, where the diesel engine filled the role of steam boiler and turbine. Later developments greatly simplified the transmission process by using a conventional boiler to generate steam that was admitted to a turbine coupled through reduction gears direct to the driving axle – a layout paralleled in the diesel-mechanical locomotive.

In marine and industrial locations, it is comparatively easy to isolate the 'dirty' process of steam generation from the 'clean' turbine and its electrical ancillaries. This luxury is denied a turbo-electric locomotive as the dirty and clean elements must co-exist in close proximity, with the entire ensemble constrained by the loading gauge. With many individual components to be accommodated, it was necessary to employ a single carrying frame longer than normal, or to adopt some form of articulation.

Early efforts attempted the 'power-station-on-wheels' idea, but by 1930 it was evident that this concept was complex, expensive, and unlikely to assume commercial viability within a reasonable timescale. Although these efforts advanced technical know-how and produced some ideas that had application elsewhere, the steam turbine/electric combination in the British context proved a blind alley. Later, the idea was revived in the United States in experiments that were less impeded by size constraints. Also, they were backed by commercial parties interested in alternative energy sources to the diesel-electric type then rapidly penetrating the railroad sector. Broadly speaking, these initiatives foundered through factors similar to those encountered in Britain.

The Reid-Ramsay Steam-Turbine Electric Locomotive
The earliest British attempt with turbine drive stemmed from a partnership between Hugh Reid and David McNab Ramsay. Reid had been the senior partner of locomotive manufacturer Neilson, Reid & Co, which merged in 1903 with two other Glasgow-based businesses (Sharp, Stewart & Co and Dübs & Co) to form the North British Locomotive Co. Reid was appointed Deputy Chairman and Chief Managing Director of the combined venture, which was then the largest British commercial locomotive manufacturer. In that position, and with extensive resources at his disposal, he was well placed to sponsor novel ideas.

Ramsay, born in Perth in 1871, started work as an engine fitter in 1891 and ten tears later had risen to become a locomotive engineer and assistant manager at Neilson, Reid. In 1905 he jointly registered a patent with Hugh Reid for an invention known as the 'Reid-Ramsay Steam-Turbine Electric Locomotive'. This machine combined the processes used in coal-fired electricity generating power stations mounted on a single chassis. Completed in 1910, the locomotive comprised a girder frame, about 67 feet long over buffers, carried by two compound bogies equidistantly placed with about 40 feet between the pivot centres. Each bogie had two leading carrying wheels, acting as a sub-bogie, and two driving wheels of about 4ft 6in diameter, creating a 4-4-0+4-4-0 wheel arrangement. Hung on each of the four driving axles was a 275hp

TURBINE LOCOMOTIVE DEVELOPMENT

One of the few full photographs of the Reid-Ramsey Steam-Turbine Electric Locomotive built by the North British Locomotive Company in 1910. It was intended to operate in cab-forward mode – the front of the engine is to the left – with the bogies leading in the 4-4-0+4-4-0 wheel arrangement. *The Beyer-Peacock Quarterly Review*

The rear (boiler) end of the Reid-Ramsay locomotive.

series-wound electric motor. Below solebar level, the machine thus resembled a long electric locomotive but with an unusual disposition of carrying and powered axles.

The locomotive worked in cab-forward mode with the condenser mounted on the solebars immediately above the leading non-powered sub-bogie. Behind the condenser was a long cab-like structure that covered the central section and extended back to the firebox. The cab accommodated the crew and a dynamo capable of producing between 200 and 600 volts dc, driven by an impulse turbine running at 3,000rpm. Fuel was stored immediately behind the turbine and forward of the boiler, which was flanked by side tanks and located over the trailing compound bogie.

In a long articulated locomotive lengthy steam passages can cause problems, but in this case live steam made a comparatively short journey to the turbine. Exhaust steam passed from the turbine direct to the ejector-type condenser where it was sprayed with cold water drawn by centrifugal pumps (driven by auxiliary turbines) from the side tanks. The mixture of steam and cold water then passed into a hotwell from which it was extracted by means of a second pump into cooling tubes at the front of the locomotive, then piped back to the side tanks. As the steam/water circuit was closed and used no mechanical moving parts, it operated entirely

The condensing equipment of the Reid-Ramsey machine was located at the front end, ahead of the cab. This end-on view illustrates the size and complexity of the condensing equipment, and emphasises the importance of the airflow in providing the requisite cooling. This arrangement and its effect would have been similar to that of an enormous motorcar radiator, which begged the question as to its practicability during extended periods of working in reverse, i.e. with the boiler leading. There was a similar problem in cooling the engines of early internal-combustion-powered railcars that were in reality rail-borne versions of contemporary road motor omnibuses.

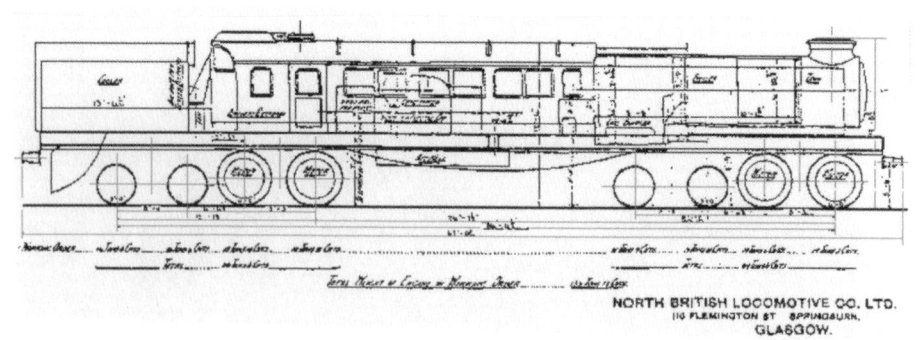

A sketch of the Reid-Ramsay Steam-Turbine Electric Locomotive. *North British Locomotive Co*

The rear (smokebox) end of the Reid-Ramsey machine displays a conventional Westinghouse brake pump, the air vent above the buffer beam, and the chimney. The purpose of the enormous-diameter chimney is unknown – purely for styling, or was it intended to improve the smokebox draught? Also, the vent is the same as that at the condenser end, but does not appear to have served any purpose.

Right: The Reid Ramsey impulse turbine. In operation this ran at 3,000rpm.

Excluding the electric generator, turbine transmission and condensing equipment, the Reid-Ramsay engine shared some characteristics with the Meyer/Kitson-Meyer genre, as exemplified by Cape Government Railways Kitson-Meyer 0-6-0+0-6-0 No 800 (Kitson Works No 4197), built in 1903 and withdrawn in 1911. A conventional Meyer usually, but not exclusively, had the cylinders of both bogies facing inwards, near the centre of the locomotive, sometimes with the rear cylinders uncomfortably close to the firebox. With the Kitson-Meyer, the rear bogie was reversed thereby allowing more room beneath the running plate. The CGR locomotive had the curiosity of an auxiliary chimney for the rear cylinders, set within the coal bunker. The rear power bogie thus contributed nothing to the smokebox draught, making the engine a poor steamer, being effectively 'under-boiled' for its four cylinders. This problem recurred fifty years later with South African Railways Class '25', which required induced draughting equipment to make the condensing tender function properly. No 800 also had an axle-loading problem, which was circumvented by the attachment of a tender that carried water only. This issue recurred from 1938 onwards with the successful 4-8-2+2-8-4 Beyer Garratts of the 'GM'/'GMA'/'GMAM' family, each of which was permanently coupled to an auxiliary tank car that carried 6,750 gallons.
Locomotive Publishing Co

oil-free although lubrication of shaft bearings, which did not come into contact with steam, was necessary.

The primary purpose of the condenser was to optimise the exhaust, rather than specifically to conserve water, and this meant that the usual blast-pipe arrangement was impracticable. The auxiliary pump that directed air through the cooling tubes apparently also fed heated air into the firebox. Presumably there was a mechanism in place that automatically closed off this air feed prior to opening the firebox door, otherwise this action would have resulted in emission of flames and hot air into the footplate area.

The locomotive was initially tested on a works siding, but later worked over Caledonian and North British rails, hauling a single coach. There is little information about how it performed, but it is understood that it was not particularly successful, with most problems allegedly coming from the axle-hung motors. Contemporary commentators apparently concluded that the configuration was too complicated. In view of the direct involvement of the company's chief executive, the failure was presumably treated with discretion, so as to minimise embarrassment. The locomotive was set aside and apparently dismantled, but not actually scrapped.

The Reid-Macleod Steam Turbine Locomotive

With (by now Sir) Hugh Reid's continuing interest in turbines, components from the Reid-Ramsey Steam-Turbine Electric Locomotive were reused in the creation of this machine, under patents held jointly by Reid and James MacLeod. The frame structure, boiler, wheels and bogies were retained, but the dynamo, main turbine, auxiliary turbines and pumps, and the axle-hung motors were discarded in favour of mechanical transmission. The bogie below the boiler was reversed, thereby changing the wheel arrangement to 4-4-0+0-4-4. The locomotive was identified by the number 23141, carried on its buffer beams, which was the works number from the 1924/25 North British series, rather than the 1910 period that applied to its earlier manifestation.

The superstructure was significantly changed while retention of the long rigid girder frame and removal of the centrally mounted turbine and dynamo meant that there was space to spare. The boiler was moved towards the centre by about 7 or 8 feet while keeping the large-diameter chimney. The drawing indicates a blast-pipe of more or less normal proportions, but this did not operate in the normal fashion. An auxiliary steam turbine drove a fan that provided draught either to the ashpan or up the chimney. A safety mechanism ensured that the latter mode was engaged before the firebox door was opened, to prevent blowback. Thus, with the firebox door closed the draught was forced, and induced with the door open.

The spaciously proportioned driving cab was placed centrally, roughly where the turbine had previously resided. The driving controls were simple and well laid out, allowing convenience and comfort superior to that of normal locomotives. Long reprofiled side tanks flanking the boiler extended from the cab to the end of the frames but about one-third of this length, adjacent to the cab on each side, served as a coal bunker. The condenser together with its associated equipment was apparently unchanged from the Reid-Ramsay machine, but was moved towards the centre by roughly the same distance as that for the boiler. The condenser was enclosed within shrouding whose lower profile matched the side tanks; a stylised cowling covered the upper part.

Each driving bogie carried a single impulse turbine mounted longitudinally and connected through reduction gears with a short longitudinal countershaft. This shaft was connected at either end by a bevel pinion with a large bevel wheel on a quill, which in turn connected with the driving axle, and all gearing operated within a

The second attempt involving North British was the Reid-MacLeod Steam Turbine Locomotive, in which many key components were evidently recycled from the Reid-Ramsey experiment of 1910. The Reid- MacLeod engine was technically less complex than its predecessor, whose electric transmission had proved especially troublesome. Substitution of mechanical (geared) transmission made for a simpler layout but one that was not markedly more successful.

Two general views of the Reid-MacLeod engine were reproduced in *The Railway Gazette* **of April 1924, evidently in connection with the locomotive's display at Wembley, but before it was mechanically complete. The condenser has been styled within the profile of the side tanks and superstructure, resulting in an unusual yet impressive appearance. The number 23141 on the buffer beam was the locomotive works number from the 1924/25 NBL series rather than the 1910 period that applied to its earlier manifestation as the Reid-Ramsey engine, although the frames, boiler and wheels dated from that time.** *The Railway Gazette*

sealed oil bath. A steam driven reciprocating pump kept the lubrication circulating. By this means both driving axles on each bogie were effectively coupled without recourse to rods, thus ensuring complete balancing.

Each turbine had three sets of blades, two for forward movement and the other for reverse. Selection was effected simply by turning a handle in the cab – forward opened double 3-inch valves while backward opened a single 3-inch valve. It was calculated that the power output in reverse was 70% of that available for forward movement. This would have necessitated turning at journey's end, as was the practice with earlier turbine machines in continental Europe produced by Krupp, Zoelly and Maffei.

Apart from the draught arrangements, the superheated boiler was of conventional design. High-pressure steam at a maximum of 180lb per sq in was admitted to the turbine on the bogie below the boiler through a control valve mounted inboard of the turbine.

For comparison, this is the Reid-Ramsay steam-turbine electric loco again with the condensing equipment on view – see illustration page 17. Forward visibility could not have been good.

On emission the steam was piped to a matching control valve on the leading, low-pressure turbine, making the locomotive a compound. The low-pressure turbine was rated as having a similar power output to that of its high-pressure companion. On exhaust from the low-pressure turbine, steam passed to the condenser to be recycled into

538   THE RAILWAY GAZETTE.   APRIL 11, 1924.

Interior View of Driver's End of Cab.
Showing Westinghouse and Vacuum Brake Valves and Turbine Steam Control and Reversing Wheel (left-hand), Controls for Condenser Fan at the back and Turbine therefor at the front (centre), and Hand Brake Wheel (right-hand).

Interior View of Fireman's End of Cab.
Showing Weir Feed Pump (left-hand), Lubrication and Water Spray Arrangement for Condenser Auxiliaries (under window, left-hand), Boiler Head with Forced Draught Control (centre), and Forced Lubrication Pump for Turbines and Gear (right-hand).

CAB VIEWS, "REID-MACLEOD" GEARED TURBINE LOCOMOTIVE.

The cab was divided between the 'driver's end' (adjacent to the condenser) and the 'fireman's end' (the boiler); the space and general layout impressed visitors to the 1924 British Empire Exhibition. *The Railway Gazette*

THE LMS TURBOMOTIVE

GLASGOW-BUILT LOCOMOTIVE FOR WEMBLEY

Reproduced above is a photograph of a new locomotive which has been built by the North British Locomotive Company (Limited), Springburn, Glasgow, and is to be on view at the British Empire Exhibition. The first geared turbine condensing locomotive constructed in Great Britain, it has been built on the Reid-MacLeod (patented) system, whereby there are incorporated in the design of the engine important advantages, mechanical, thermal, and economical, as compared with the ordinary non-condensing locomotives fitted with reciprocating engines. In geared turbine locomotives as built on this system, the turbines are placed longitudinally (without coupling rods), and, as all the motion is rotary, the engine is completely balanced. There being no reciprocating parts, the damage to rails, roadway, and bridges hitherto caused by imperfections in the balancing of steam locomotives, will be entirely obviated, and heavier weights on the driving wheels should be permissible. As there is a uniform torque on the driving wheels of the turbine locomotive at any position, rapid acceleration equal to that of electric traction is always obtainable. The condenser provides a vacuum for the exhaust from the turbine and a continuous supply of hot feed water, free from all impurities, to be returned from the hot well to the boiler. The combination of two-stage turbines with a condenser secures expansion of the superheated steam from boiler pressure to condenser vacuum, and an estimated economy of 50 per cent. in fuel and water should be obtained. The forced draught apparatus ensures steady combustion in the firebox, also that the rate of combustion is under complete control, and that it can be adjusted to meet all conditions of varying load and speed. The closed system of lubrication not only effects a substantial economy in labour and in oil, but also ensures that all the parts in motion are adequately lubricated, reducing the wear and tear to a minimum.

Under the headline 'GLASGOW-BUILT LOCOMOTIVE FOR WEMBLEY' this side view appeared in the Glasgow Herald of 3 April 1924. *Glasgow Herald*

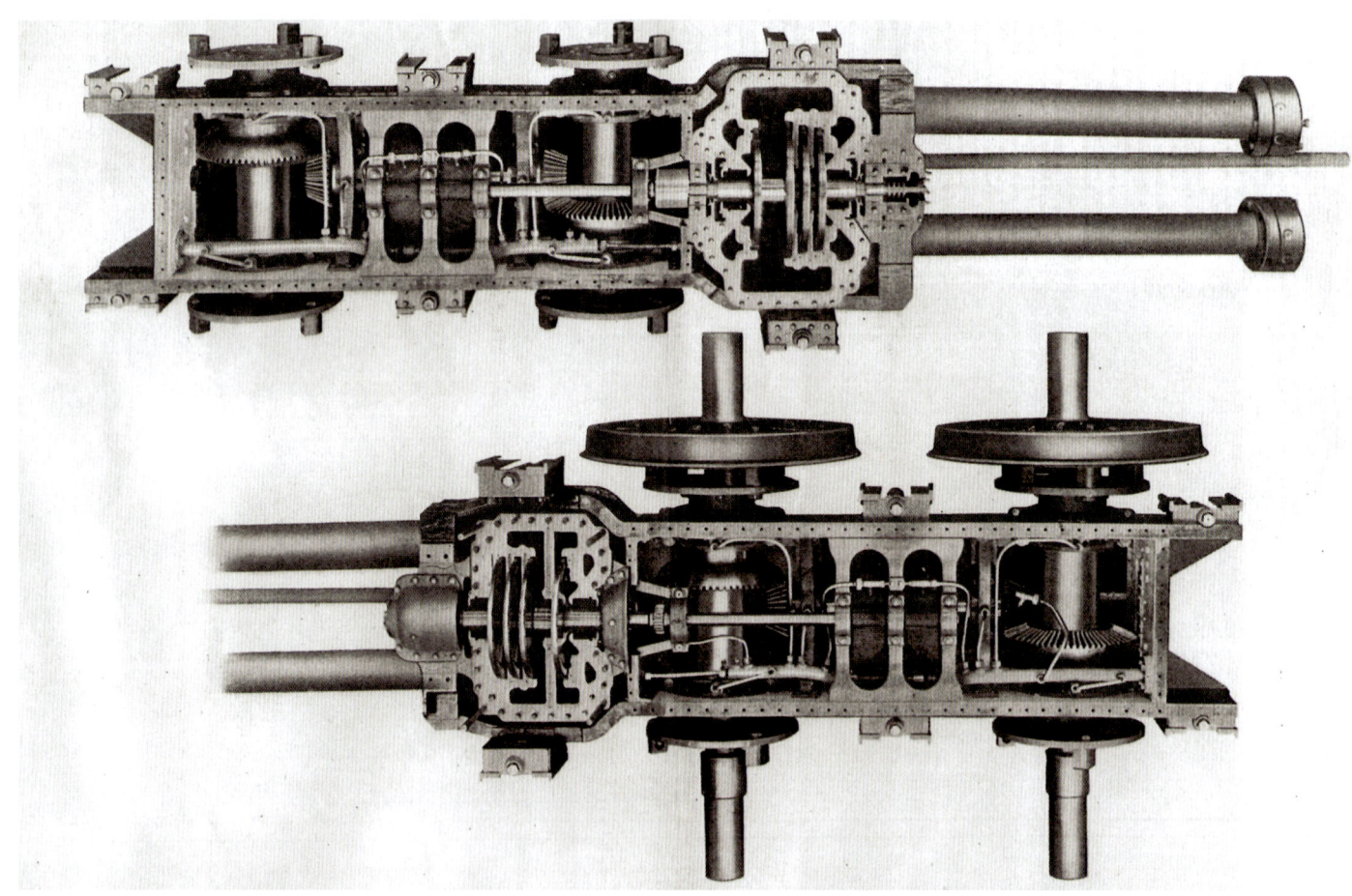

The turbine and gearing arrangements for the high- and low-pressure bogies. *The Engineer*

TURBINE LOCOMOTIVE DEVELOPMENT

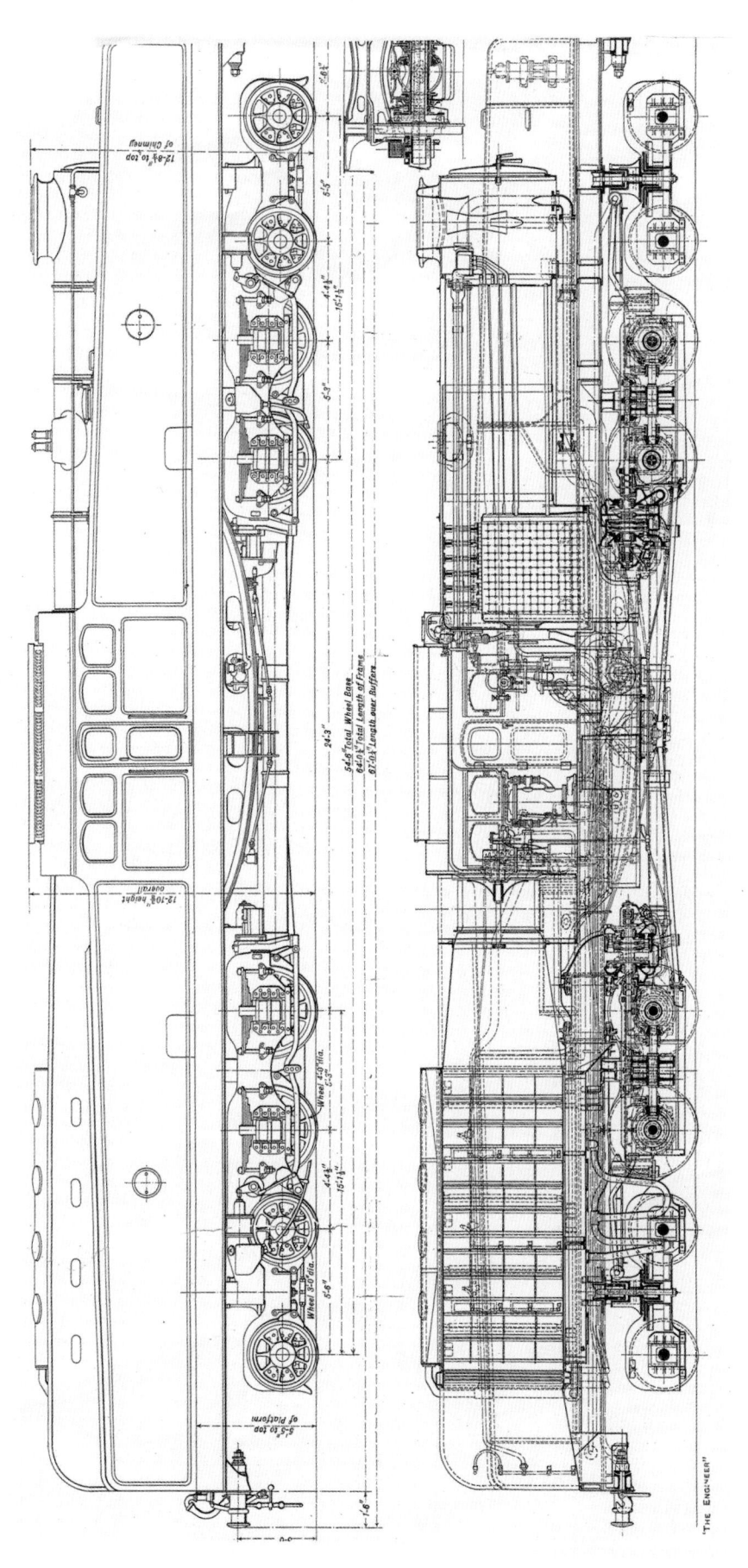

A line drawing of the Reid-MacLeod Steam Turbine Locomotive. *The Engineer*

THE LMS TURBOMOTIVE

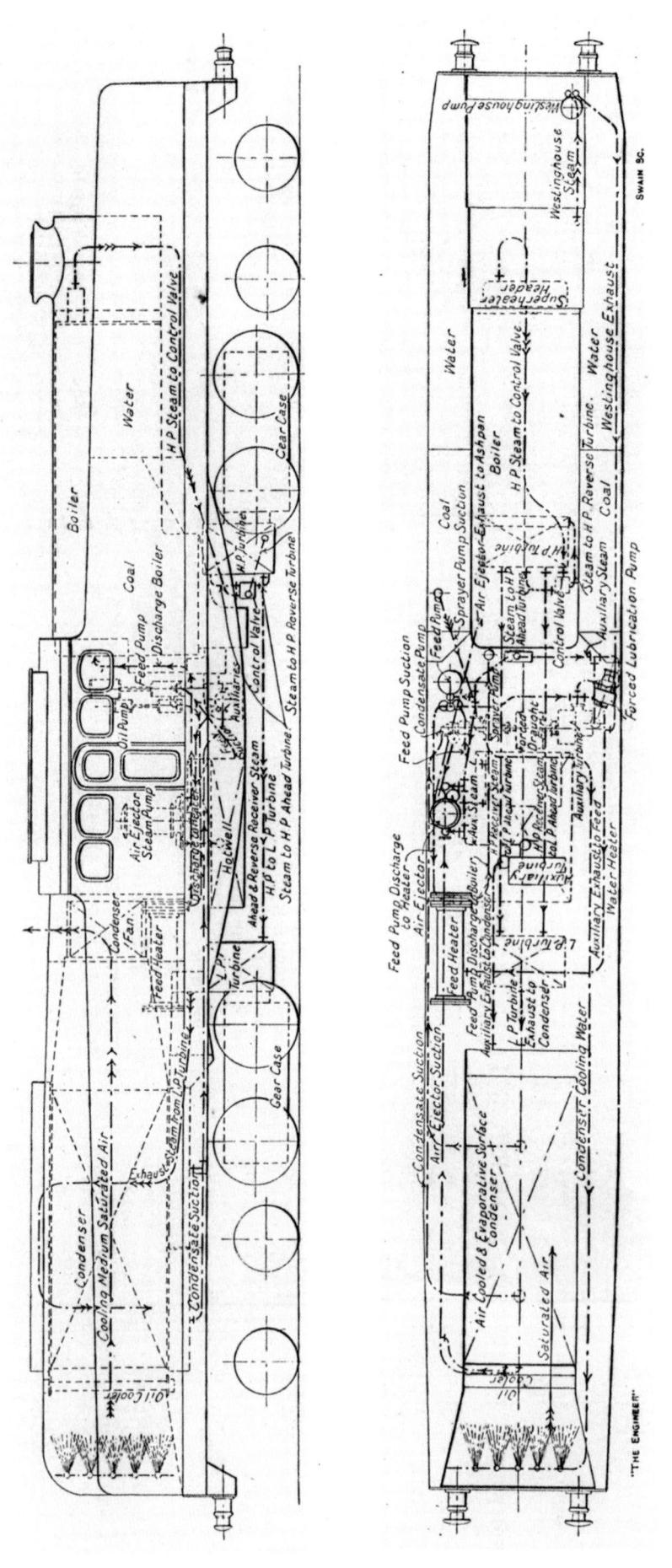

A diagram of the locomotive showing the steam flow through the turbines and condenser. *The Engineer*

Published key dimensions of the Reid-Macleod Steam Turbine Locomotive

Turbine power rating	Forward, two x 500hp; reverse, two x 350hp
Gear ratios	First stage: 8:1 double helical; second stage: 2.38:1 bevel (total reduction approximately 19:1)
Turbine speed (at 60mph)	8,000rpm
Boiler pressure	180 lb per sq in
Tractive effort	15,000lb (measured on a dynamometer at Hyde Park Works)
Driving wheels	4ft 0in
Carrying wheels	3ft 0in
Bogie wheelbase (carrying wheels leading)	5ft 6in + 4ft 4½in + 5ft 3in
Length:	
Between inner driving axles	24ft 3in
Total wheelbase	54ft 6in
Frame	64ft 0in
Over buffers	67ft 0in

water within the closed, contaminant-free circuit in similar fashion to that applied in the earlier Reid-Ramsay version.

Prior to road testing, the locomotive was tried out with a 280-ton freight train on a works siding. The rails were greasy and the locomotive slipped badly, but nonetheless drew the train steadily. Light engine tests showed that the forward and reverse gears could be engaged simply and efficiently, and performance generally was impressive

It was intended that the locomotive should be capable of hauling a 225-ton passenger train at 60mph, and of maintaining an average of 50mph over an extended distance. The capital cost was not disclosed but the manufacturer believed that substantial savings in fuel and running expenses would be possible compared with a reciprocating locomotive of similar power. It was estimated that over a fifteen-year period these savings could exceed the construction cost of a reciprocating locomotive, 'after allowing for depreciation and the return of the initial capital difference between the turbine and reciprocating locomotives at 5% interest'. This definition seems ambiguous but, assuming an expected operating life of 30 years, the estimated benefits seem ambitious. However, financial advantage on this scale would have been necessary to justify substantial investment in turbine-driven machines, but the projected superiority had first to be proven.

Use of the girder frame and other major components from the Reid-Ramsay locomotive made this machine more a test bed than a design prototype, being substantially longer than necessary and rather poorly proportioned. As the basis for an express passenger locomotive it appeared underpowered with a nominal rating of 1,000hp developed by the two forward turbines. A further drawback lay in reverse running, where performance was restricted by the smaller turbine and by the reduced efficiency of the condenser as exposure to air as a cooling agent was essential. No information is available on this aspect, but it is notable that photographs of the locomotive on the move all show it working with the condenser leading. Nevertheless, had the concept proved feasible the length would have allowed for a larger boiler, uprated turbines, a 4-6-0+0-6-4 wheel arrangement, and modified condenser layout.

No 23141 was regarded significant enough to be displayed on the North British stand at the 1924 British Empire Exhibition at Wembley. It was apparently internally incomplete at that time, although a number of components and structural features were filmed by British Pathé News. This level of publicity might have been unwise given the risk of teething troubles and possible embarrassment in the event of failure.

The incomplete nature of the construction was evident in the interval before working trials commenced in March 1926. The locomotive immediately impressed with its minimal vibration, oscillation and rail pounding. On the first test run between Glasgow and Edinburgh problems were experienced with the condenser pumps. The second trial, reportedly in April 1927, was blighted with axlebox problems and then significantly by turbine failure. It is surmised that the latter was crucial to viability in revealing key metallurgical shortcomings, i.e. the inability to produce a turbine capable of safely absorbing the stresses generated. Whatever the reasons, this evidently marked the experiment's conclusion, as No 23141 does not appear to have been steamed again. It was placed in store, and broken up in 1940 at a time when scrap metal was in high demand.

Although most turbine machines were experimental one-offs that had little impact on mainstream development, it seems that certain features of the Reid-Macleod locomotive were put to commercial use. For many years, the railways of South Africa had been important customers for North British and its predecessors, with the main competition coming from Baldwin and Alco. Then in 1914 a new type of articulated locomotive was ordered from Beyer Peacock, although not delivered until 1919. The prototype Garratt Class 'GA' 2-6-0+0-6-2 was tested against SAR's most modern Mallet (of broadly similar power) with profound results. Thereafter, SAR bought no more Mallets and became a major customer for the Garratt type.

Protected by patents, Beyer Peacock's products were a serious threat, inducing North British to respond with its own articulated design, known as the Modified Fairlie. Above the footplate the superstructure resembled a Garratt, but the leading tank, boiler, cab, bunker and rear tank were all carried on a single girder frame supported by power bogies fore and aft. Technically, it was a variant of the Kitson-Meyer type, as was also the Reid-MacLeod engine and its predecessor. The SAR Class 'FC' 2-6-2+2-6-2 was the first Modified Fairlie, and was a direct challenge to the Beyer

South African Railways 2-6-2+2-6-2 'Modified Fairlie' Class 'FC' No 2310 of 1924 was superficially similar to a Garratt, but the entire superstructure was carried on a single rigid frame. This variation on the Meyer layout (with both cylinder sets located outwards from the centre) used frame construction and cab style similar to that of the Reid-McLeod machine. This challenge to the ascendancy of Beyer Peacock's products in Africa was unsuccessful, being withdrawn in 1939. Undue stress on the bogie pivots led to heavy maintenance costs, highlighting a potential limitation had development of the Reid-MacLeod engine continued. *B. Jackson*

Peacock monopoly. In some respects it resembled the Reid-Macleod Steam Turbine – specifically in the massive frame structure and the styling of tank profile and cab.

Eventually, there were sixteen Modified Fairlies in service with SAR in three classes (including eleven built by Henschel), but all suffered from excessive wear of the bogie pivots, caused in part by oscillation induced by water movement in the tanks. Similar problems arose with the so-called Union Garratts, which had the usual Garratt leading bogie arrangement but with bunker and rear tank cantilevered out from the cab, supported by a Modified Fairlie-type pivoted power bogie. Neither the Modified Fairlies nor the Union Garratts matched the success of the classic Beyer Peacock design. These experiences highlighted a possible problem area, had enlargement and development of single-frame condensing turbine locomotives continued.

The Ramsay Turbo-Electric Condensing Locomotive

Chronologically, this locomotive (also referred to as the Armstrong-Whitworth Turbine-Electric Locomotive) was the second British attempt at a steam-turbine-electric locomotive and followed the 'power-station-on-wheels) theme. It was built by Armstrong-Whitworth at its Scotswood works to the design of D. M. Ramsay, who, having parted company with North British, had formed the Ramsay Condensing Locomotive Company based in Glasgow. A key objective was to exploit the advantages of electric traction without recourse to overhead or third-rail supply networks. It was hoped that the condenser's closed circulation system using pure water would greatly reduce boiler maintenance costs and also attract export sales to countries with sub-standard water supplies.

The locomotive comprised two six-coupled driving sections, articulated and coupled by a universal joint, creating a 2-6-0+0-6-2 wheel arrangement. The front section carried boiler, two turbines, generator, two electric motors, and driving cab. The rear section carried coal and water supplies, as with a normal tender, together with condenser, fans, hotwell, and two electric motors.

The boiler had a comparatively modest diameter, made necessary by being pitched at 10ft 3in above rail level to allow room for the main turbine installed immediately below. Combustion was assisted by a fan placed in the cab to provide forced draught. An electric generator was coupled to and immediately in front of the main turbine to feed two electric motors that were mounted on a centre stretcher between the frames (and also two similarly placed electric motors on the rear unit). These motors engaged with a transverse drive shaft that carried flywheels, and also spur wheels at both ends that were connected to the driving wheels by coupling rods. The drive shaft on the front engine unit was located between the leading and centre driving axles, and on the rear unit between centre and trailing driving axles.

The transmission layout on the rear unit (electric motors, drive shaft, flywheels and coupling arrangements) was identical to that on the front unit, except that it was reversed. Above the solebar, the rear unit comprised a coal bunker (capacity 4 tons), a water

The Ramsay Turbo-Electric Condensing Locomotive, newly constructed by Armstrong-Whitworth in 1922.

The Ramsay locomotive hauling a test train. *The Railway Gazette*

Right: **This three-quarter rear view of the Ramsay Turbo-Electric Condensing Locomotive reveals the amount of space needed for the condenser and ungainly air scoop. Despite these elaborate arrangements, the condenser vacuum failed to exceed 70% of the level considered necessary to achieve acceptable performance levels.** The Railway Gazette

tank (capacity 2,500 gallons), and a hotwell beneath. The condenser was located centrally in this unit with an air scoop at the rear that projected out over the buffer beam.

The main turbine was a nine-stage impulse type. There was also a single-stage auxiliary impulse turbine that drove a direct current dynamo to excite the main turbine. It also provided dc current to the condenser fan, rotor and pump, as well as driving the auxiliary fan in the cab, and powering the train lighting circuits.

The ac/dc power circuits together with the turbine, generator and electric motors were indeed complex. However, contemporary accounts seem to have focussed on the design and layout of the condenser, the system of closed water/steam circulation, and the means of optimising the resultant vacuum to induce draught. The main emphasis appears to have been placed on leakage minimisation, exclusion of poor water that could cause boiler deterioration, and optimisation of water consumption. This gives the impression that the main objective was to produce a more efficient steam locomotive boiler, with the development possibilities of turbine power and electric transmission systems a secondary consideration.

The starting procedure reflected the design's complexity. Once sufficient steam pressure had been raised, the auxiliary turbine was started and run up to full speed, thereby producing excitation to start the main turbine, which in turn was run up to half speed (about 1,800rpm). At that point the electric motors were connected in series and exerted 1½ times the usual running torque to enable the locomotive to start. Once under way, the electric motors were switched to working in parallel, and thereafter the torque level was reduced progressively as speed increased. Tractive effort at the wheel was calculated as follows:

THE LMS TURBOMOTIVE

On starting	22,000 lb
15mph	22,000 lb
30mph	11,050 lb
60mph	8,600 lb

Normal running mode at 60mph, electric motors in parallel – 6,000 lb

Published dimensional details of the Ramsay Turbo-Electric Condensing Locomotive

Length:	
Overall	69ft 7in
Wheelbase (two units)	59ft 4in
Over rigid wheelbase	16ft 4in
Boiler pitch	10ft 3in
Maximum width	8ft 11in
Driving wheel diameter	4ft 0in

Heating surfaces:	
Total (inc superheater)	1,453sq ft
Grate area	28.4sq ft
Boiler pressure	200 lb per sq in
Superheater	300°F
Turbo-generator	890kW at 3,600rpm, 600v ac

Weights (published):		
Front unit	empty	63 tons 5 cwt
	laden	67 tons 5 cwt
Rear unit	empty	48 tons 3 cwt
	laden	63 tons 10 cwt
Average adhesive weight		18 tons

The Ramsay locomotive was completed in early 1922 and delivered in April to the Lancashire & Yorkshire Railway at Horwich for road trials. Weight was immediately a contentious issue as the manufacturer's diagram had indicated 122 tons (laden) whereas the locomotive turned the scales on the LYR at almost 156 tons, with a maximum axle loading of 24 tons. This appears to have been formally acknowledged as later disclosures stated that the adhesive weight of each unit was 65 tons. Any perception that the manufacturer had tried to mislead could have induced the railway company to be less cooperative. Restrictions were certainly placed on the routes available for testing, which were limited to the Bolton area, although weight was of little significance as performance was disappointing.

The turbine and associated electrical equipment apparently proved reliable and trouble-free, but difficulties were experienced with the steam and condensing cycle. The forced draught was inadequate, and the maximum condenser vacuum was little more than 70% of the targeted level. Coal and water consumption was high, presumably partly due to the modestly sized boiler. Following modifications that included a revised chimney, installation of a brick arch, and a new condenser that was about 2 tons lighter, there was some improvement. The condenser vacuum rose to about 93% of target and a speed of 48mph was achieved hauling a 230-ton train. Dynamometer tests nonetheless revealed poor efficiency below 30mph. In November 1922 a speed of 59mph was reached, but hauling only 65 tons while consuming 40lb of coal per mile. Again, boiler performance was problematic as the prescribed working pressure was 200lb per sq in, but the maximum achieved was 170. By way of comparison, an LYR 4-6-0 (not regarded as an especially efficient type) could haul 400 tons with a similar coal consumption rate.

A side view of the Ramsay locomotive, with the air scoop removed.

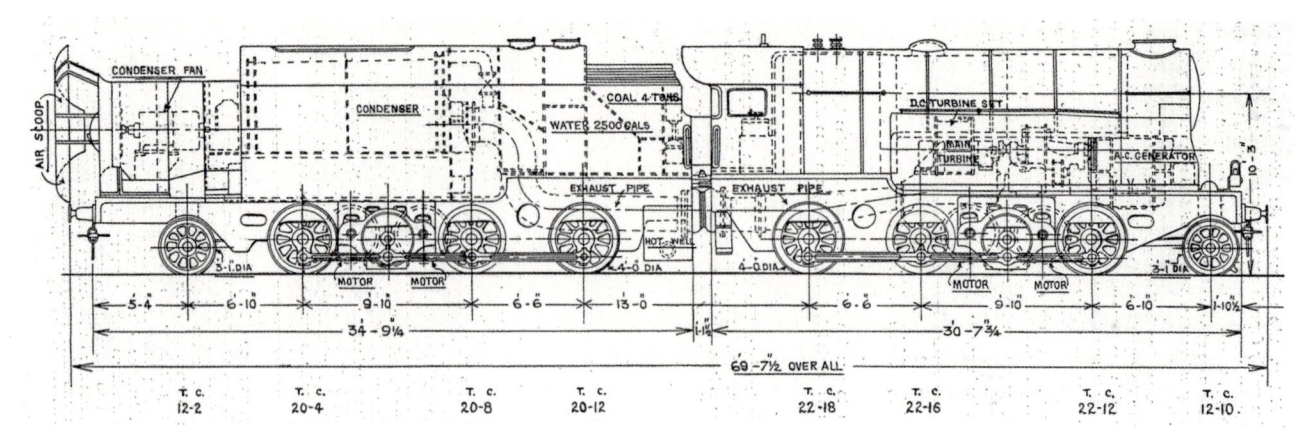

A diagram of the Ramsay Turbo-Electric Condensing Locomotive. *The Railway Gazette*

TURBINE LOCOMOTIVE DEVELOPMENT

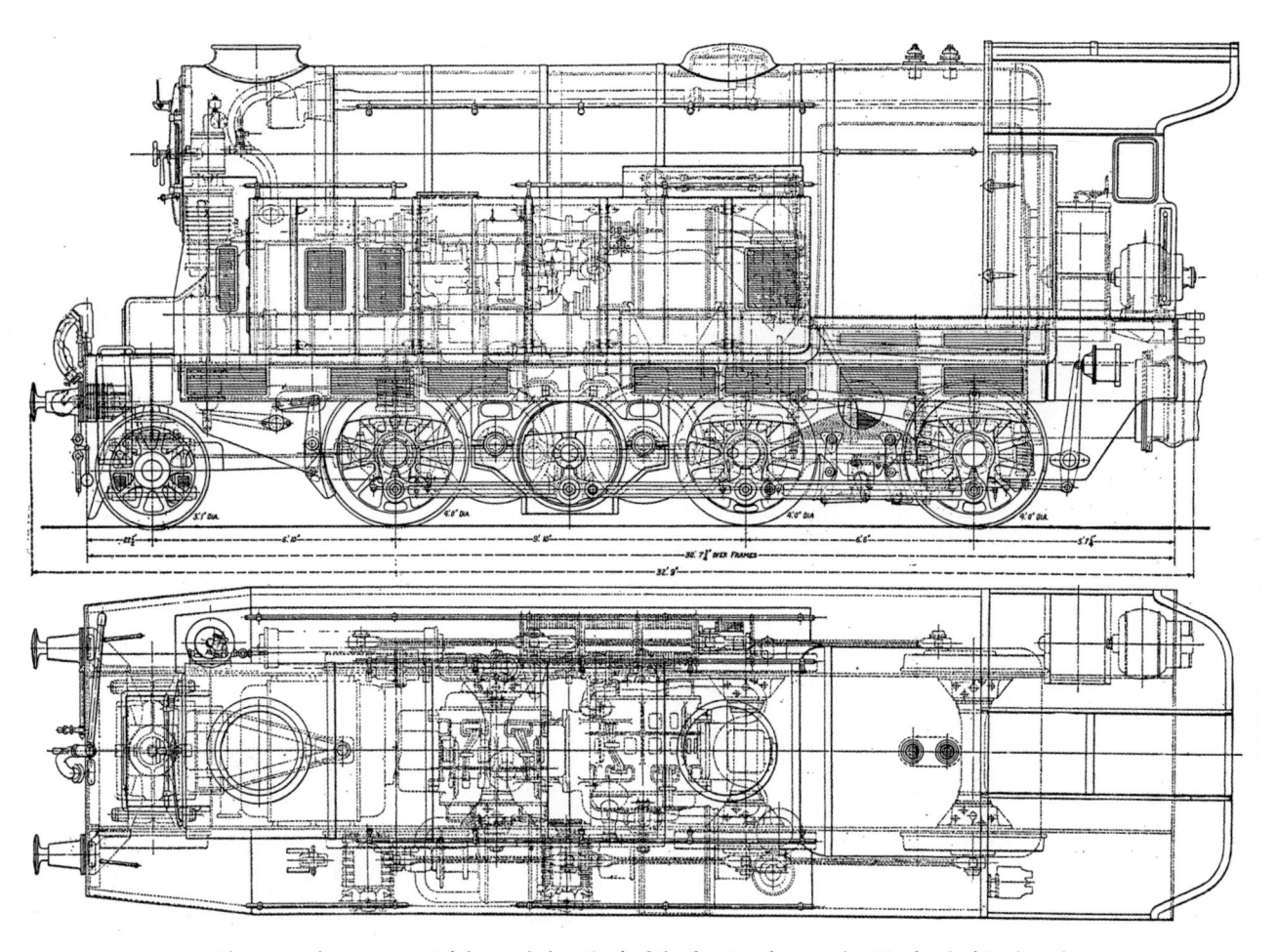

The general arrangement (plan and elevation) of the front and rear units. *Mechanical Engineering*

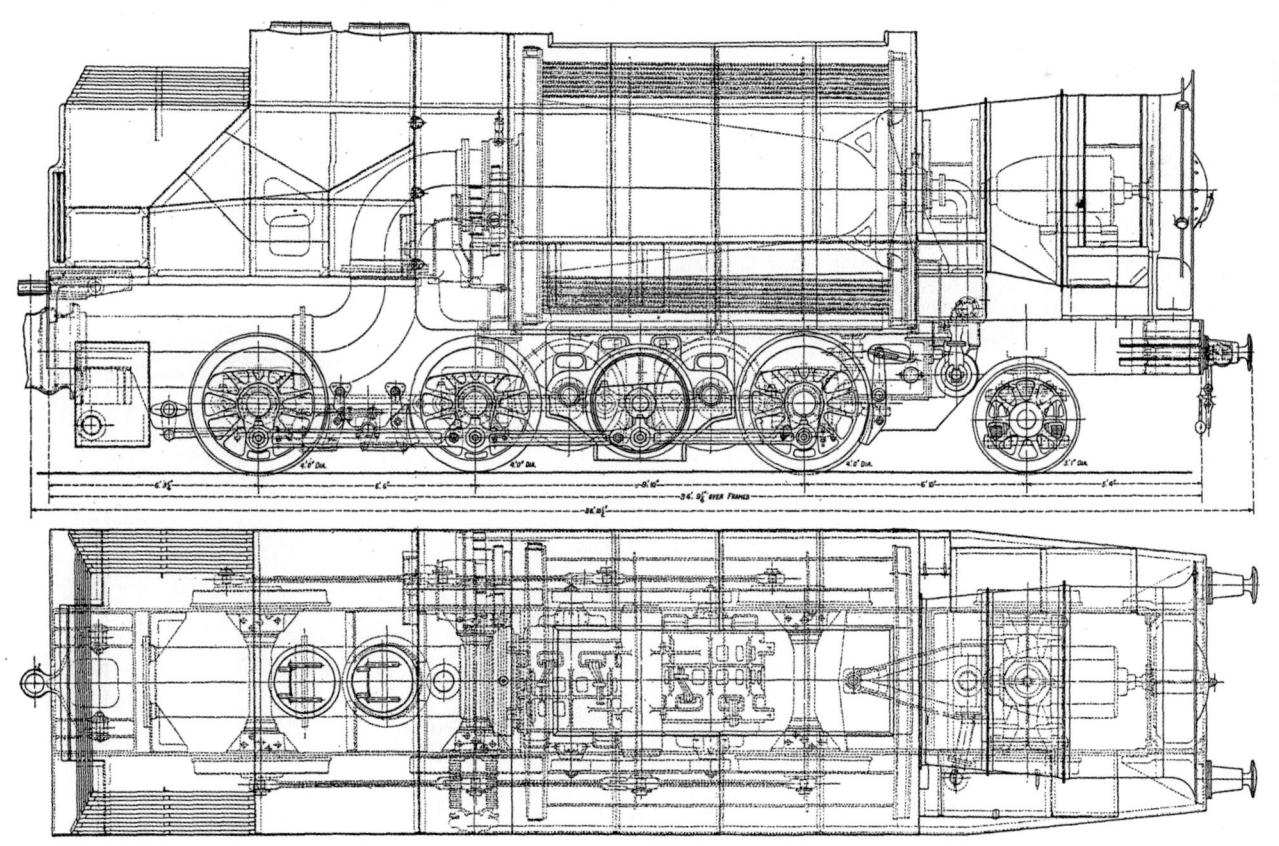

29

More tests were held in May 1923, presumably following further modifications, details of which do not seem to have survived. The results proved even more disappointing, failing to match the performance of a small LYR 2-4-2T. The project was then terminated and the locomotive returned to Newcastle, where it was broken up.

Summary

It was apparent by 1927 that all-British experimental machines had achieved little in the cause of rail-borne turbine power. Despite the backing of two major industrial manufacturers, test results displayed no discernible features to support the contention that a turbine locomotive would be a feasible proposition. In an operational sense, the Reid-McLeod locomotive demonstrated the attractions of smooth torque, vibration-free running and absence of hammer blow, but the incidence of component failure was high during its brief road trials. In particular, the failure of its turbine after so little use suggested that the technological competence then available was inadequate for the task.

The Armstrong-Whitworth machine proved less prone to turbine failure, but the lacklustre performance of boiler and condensing equipment was a severe handicap. Further, it was apparent that articulation did not relieve the issue of excessive weight, and it is hard to see how matters could have been improved without radical redesign for which there was no evident appetite.

Above all, the three machines were vastly more complex than conventional steam locomotives, which implied substantially higher construction costs as well as more complex maintenance regimes. Details of the actual costs incurred do not seem to have been released. Projected financial benefits are also unclear, except for the vague definitions presented in connection with the Reid-McLeod engine, which were more an expression of hope.

Any initiative relying solely on domestic expertise alone thus had little chance of substantive progress. The next stage in the story relied on reference to development overseas, a practice that sadly was all too infrequent in the annals of British steam.

A significant step in the development of turbine locomotives was elimination of the condenser. The weight and space penalty imposed by such equipment is illustrated by the size of the condensing tenders fitted to the otherwise conventional South African Railways 4-8-4 Class '25' locomotives, built by North British and Henschel in 1953-55. These engines were also fitted with electrically powered fans to induce draught, as exhaust steam was not emitted from the chimney. They were condenser-fitted to traverse the Great Karoo, an extensive region of semi-desert north of Cape Town, and an 85% reduction in water consumption was achieved.
The locomotive was 50ft 9in long over couplers and weighed 120 tons 3 cwt; the tender was 56ft 9in long over couplers and weighed 113 tons 18 cwt.

CHAPTER THREE

The Ljungström Turbine

FREDRIK LJUNGSTRÖM was a Swedish engineer, technical designer and industrialist who, working with his older brother Birger, developed a new form of high-pressure steam boiler in the 1890s, and then in 1894 produced the Ljungström radial steam turbine. Turbine manufacturing was absorbed into AB Ljungström Ångturbin (ALÅ), a company formed for the purpose in 1908. In 1913 the brothers formed a second company to take over manufacturing, and this was acquired three years later by electrical manufacturer Allmänna Svenska Elektriska Aktiebolaget (ASEA). ALÅ retained control of the patents and continued to operate under Ljungström ownership for the purpose of research and development, together with promotion of the technology in other fields.

In 1922 Nydqvist & Holm AB (NOHAB) built a turbine condenser locomotive in accordance with the Ljungström patents. This worked a number of test runs on Swedish State Railways, proving its potential to a greater degree than had the British ventures. There were initial problems with the preheater located below the smokebox, which channelled air for the firebox past waste combustion gases, but this was soon improved with a modified system of greater capacity. An estimated 10-12% reduction in coal consumption resulted and it was concluded that there was a basis for continued development.

The Beyer-Ljungström turbine locomotive

The first issue of *The Beyer-Peacock Quarterly Review* appeared in January 1927 and its lead article (in four parts) reviewed progress in Britain and continental Europe with turbine-drive locomotives. The fourth instalment (October 1927) dealt at length with the design and construction of 'The Turbine Condenser Locomotive', following collaboration with Ljungström. That this article took precedence over progress with Garratt locomotives indicates the importance that Beyer Peacock attached to the possibilities.

The first Ljungström Turbine-Driven Locomotive was built in 1922 and tested with Swedish State Railways. Once again the space-consuming characteristic of the condensing unit is evident.

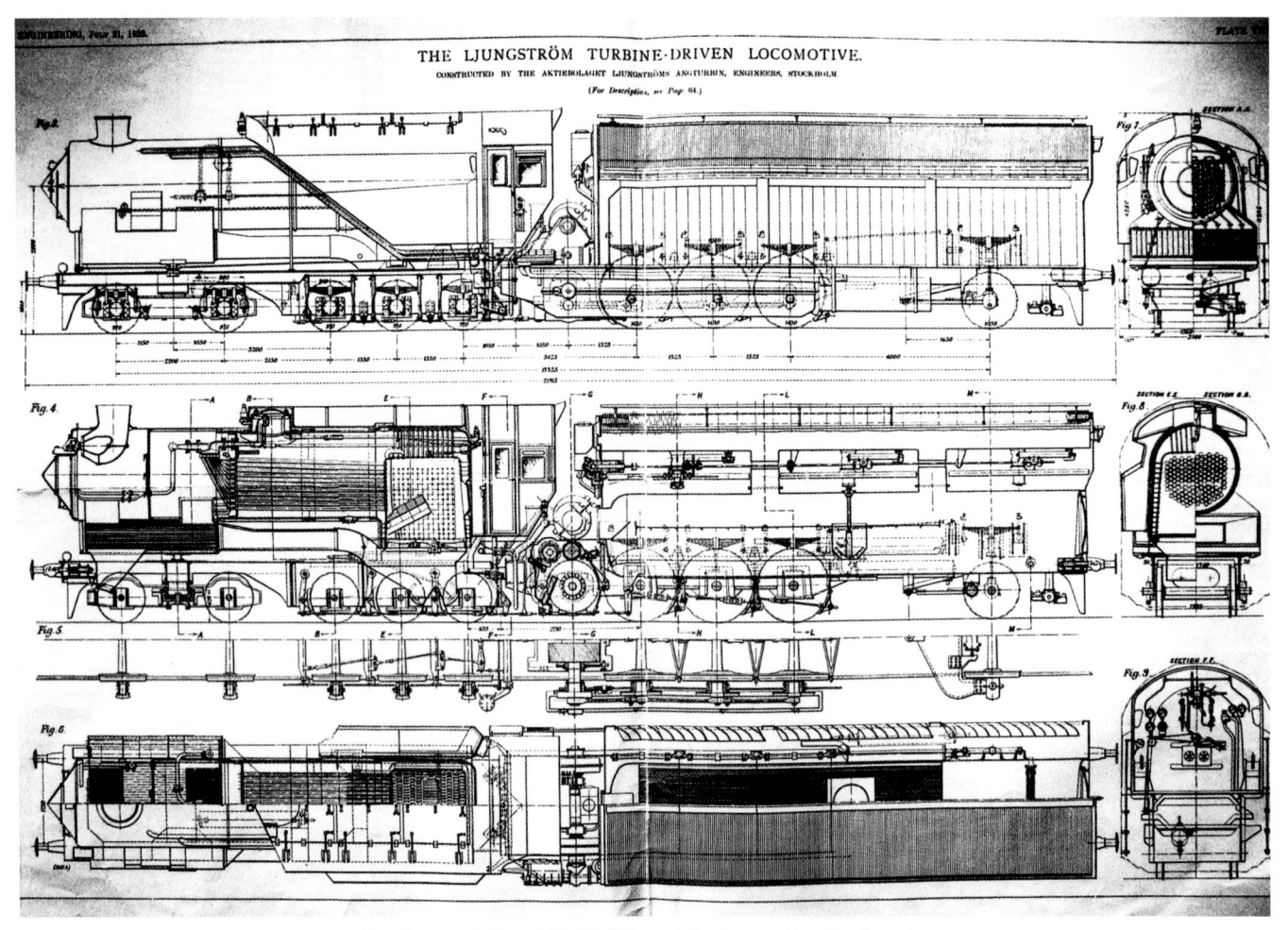

Elevations and plan of the first Ljungström locomotive. *Engineering*

The account opened with a technical and commercial explanation of the reasons for the project. It was noted that compounding, superheating and very high boiler pressures could have only marginal impact on thermal efficiency, while the impressive performance levels of steam turbines in marine and industrial use offered a chance to redress energy loss between the firebox and the driving axle. It was also believed that a large condenser combining air-cooling and water recirculation could substantially reduce water consumption, perhaps allowing a turbine locomotive to cover 1,000 miles without the need to replenish its tank. This was seen as an export sales aid to arid parts of the British Empire, or in regions where indifferent track militated against the use of large tenders.

Beyer Peacock obtained a provisional licence for manufacturing rights in 1923. As the prototype on test with Swedish State Railways was unsuitable for British conditions,

The last attempt at a condenser turbine locomotive in the United Kingdom took the form of the Beyer-Ljungström locomotive that appeared in 1926. The general configuration followed that used with the Swedish locomotive of 1922, retaining the principle of dividing the mechanical equipment between locomotive and tender. This locomotive had a less bulky superstructure than the prototype of four years earlier, suggesting significant progress in the interim, especially regarding condenser design.

THE LMS TURBOMOTIVE

Table 3.1: Eight-coupled fleet of the Grängesberg-Oxelösund Railway

Running Nos	41-45	46-50	61-63	64-70	71-73	95, 96
Type	0-8-0	0-8-0	0-8-0	0-8-0	2-8-0	0-8-0
Built	c1905	???	???	???	1930/1936	1942
Cylinders	2 (inside)	3*	3*	2 (outside)	turbine	2 (outside)
Cylinder dimensions	???	???	500mm x 600 mm (20"x 26in)	600 mm x 660 mm (24"x 26in)	n/a	600 mm x 660 mm (24"x 26in)
Valve gear	Stephenson	Stephenson (inside) Walschaerts (outside)	Stephenson (inside) Walschaerts (outside)	Walschaerts	-	Walschaerts
Boiler pressure	???	???	13KP/sq cm (184lb per sq in)	14KP/sq cm (198lb per sq in)	13KP/sq cm (184lb per sq in)	14KP/sq cm (198lb per sq in)
Driving wheels	1,350mm (4' 5")	1,350mm (4' 5")	1,350mm (4' 5")	1,350mm (4' 5")	1,350mm (4' 5")	1,350mm (4' 5")
Tractive effort	???	???	15,000 K (34,171 lbs)	16,000 K (35,273 lbs)	18,000 K** (39,683 lbs)	16,000 K (35,273 lbs)
Weight	???	???	72,000 K (71 tons 17 cwt)	70,000 K (68 tons 17 cwt)	81,800 K (80 tons 10 cwt)	70,000 K (68 tons 17 cwt)

* Divided drive: inside cylinder to 2nd and outside cylinders to 3rd axle
** Assumed to be notional
NB Imperial equivalents have been rounded to the nearest inch/ pound/ hundredweight

Railways in 1922. With Grängesberg-Oxelösund No 71, combustion air was drawn into the firebox through dampers below the grate, and the steam generated then passed through a regulator located in the dome. The regulator acted as the main stop valve and was left fully open while the engine was in use. Steam then passed through the superheater and was admitted to the turbine by a five-nozzle valve attached to the turbine casing. This arrangement governed the volume of steam admitted and was controlled from the cab. Having passed through the turbine, steam was then exhausted through the blast-pipe, thereby providing the requisite draught. The steady flow of steam through the turbine yielded an even draught and backpressure was greatly reduced.

Other modifications included an increase in the superheating surface, although details have not been ascertained. The pitch of the boiler was raised to permit access to the smokebox (which was through an asymmetrically placed smokebox door). This change

Non-condensing Ljungström steam turbine 2-8-0 No 72 of the Grängesberg-Oxelösund Railway (TGOJ).

Problems emerged on these more onerous duties. The reversing gear tended to leak steam, but this was soon corrected. More serious was a significant drop in condenser vacuum when traversing long tunnels. This was initially attributed to soot, disturbed from tunnel roofs, clogging the condenser fans, but inspection revealed no undue accumulation of dirt. It was concluded that the cause was aerodynamic – when passing through a tunnel, air pushed in front of the engine reduced the pressure behind, thus restricting flow to the condensers and leading to sluggish running. There does not seem to have been any attempt to address this issue.

A more persistent problem lay in the propensity for the carrying and driving axleboxes to run hot, believed to have been caused by an excess of fast running. The engine steamed well and was capable of speeds of up to 85mph and more while maintaining a comfortable ride. In the absence of the noise and vibration associated with a conventional locomotive, it was hard to judge speed. The absence of a speedometer was unfortunate, and it is surmised that No 6233 habitually ran faster than the intended maxima, and beyond the capacity of the lubrication systems.

The initially identified advantage of reduced water consumption was realised and this led to discussions with representatives of the Commonwealth of Australia Government Railways in July 1927. Condensing turbine locomotives were proposed as suitable for the transcontinental route across the arid Nullarbor Plain, and there were plans to show the locomotive to the Australian Prime Minister at St Pancras. Unfortunately, shortly before this demonstration the locomotive suffered a hot axlebox. Hasty repairs were instituted at Derby before running the engine up to London, but the demonstration was cancelled at the last moment. It was decided that the recurrent nature of this problem presented an unreasonable risk in regions where ambient temperatures were considerably higher than in the UK.

Following this setback, the engine returned to Gorton for overhaul and further modifications. More tests were conducted in March/April 1928 and a number of minor problems were encountered. These notwithstanding, the locomotive was generally able to work trains to schedule, but comparison of test results against those of a Horwich 2-6-0 (the 'Crab') were not encouraging. Water usage was significantly lower, but coal consumption on a drawbar horsepower per hour basis was higher. Most importantly, No 6233 had cost £37,000 to construct while a conventional locomotive of similar power could be built for about £6,000.

Loss of the Australian opportunity was a blow, but other negative factors were also in play. Technical complexity and associated high maintenance costs outweighed the benefits of the marginal increase in thermal efficiency, undoubted haulage capacity, and smooth riding. Further, difficulties arose over the licensing arrangements, and Beyer Peacock Chairman Sir Sam Fay was unhappy with his company's trading performance. In 1928 he noted that while the order book was full, this had been achieved with some under-pricing, so profitability was unimpressive. Matters improved during the next two years, but trading was very difficult from 1931 onwards (the company sold only six locomotives in 1934). No more development work or modifications were undertaken after 1928 and No 6233 was placed in store. The boiler was adapted for stationary use at Gorton in 1940; the remaining parts lingered on and were finally scrapped in 1953.

The performance of the Beyer-Ljungström engine exceeded anything achieved with the earlier experiments. The steady continuous torque and absence of hammer blow emphasised the potential for a larger machine. Also, an advantage perhaps peculiar to Beyer Peacock lay in that company's expertise with flexible pipework arising from its experience with Garratts. With the need for a condenser borne by a separate chassis, specialist skills learned with articulated engines would have been helpful, although imminent developments were to make this aspect redundant.

There was a limit to the financial and technical resources that an organisation such as Beyer Peacock could devote to an essentially speculative venture. The only other possible sponsor could have been the LMS, but the condition of that company's motive power management in the late 1920s was not conducive to research and development on the scale necessary. Nevertheless, the Beyer-Ljungström engine marked a considerable advance over earlier British experiments, consistently proving its operational, if not commercial, feasibility. The locomotive's positive features undoubtedly left a lasting, favourable impression.

Breakthrough: the Ljungström 2-8-0s

The Beyer-Ljungström locomotive had proved to be the most successful turbine type to operate in Britain, demonstrating enticing performance capacity. However, the capital and maintenance costs over a conventional locomotive outweighed the realised and potential advantages. Multiplication of the type could generate some scale economies, but insufficient for commercial viability. The Ljungström brothers recognised these constraints and their continued research led to the elimination of the condenser and associated ancillaries.

The first Ljungström non-condensing turbine locomotive appeared in 1930 for service as a heavy freight hauler for the 159-mile Grängesberg-Oxelösund Railway (TGOJ) in Sweden. This privately owned line had been built to move iron ore southwards from the major deposits at Grängesberg to the steel works at Oxelösund, and also for export from that port in raw form. This was a major industrial undertaking, and for many years Sweden's most profitable corporation; the mine closed in late 1989 with the last ore train operating in January 1990. Prior to electrification in the early 1950s, ore traffic was hauled by a fleet of eight-coupled tender locomotives that was developed from around the First World War until 1942. The composition of the fleet (perhaps not exclusively) is described in the Table 3.1.

Visual inspection of a preserved example indicates that 0-8-0s Nos 61-63 (classified 'M3b:s') formed the design base for the turbine trio (classified 'M3t:s'), using the same boiler size and coupled wheelbase. The frame was lengthened at the front end to enable the turbine and triple reduction gearbox to be carried in front of the smokebox and connected with the driving wheels by means of a jackshaft; the extra front-end weight was borne by the pony truck. The Class 'M3b:s' coupled wheelbase was chosen so that should the turbine drive prove a failure, the locomotive could be readily modified to reciprocating form.

The turbine was similar to that used in the Ljungström condensing locomotive that had been tested with Swedish State

THE LMS TURBOMOTIVE

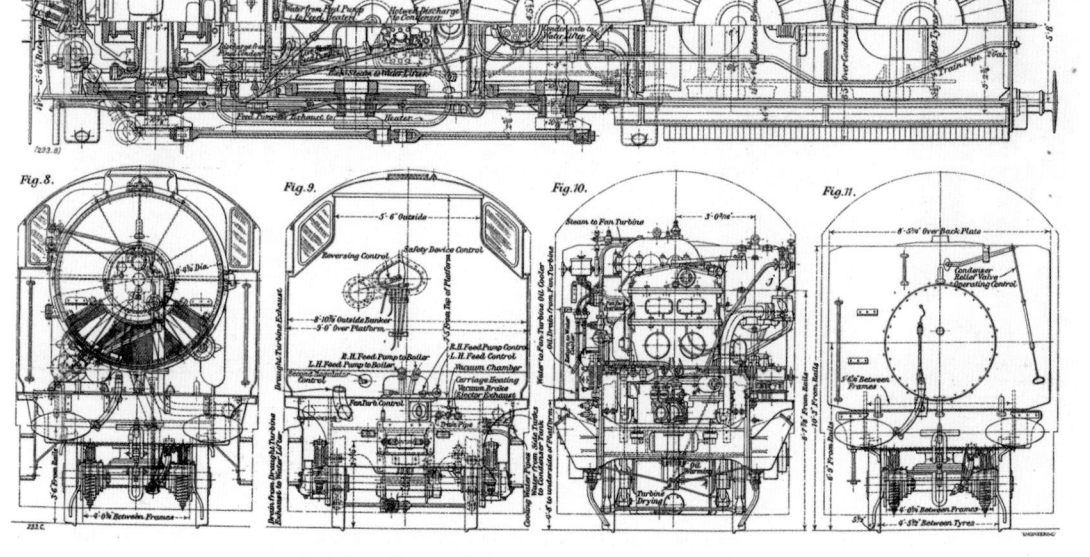

Detailed elevations and plans of the Beyer-Ljungström locomotive.

The locomotive on test with a rake of vintage coaches.

The locomotive on a test train, in this case working in reverse. The design seems to have been more flexible than previous condensing turbine locomotives, being capable of operation in either direction without limitations imposed by cooling, draught or gearing.

Showing obvious signs of usage, the Beyer-Ljungström locomotive stands on shed.

Below: **A diagram of the Beyer-Ljungström locomotive.**

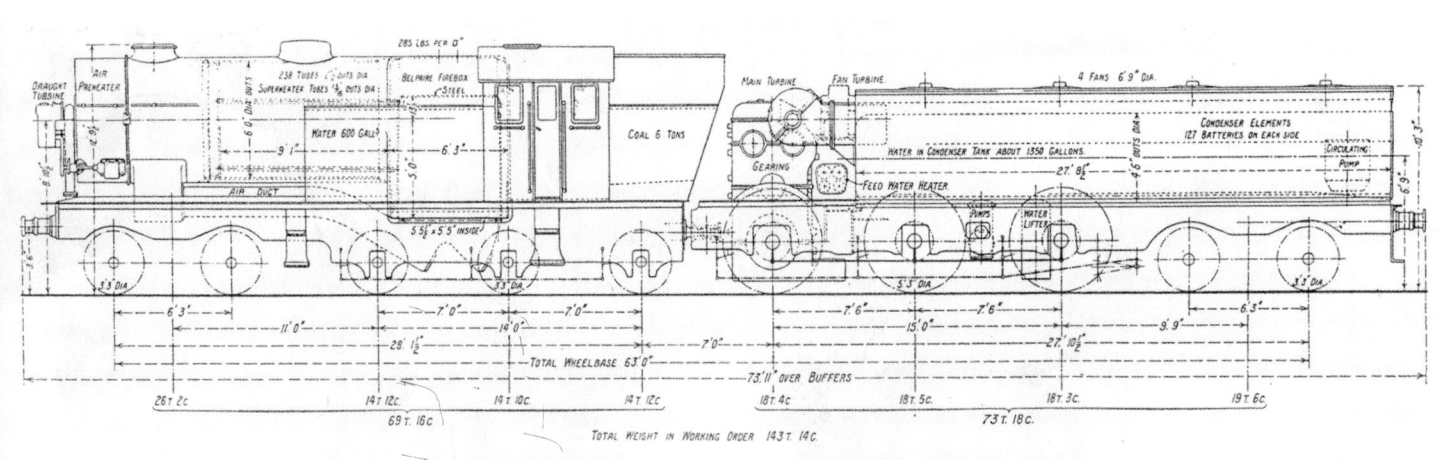

between Derby and St Pancras, although apparently only with special permission. (According to Col H. Rudgard, member of the Institution of Locomotive Engineers, No 6233 was regarded with suspicion by operating personnel and taken out of traffic at the slightest sign of trouble, whereas a more relaxed attitude was adopted with the Turbomotive a few years later.)

35

Table 3.2: Comparison between the Ljungström 2-8-0 (non-condensing) and Beyer-Ljungström (condensing) locomotives

	Ljungström 2-8-0	Beyer-Ljungström
Length (locomotive and tender) over buffers	58ft 7in	73ft 11in
Locomotive wheelbase	9ft 9in + 5ft 5in + 5ft 5in + 5ft 5in	n/a
Power tender driving wheelbase	n/a	7ft 6in + 7ft 6in
Overall wheelbase (locomotive and tender)	46ft 11in	63ft 0in
Driving wheel diameter	4ft 5in	5ft 3in
Boiler pressure	185 lb per sq in	300 lb per sq in
Steam pressure after turbine	4lb per sq in	not recorded
Heating surface	1,604sq ft	1,620sq ft
Superheater heating surface	1,076sq ft	640sq ft
Grate area	32.3sq ft	30sq ft
Steam temperature	400°C	
Turbine rating, nominal	1,370hp	2,000hp
maximum		2,000hp
Weight (locomotive and tender), empty	90 tons 1 cwt	
working	115 tons 3 cwt	143 tons 14 cwt
Adhesive weight	70 tons 17 cwt	54 tons 12 cwt
Adhesive weight as % of total working weight	61.5%	38%
Coal capacity	5 tons	6 tons
Water capacity	3,300 gallons	c2,000 gallons (side tanks and tender)
Maximum speed	37mph	75mph*

* Notional maximum; in service higher speeds were recorded

This press photograph of the TGOJ trio of non-condensing Ljungström turbine locomotives was taken in 1936. The prototype (No 71), which had been introduced in 1930, is on the right.

was evidently possible without compromising the more generous Swedish loading gauge.

The turbine was of the combined impulse and reaction type, as had been used earlier by Ljungström. With a full load and the boiler developing 17,600lb of steam per hour at a pressure of 185lb per sq in, it was estimated that a 78% efficiency factor at 23mph would be achieved, whereas on test the proven figure was 80%. It was noted that there was little diminution in available tractive effort as speed increased. Dynamometer trials showed that, when hauling 1,687 tons up a 1 in 100 gradient, a drawbar pull of 21.7 tons was recorded, whereas a three-cylinder reciprocating engine of comparable adhesive weight could only manage 16.7 tons with a similar load.

The progress achieved over the earlier Beyer-Ljungström machine was apparent in the dimensional comparison, outlined in Table 3.2.

The overall working weight and length had both been reduced by about 20%, with an improvement in the proportion of adhesive weight to the whole. The two designs were intended for quite different types of work, as apparent in the notional speed maxima, yet there was only an 10-inch difference in driving wheel diameter. This particular dimension was traditionally considered critical in determination of relative speed and haulage characteristics of reciprocating steam engines, but was no longer relevant with turbine drive; performance parameters could be varied by adjusting the reduction gearing between the turbine shaft and the driving axle.

Forming the prototype of Class 'M3t:s', No 71 (maker's No 1871) was built in 1930 by NOHAB, a manufacturing company specialising in steam (and later diesel) locomotives, turbines and aircraft. This locomotive received a modified blast-pipe and enlarged superheater in 1933, but its performance in original

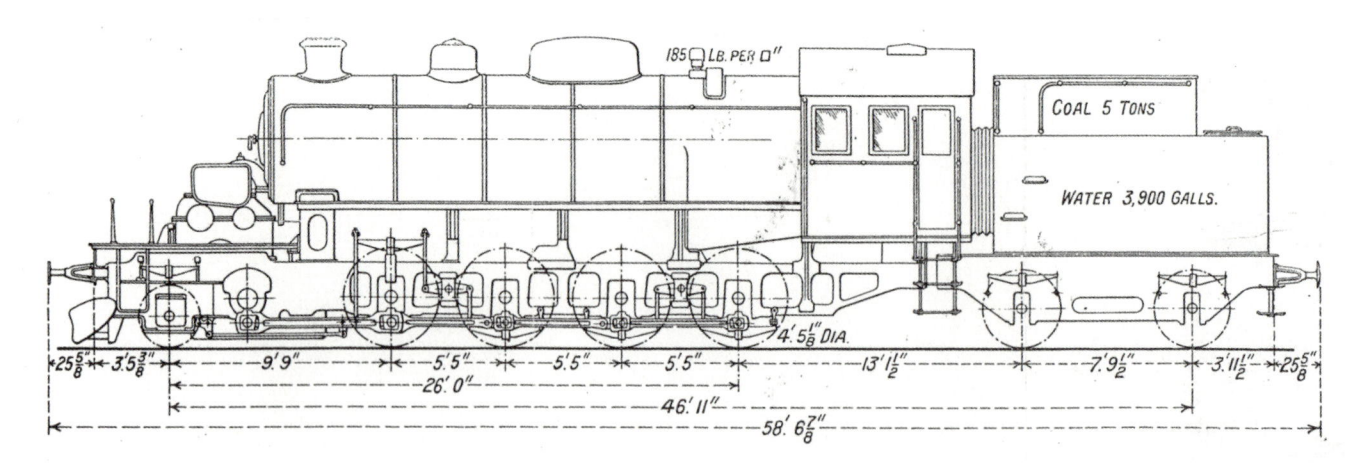

A diagram of the non-condensing Ljungström turbine locomotive.

All three Swedish turbine engines survive and are presently stored at the Grängesberg Locomotive Museum. At the time of writing (2015) efforts were being made to bring No 73 (right) back to running order. Externally the engines are almost identical with only minor differences between them – note the connecting rod on the front framing of No 72 (left), which had been removed to facilitate shunting. The high pitch of the boiler was necessary to allow for a high smokebox to clear the turbine housing, which is mounted on the front framing. This in turn required a leading pony truck to prevent overloading of the front axle. The engines were intended for sustained slow to moderate speeds and consequently stability was not a problem. The boiler and smokebox are central upon the frames; it is the lack of symmetry on either side of the front framing that affords the illusion of these being off-centre.

condition had already excited the interest of William Stanier. Nos 72 and 73 were added to the fleet in 1936 (NOHAB maker's Nos 2000 and 2001); these embraced some small modifications, which appear to have been of an internal nature. They were found capable of hauling 1,830 tons unassisted up 1 in 100 gradients with a 10% fuel saving compared with the 0-8-0s.

These locomotives hauled ore trains typically weighing around 1,700 tons over the difficult 64-mile section from Eskilstuna to Oxelösund, with conditions even more demanding during the Scandinavian winter. Significantly, eight of the 0-8-0s were three-cylindered and clearly the even torque justified the extra cost and complexity. In this vein, the similar attributes of turbine drive

Front-end detail of No 71. Physical examination revealed that there was plenty of room between the frames for a chute to have been provided from the base of the smokebox, which would have allowed ash to be cleared; in return for this minor addition the major issue of boiler pitch might have been addressed. Although not apparent from the front the driving cabs were well insulated, as well they might be to deal with the Scandinavian winter. On all three engines coal and water were carried in a simple four-wheel tender, the length of run regularly undertaken dictating that this was sufficient. All three were fired manually and there is no evidence that oil-firing had ever been resorted to.

The connection between the turbine and the coupled wheels is seen here; note also the builder's plate on the framing. All three engines are well cared for and clearly revered, for while the Grängesberg site is extensive and some of the museum stock, stored outside, is suffering from the ravages of the weather, Nos 71-73 appear to have always been kept indoors. The museum comprises probably in excess of 100 locomotives and items of rolling stock and is well worth a visit. It is open to visitors between mid- June and mid-August. (Do not confuse it with the official Swedish Railway Museum located at Gävle, approximately 168km distant.) Visit
http://mittgrangesberg.se/portfolio/lokmuseet and
http://www.bjorns-story.se/private/Lokmuseethtm/Lokmuseet_eng.htm.

would have encouraged the experiment, and on test the performance was superior to that of a three-cylinder 0-8-0. Also, maintenance costs proved moderate, largely due to the fully enclosed gearbox lubrication. Surmised performance comparisons are shown in Table 3.3.

After some modifications to rectify early problems with the gear set, No 71 ran 100,000km without interruption before general inspection and repair, at which point no wear was found in the turbine or transmission. Reliability continued to be very good with mileages and major overhaul intervals as shown in Table 3.4.

For locomotives dedicated to slow-speed haulage of very heavy trains over a comparatively short section of route, these were impressive mileages that vindicated the competence of the Ljungström system. Reportedly the only major failure occurred with No 73 when an oil pipe supplying lubrication to the main bearing burst. The bearing overheated and turbine damage was sustained, although repair costs were apparently not excessive.

Another problem arose from driver error when one of the turbines slipped on greasy rails and sand was applied before the steam supply was shut off. The turbine and gears were thus rotating at a higher speed than the driving wheels when the sand enabled the latter to regain traction on the rails, generating enormous conflicting forces that totally destroyed the coupling rods.

Overhead electric power was installed throughout the Grängesberg-Oxelösund Railway system in the early 1950s, but the precise date that the turbine trio was taken out of service has not been established. They were formally withdrawn in 1957, but had been held for a period in store as part of a strategic reserve. Happily, all three survive in preservation and at the time of writing are in the roundhouse adjacent to the yard that served the now defunct iron ore mine at Grängesberg. The custodian body is the Grängesbergbanornas Järnvägsmuseum, owner of Nos 71 and 73, while No 72 is owned by the Swedish National Railway Museum. The facility at Grängesberg is open to the public during summer weekends. All three locomotives are well maintained and obviously a source of great pride.

Summary of advantages
There were other experimental efforts to apply steam turbine technology to railway locomotives in Europe during the interwar years, but the British experience, aided by the strong Swedish influence, led to significant conclusions about the technology's potential benefits:

> **1.** Use of a condenser offered theoretical efficiencies in recycling steam exhausted from the turbine to aid draught, but any gain was offset by the resultant space and weight

Table 3.3: Summarised performance comparisons between the Ljungström 2-8-0 turbine and a three-cylinder reciprocating 0-8-0

	Ljungström turbine	Three-cylinder reciprocating 0-8-0
Mileage since shopping	22,000	3,000
Train weight	1,726 tons	1,415 tons
Overall time	3hr 26min	3hr 48min
No of stops	2	2
Total duration of stops	18min	13min
Average speed excluding stops	20.2mph	17.7mph
Work at drawbar	1,313hp	1,135hp
Water consumption	2,500 gallons	2,670 gallons
Coal consumption	3,800lb	4,340lb
Certified calorific value of coal	12,550 BTU per lb	12,400 BTU per lb
Coal consumed per 1,000 metric ton-miles	32.1lb	41.5 lb

Table 3.4: Performance reliability of the Ljungström 2-8-0s

Loco No	Introduced	Distance worked (km)	Miles (say)	Years overhauled	Years in service*	Estimated annual average mileage
71	1930	688,446.00	430,279	1937/1943/1952	23	18,708
72	1936	583,825.00	364,891	1939/1942/1952	18	20,272
73	1936	685,588.00	428,493	1939/1944/1951	18	23,805

* Precise withdrawal year is unknown; for these purposes it is assumed to have been 1954.

penalties, and by the complexity of the associated auxiliary systems. Elimination of the condenser improved viability in reduced construction and maintenance costs.

2. Advances in lubricants and lubrication systems made high-degree superheat practicable thereby improving thermal efficiency in reciprocating engines, but the risk of carbonisation of pistons and valves remained. With a turbine, high superheat was obligatory to prevent turbine blade damage and practicable because gears and bearings were enclosed in an oil bath, and not in direct contact with ultra-hot steam.

3. A major cause of inefficiency with an external-combustion engine is the inevitable energy loss between the throatplate, the hottest part of the boiler, and the cylinder, where steam is put to work. With a non-condensing turbine, steam is delivered from superheater to turbine blade by a less circuitous route.

4. It had long been recognised that slide or piston valves actuated by traditional types of valve gear, typically Stephenson's Link Motion or Walschaerts, were inherently inefficient. Valve ports must exhaust a greater volume than is admitted at the commencement of the cylinder piston stroke, and the inadequacy of the exhaust port's dimensions at this stage effectively throttled steam flow. More or less contemporaneously with turbine systems, cam-driven valve actuation had been under development. Most prominent were the Caprotti and Lentz systems, both of which used two sets of poppet valves, those for exhaust having larger ports than those for admission. These systems recognised the superiority of rotational movement over reciprocation, but the turbine exploited this benefit to greater degree, while eliminating all the intricacies of valve design.

5. Traditional valve motion required frequent maintenance and adjustment, which was usually within the competence of local shed personnel. Poppet valves required less attention but, when adjustment was necessary, a higher level of expertise was required. Totally enclosed turbines and associated reduction gear sets demanded even less routine maintenance beyond that necessary during works visits.

6. With a reciprocating engine, regardless of the method of valve actuation, the delivery of steam to the cylinder piston varies in intensity through the cycle, which in turn imparts uneven torque to the driving axle. This phenomenon is accentuated by the perpetually changing angles of cranks and connecting rods, and by the extent to which the total mass of the reciprocating parts remains unbalanced. It is possible to reduce the unbalanced element with the use of three or four cylinders, but such measures result in further complications in multiplicity of valve gears, reduced access to moving parts, and greater frame stresses. All these elements are eliminated with turbine drive.

7. As the amount of power applied to the driving axle is directly related to the volume of steam admitted, it follows that a turbine locomotive enjoys constant, steady torque throughout each rotation of the driving wheel. Freedom from the peaks and troughs in torque suffered by a reciprocating locomotive means that the risk of slipping is substantially reduced.

8. The Beyer-Ljungström locomotive had shown that small driving wheels were no barrier to high speeds. Hitherto it had been generally thought that driving wheel diameter should be correlated to each class's intended duties, e.g. 4ft 6in to 5ft – heavy freight; 5ft to 6ft 3in – mixed traffic; over 6ft 3in – express. It was not until late in the steam story that the heavy freight British Railways Class 9F 2-10-0s with 5-foot driving wheels disproved these maxims by reaching 90mph in ordinary passenger service. Nevertheless, the Beyer-Ljungström's regular achievement of this speed level with its 5ft 3in driving wheels amply demonstrated the impressive flexibility of turbine drive some thirty years earlier.

9. It followed that small driving wheels could allow installation of a boiler of greater than normal diameter without compromising speed potential. The British loading gauge could significantly constrain locomotive development, as with the space problems encountered with the first Gresley three-cylinder locomotive No 461 (LNER 2-8-0 Class 'O2'). Until an ingenious rearrangement of the valve gear was introduced, it would not have been possible to use conjugation with a larger-diameter boiler. Unfortunately, the combination of small driving wheels and maximised boiler diameter was an option that was never fully exploited in a turbine design.

10. When officialdom became aware of them, the previously mentioned high-speed exploits with the BR Class 9F 2-10-0s were firmly prohibited. One reason was the intense hammer blow imparted by the high proportion of unbalanced reciprocating mass in these two-cylinder locomotives. Hammer blow is significantly reduced in a multi-cylinder engine, but changing operating conditions and higher maintenance costs militated against this complexity. In this context, the zero-hammer blow characteristic of a turbine locomotive was inherently attractive.

Nearing the end of the climb from Shepton Mallet to Masbury summit, a BR '9F' No 92206 powers through the station on a northbound Somerset & Dorset line passenger working. The S & D line was where the class was most frequently seen on passenger trains, although infrequent examples also occurred on the WR, ER and SR. Intended primarily for freight, the type were well capable of keeping up to and even exceeding the schedules of most passenger workings provided that is the fireman did not mind 'bending his back'. In order to accommodate a wide firebox over the trailing driving wheels able to burn all grades of fuel, the boiler was pitched high which have might been expected to induce roll but any such cases were rarely reported. The class proved large diameter driving wheels were not necessary to achieve high speed, 90 mph plus on the ER, although the associated high piston speed could have been avoided if a turbine drive had been provided.

CHAPTER FOUR

Stanier at the LMS

DESPITE being large businesses by any standard, the character and reputation of the principal British railway companies was often intimately associated by employees, enthusiasts and better-informed elements of the travelling public with that of the contemporary Locomotive Superintendent or Chief Mechanical Engineer. The pre-eminence enjoyed by these officers was well demonstrated in the case of Sir Ralph Wedgwood who, as Chief Officer, led the London & North Eastern Railway with enthusiasm and enterprise through sixteen challenging years, yet his period in office is indelibly associated with the 'Gresley era'.

The prestige and command independence enjoyed by the CME could generate resentment among directors and other senior officers. The Board of the GWR once had the temerity to challenge Churchward over the construction cost of his locomotives in comparison with those of the LNWR. There was ample justification for his design policy but his famously robust rebuttal could not have been well received among the more august members of the directorate. Remuneration was another thorny topic; for example, F. W. Webb's salary rose to £3,000 per annum in 1872 after twelve months as Locomotive Superintendent of the London & North Western Railway (equivalent to more than £400,000 at 2015 values). There were other cases of conflict between CMEs and directors, but few contretemps had such impact as did certain affairs at Derby in the 1900s, the effects of which were still being felt fifty years later.

The authority enjoyed by senior officers was derived through careers as long-term employees, whose climb of the corporate ladder had imbued them with the prevailing company management culture. A notable exception occurred with the appointment in 1900 of (later Sir) Guy Granet (1867-1943) as secretary to the Railway Companies' Association. He was a barrister by profession, with superb organisational skills, a keen analytical mind, and what has been described as a Machiavellian ability to get what he wanted. In 1905 he was appointed Assistant General Manager of the Midland Railway, becoming General Manager the following year. In conjunction with his protégé Cecil Paget in the role of Chief Superintendent, he revolutionised that company's mode of operations with a view to improved efficiency and profit maximisation.

Either then or through his earlier employment, Granet became antipathetic towards the power enjoyed by the locomotive superintendent, an attitude believed to have contributed to the departure of R. M. Deeley in 1909, under contentious circumstances. One aspect concerned Granet's refusal to countenance proposals for a new generation of motive power that included eight-coupled freight locomotives and four-cylinder de Glehn compound 4-6-0s. Deeley's replacement was Henry Fowler, a man of broad interests that embraced some aspects of locomotive practice (e.g. superheating and metallurgy) but without great experience in steam design or operation. He could be described as a well-informed generalist with a congenial attitude and, significantly for Granet's needs, a malleable temperament. Certainly, rejection of Deeley's proposals marked the commencement of what came to be known as the Midland's 'small engine policy'.

During the First World War Granet held government appointments mainly focussed on management and deployment of railway activity, but did not resign as General Manager until 1918 when he was given a seat on the Midland board. With his past experience and governmental contacts, he played a critical behind-the-scenes role in the formation of the LMS, and in the manoeuvring needed to protect Midland interests within the enlarged organisation. He was appointed Deputy Chairman of the new company, then held the position of Chairman from 1924 until 1927, when he left the industry for a new career in the City of London.

Evidently reflecting his own entry into the industry and possibly aware of the damage that his partisan approach had caused, Granet opted for neutrality by ensuring that his successor would be an outsider. Sir Josiah (later Lord) Stamp came from a gifted family and was an extraordinary individual who had commenced his career as a civil servant, later becoming an industrialist, economist, statistician, writer and banker. As an accomplished polymath, his knowledge extended into many fields and he could expound at will and with authority on a remarkably wide range of complex, technical topics. With a strong sense of public duty he was regularly called to serve upon public commissions, committees and boards, and on these grounds he was an obvious candidate for command of a vast organisation with internal troubles.

However, Stamp's capacity for decisive action reputedly fell short of his intellectual gifts and academic accomplishments, preferring quiet negotiation in resolution of conflicts to determined face-to-face confrontation. The range of his interests brought him international recognition and in the 1930s he made several low-key visits to Germany in his capacity as a founder member of the Anglo-German Fellowship. These activities reflected his preference for compromise, and led to his later identification as a leading 'appeaser' of the immediate pre-war period. With dreadful irony he was killed in 1941 together with his wife and eldest son by a direct hit on his home at Shortlands, Kent, in an air raid.

Stamp had to deal with factional rivalries that stemmed from the pre-Grouping period and were exacerbated by a management structure where two officers of similar seniority supervised locomotive and rolling stock matters – Fowler as Chief Mechanical Engineer and Anderson as Chief Running Superintendent. Given the LMS's size and geographic diversity this division of responsibility was necessary and logical, but it was unfortunately complicated by the awkward relationship between these two ex-Midland Railway men.

By 1926 Anderson appears to have acknowledged the need to revise the small engine policy. There was mounting evidence that lighter, frequent passenger trains in the Midland tradition were no longer viable on routes that carried dense freight traffic. Regular recourse to double-heading was expensive and inconvenient, while small tender locomotives prevented regular through running between London and Glasgow. Further, the Gresley large engine policy was increasingly yielding operational and reputational benefits for the LNER. The need for something larger and better was needed for front-line passenger work.

Anderson borrowed a GWR 'Castle' for comparative assessment, then quite unrealistically made overtures to acquire a fleet of this type without prior reference to Fowler. This behaviour reflected serious management dysfunction, and the outcome might have been more extreme but for the latter's amiable acquiescence of this undermining of his authority. The arrival of the 4-6-0 'Royal Scots', conceived and constructed in rushed circumstances in 1926/27, relieved a motive power crisis, but it was evident that the malaise was deep-seated.

These events provided confirmation of matters amiss in motive power management but, while these were significant, their resolution formed only part of the broad range of issues facing Stamp. In his Presidential Address to the Railway Students Association at the London School of Economics in December 1927, he remarked that he was trying 'to realise some of the economies of amalgamation in an earnest endeavour to justify some of the glibly given and blithely estimated promises of politicians'.

Nevertheless, there was delay in addressing what was ostensibly the most pressing issue in the company's mechanical engineering affairs. It is hard to determine whether this was due to vacillation over uncomfortable face-to-face meetings, or simply that the appointment of a new motive power man was one of a number of high-priority matters needing attention. In the event, Fowler was not moved sideways into Research until 1929, to be replaced by E. J. Lemon. The latter was a brilliant administrator who had been mainly engaged since 1911 in carriage and wagon matters, where he had successfully transformed vehicle construction from a labour-intensive craft-based activity into a modern production line. However, Lemon's experience of locomotive design and construction was slight, and in this respect it was doubtful whether he had much more to offer than had

The principal product of the Fowler-Lemon interregnum was the 0-8-0 7F heavy freight class, introduced in 1929 and intended as an improvement on the redoubtable LNWR Bowen-Cooke 0-8-0s of Classes 'G1'/'G2'. The advantages bestowed by an improved front end, yielding better fuel consumption, were offset by sub-standard axleboxes. By the time of its introduction the concept of an inside-cylindered 0-8-0 was definitely anachronistic. No 9569 is recorded at an unknown location.

George Hughes's 2-6-0 (the 'Crab') was symbolic of the factional rivalry that plagued the LMS in the 1920s. It was designed at Horwich in the face of determined efforts by the Derby camp to have it 'Midlandised' – most prominently in the use of the Midland-type tender, which was too narrow for the cab. Five of the class became guinea-pigs for experiments with rotary cam valve gear, but there was otherwise little significant change to these engines during their long and useful careers, as apparent with BR No 42817 in the mid- 1950s. *Lens of Sutton*

'Crab' No 13124 was experimentally equipped with Lentz rotary cam valve gear in 1931. *British Railways*

Another sound class that avoided the Midland-based strictures on valve dimensions was the 'Fowler' 2-6-4T of 1927. The plans, drawn up by staff of non-MR origin, relied heavily upon the design of the South Eastern & Chatham Railway Class 'N' 2-6-0 introduced during the First World War and endorsed by the Association of Locomotive Engineers as the basis for a standard design in the event of post-war nationalisation.

The essential soundness of the Fowler-era 2-6-4T was endorsed by two taper-boiler versions introduced under Stanier. The three-cylinder variant was designed for commuter services but its greater complexity added to the construction cost. Later 2-6-4Ts reverted to the two-cylinder format with a taper boiler, as seen here with No 42641 in early BR livery at Wigan on 13 September 1950. *H. C. Casserley*

Before rebuilding, the 'Royal Scots' underwent a number of visual changes. No 6101 *Royal Scots Grey*, seen at Camden in August 1935, has received smoke deflectors but retains its original tender.

No 6399 was rebuilt in 1936 as 4-6-0 No 6170 British Legion with a Type 2 taper boiler and new cab, as seen here at Crewe Works on 19 July 1936. The LMS had carried little financial risk in the joint venture with North British to produce this experimental locomotive, as its contribution was limited to provision of chassis and tender. *H. F. Wheeller collection*

Fowler. This question soon became academic as he was promoted to Vice-President Railway Traffic, Operating and Commercial, in 1931, following the unexpected retirement through ill health of J. H. Follows.

Identification of a suitable replacement for Fowler must have been no easy task. Promotion from within the existing ranks of a team plagued with dissent would have exacerbated partisan feelings. Tradition had bred xenophobia that made the appointment of a foreigner, however technically accomplished, unlikely. Management of private firms possessed manufacturing/factory cultures but little experience of coping with geographically diverse and extensive transport undertakings. Within the 'Big Four', the Southern Railway was a much smaller operation where steam development had taken a back seat, and thus offered no obvious candidates. On basis of size and diversity, the LNER might have seemed a recruitment source, but Gresley's deputy, Edward Thompson, had an acerbic personal style that would have been incompatible with mending fences. The other possible candidate from that stable was Bulleid, whose reputation for creative, if eccentric, brilliance was by then emerging.

Just how long it took to secure the services of William Stanier is not known, but the process might have been complicated. It seems that negotiations took place in the autumn of 1931, although there is some evidence to suggest that his candidacy had been under consideration for most of that year. In the pre-Grouping era, movement of senior engineering personnel between companies for career advancement was quite common, but the market had since narrowed. Collett had succeeded Churchward on the GWR in 1921 (to the surprise of some observers), and Stanier, who was his immediate subordinate and five years younger, had already demonstrated superior leadership qualities. On the GWR he never rose above Principal Assistant, whereas Collett had been Deputy CME to Churchward. It has been speculated that Collett feared Stanier being accorded too much seniority as this could threaten his position. On the other hand Collett was a closed and complex character, and might have prevaricated over release of such an able assistant.

Whatever factors were in play, the events of 1926/27 had underlined the pressing need for change on the LMS, and the four-year hiatus before Stanier's appointment was unfortunate. Churchward had set about restocking the GWR locomotive fleet in 1902 and this task was complete with regard to basic design features and prototypical proving by 1908. With construction programmes then well under way, Churchward was providing for traffic expansion and heavier trains anticipated to develop over the next ten to fifteen years. In contrast, Stanier had to restock a larger fleet, the need for which had become overdue during the preceding eight to ten years. The delay thus added further urgency to a massive task.

The post-1927 Fowler-Lemon interregnum had produced three classes that were significant, although not all for the most positive reasons. Two new freight classes – the Class 7F 0-8-0s and the Beyer Garratts – reconfirmed the inadequacy of traditional Midland axlebox dimensions and offered no particular advancement over the antiquated yet sturdy and much respected ex-LNWR 0-8-0 fleet. On the other hand, the rebuilding of two 'Claughtons' as precursors to the 'Patriots', a smaller version of the 'Royal Scots', highlighted the need for medium power 4-6-0s. This gap was soon filled by the 'Black 5s' and with rather less panache, initially at least, by the three-cylinder 'Jubilees'.

The motive power fleet that Stanier inherited was thus largely an expression of Midland Railway practice. Significantly, all the most promising designs of the previous decade had benefited from non-Derby influence. The Beames 0-8-4T of 1924 was the final expression of the LNWR pursuit of large freight types that went back as far as the variegated 0-8-0/2-8-0 family and the 'Bill Bailey' 4-6-0s. The Hughes 2-6-0s of 1926 (the 'Crabs') were a Horwich creation that narrowly avoided being spoiled by Derby's policies. The 'Fowler' 2-6-4T inherited much from the 1917 Maunsell Class 'N' of the South Eastern & Chatham via the standardisation project sponsored by the Association of Railway Locomotive Engineers after the First World War. The 'Royal Scots' were the product of the North British Locomotive Co.

The other unusual presence was the Beyer Garratt, a classic 'could have been'. This type suffered through adherence to the MR-based undersized axlebox dimensions, but perhaps more significant was the adoption of the standard 4F 0-6-0 wheelbase – a tragic case of a potentially excellent engine ruined by being designed around the coupling rods. The 16ft 6in coupled wheelbase (that of the eight-coupled LNER Garratt was 18ft 10in) precluded the use of trailing axles, by then a standard Beyer Peacock feature that facilitated higher speeds. The 'Pacific' type was at the core of LMS large engine policy in the 1930s, and the leading dimensions of double 'Pacifics' built for service overseas (as shown in Table 4.1) graphically demonstrate how much latitude would have been available with a well-designed express Garratt for Crewe-Glasgow services.

A recurrent theme in this work concerns the demand for a new generation of motive power capable of greater speed and haulage capacity, and the failure in steam design practice to satisfy these needs. Express Garratts with their considerable reserves of power and excellent riding qualities were a neglected concept with significant unrealised potential –

Table 4.1: Leading dimensions of the LMS Garratt compared with similar locomotives built for overseas railways

Railway	Year	Wheel arrangement	Driving wheel diameter	No built	Tractive effort at 75%	Weight (tons)	Axle load (tons)	Gauge
LMS	1927	2-6-0+0-6-2	5ft 3in	33	40,250	181	21	4ft 8½in
São Paulo	1927	2-6-2+2-6-2 (later 4-6-2+2-6-4)	5ft 6in	6	47,270	191 tons	19.3	5ft 3in
Central of Aragon	1931	4-6-2+2-6-4	5ft 9in	6	40,880	155	15.75	5ft 6in
Algerian State	1932	4-6-2+2-6-4	5ft 11in	1	47,300	192	17	4ft 8½in
Algerian State	1936	4-6-2+2-6-4	5ft 11in	29	58,200	213	18.2	4ft 8½in

Evidence of change was found in Stanier's first design for the LMS with the adoption of a taper boiler. The Class 5 2-6-0 was a satisfactory interim design whose presence was soon overwhelmed by construction of large numbers of Class 5 4-6-0s. This view is an official photograph of the prototype, No 13245, taken after the removal of the GWR-style safety valve bonnet that had so displeased Stanier.

especially in the context of late large steam locomotives in North America.

Certain incidents during Stanier's early days on the LMS revealed a determination to be his own man. Usually corporate reorganisations on this scale would require importation of a supporting, trusted team, but he went alone to his new employer, and sought out the best talent from his subordinates. There seems to have been an expectation that matters would be re-conformed along GWR lines, but effort at ingratiation in that regard was wasted. His first design was the Class 5P5F 2-6-0 and he was annoyed to see the prototype adorned with a copper-capped chimney, which he ordered to be removed immediately.

On the other hand, GWR standards and attitudes were not forgotten. He made little secret of his dismay at poor workmanship in the finish of the first two 'Pacifics', based on what he would have expected at Swindon. Also, a story quickly made the rounds about an incident during a workshop visit early on in his tenure where he joined a group on a footplate that was discussing a firebox problem. Deciding to see for himself, he donned a set of borrowed overalls and entered through the firebox doorway to the amazement of those present. Apparently it was not expected that god-like CMEs should crawl around the inside of a firebox like a common fitter; obviously in Stanier the LMS had someone who was rather different.

However, he was unafraid to revise his opinions in the face of fresh evidence and in this respect an early experience with the Turbomotive project was to have wide-reaching effect on superheater policy, as will be discussed later. His open-minded attitude helped in establishing personal credibility in the eyes of his new team, and his competence as a diplomatist served him well. He evidently quickly established a harmonious working accommodation with Anderson. The latter was approaching retirement, but this did not necessarily reduce his influence as a leading advocate of Midland practice, especially in the matter of valve travel.

Another relationship that required sensitive handling concerned H. P. M. Beames, that most unlucky of senior British locomotive men in the 20th century. He had been appointed CME of the London & North Western in 1921 but was replaced twelve months later by George Hughes, following the amalgamation with the Lancashire & Yorkshire. He then became Divisional Mechanical Engineer, Western Division, and, following the Grouping, Mechanical Engineer at Crewe. Consequent upon Hughes's hounding from office, the Midland camp bypassed him in preferring Sir Henry Fowler, and he was to be disappointed again with the promotion of Ernest Lemon.

This appointment as CME had the hallmarks of the Midland camp again cynically looking after its own, and from his Crewe stronghold Beames must have regarded the machinations of the 1920s as frustrating and unedifying. He had risen through the ranks to become, briefly, CME of the LNWR – perhaps the most prestigious position in the pre-Grouping locomotive world. Now, at the age of 55 years he was promoted to Deputy CME and transferred from Crewe to Derby, the heartland of those elements whose partisan attitudes had stymied his own advancement. Even worse, his skills and experience were to be harnessed in support of a superior with little practical experience of motive power. Within a year, Lemon was promoted to Vice-President and his replacement by an individual recruited from outside the company could have proved the last straw.

On the other hand, Beames's promotion to CME would have been untenable for fear of reigniting the old pre-Grouping tensions. He retired in 1934 but Stanier seems to have won him over to the cause, which was no mean feat in the circumstances. As with Anderson, this was a case where Stanier's interpersonal skills were severely tested, but absolutely necessary in resolution of management issues prior to radical change.

Transport market background

There was a strong externally driven imperative for financial success in the restocking programme, as the company's trading environment was increasingly hostile. Excluding the turbulence of the 1926 General Strike, the previous decade had been a comparatively buoyant period although forensic analysis would have revealed worrying underlying trends. By 1931 the railway industry was in trouble, largely attributable to the effects of the Great Depression, and it would not be until 1934 that trading prospects for the LMS were to improve, as shown in Table 4.2.

Part of this contraction was the result of deflation (in contrast to the more readily understood inflation endemic in post-war economies). More insidious was the continuing erosion of premium-priced sales revenue industry-wide, as outlined in Table 4.3. Allowing for cost-of-living adjustments in the intervening period, the real monetary value of total passenger revenue by 1937 had just about recovered to 1923 levels.

The company's trend in goods traffic was equally disconcerting although, with less flexibility in freight rates, there was a closer correlation between tonnages transported, gross revenue and receipts per ton-mile:

Year	1923	1931	1932	1933	1937
Freight receipts	47.0	37.2	33.7	33.3	39.6
Tonnage (M)	163.9	126.6	117.8	116.8	140.0

Nevertheless, declining volumes meant that there was a need to reduce the size of the wagon fleet.

A prime cause for the revenue slump lay in the growing road vehicle population (see Table 4.4). The implications for the company's trading future were ominous. Since the Grouping the size of the railways' business base had remained static while the 300%-plus growth in road passenger vehicles had reflected

Table 4.2: LMS receipts, 1923-37

£ million	1923	1929	1930	1931	1932	1933	1934	1935	1936	1937
Passenger receipts	26.0	21.8	20.4	18.8	17.8	17.8	18.3	18.7	19.4	20.4
Freight receipts	47.0	43.8	40.4	37.2	33.7	33.3	35.2	35.9	37.9	39.6

Table 4.3: Industry-wide pattern of passenger revenue, 1923-1937

£ million	1923	1929	1930	1931	1932	1933	1934	1935	1936	1937
Tickets sold at full tariff	39.4	21.8	19.8	16	12.9	8.8	6.8	6.5	6.7	7.1
Excursion/weekend tickets	9.8	20.8	19.8	20.2	21.2	27.6	31	31.7	33	34.9
Workmen's tickets	3.4	3.2	3.2	3	2.9	3	3.2	3.3	3.5	3.7
Tourist	3.1	3.4	3	2.1	1.8	0.4	0.3	0.4	0.5	0.5
Other	4.4	3.9	4.5	4.5	4.1	3.5	3.3	4.1	4.4	4.9
Season tickets	10.2	8.6	8.3	8.3	8	7.8	7.9	8	8.1	8.4
Total	70.3	61.7	58.6	54.1	50.9	51.1	52.5	54	56.2	59.5

Table 4.4: Road vehicle growth, 1923-37 (figures in thousands)

	1923	1929	1930	1931	1932	1933	1934	1935	1936	1937	% growth, 1923-37
Motorcycles	430	731	724	627	600	563	517	517	508	488	13
Passenger vehicles	469	1,079	1,157	1,171	1,213	1,288	1,394	1,563	1,729	1,884	302
Goods vehicles	173	330	348	361	370	387	413	434	458	478	176

Table 4.5: Stanier's LMS locomotive fleet, 1933-41

Class	Wheel arrangement	Construction period	Number built	Built by
7P 'Princess Royal'	4-6-2	1933/35	12	Crewe
5P5F	2-6-0	1933-34	40	Crewe
5XP 'Jubilee'	4-6-0	1934-36	191	Crewe/Derby/North British
5MT	4-6-0	1935-38*	472	Crewe/Vulcan Foundry/Armstrong-Whitworth
4P (three-cylinder)	2-6-4T	1934	37	Derby
7P 'Turbomotive'	4-6-2	1935	1	Crewe and Metropolitan-Vickers
8F	2-8-0	1935-41**	194	Crewe/Vulcan Foundry/North British/Beyer Peacock
4P (two-cylinder)	2-6-4T	1935-41**	196	Derby/North British
3P	2-6-2T	1935/1937-38	139	Crewe/ Derby
6P 'Royal Scot'	4-6-0	1935	1	Crewe
7P 'Coronation'	4-6-2	1937-40*	45	Crewe

* Construction resumed in 1943
** Construction continued in 1942

considerable expansion in the total inland transport market – particularly among those travellers with the time and resources to choose how they travelled. The Depression years had held the market in check, but the faster growth in road transport from 1934 onwards reflected a superior ability to extract advantage from improving conditions.

Confronted with this dilemma, the capacity of the LMS to grow its market share and hence revenue base was limited. Preservation of profitable trading therefore dictated measures to improve return on capital assets by enhanced operating efficiencies. So far as the CME's department was concerned, this entailed factors such as replacement of time-expired or underpowered equipment, an increase in the usage levels of more modern items, and minimisation of periods out of revenue-earning service.

Stanier's achievements
The CME bore responsibility for a wide variety of mechanical engineering activities, but reinvigoration of the motive power fleet was at the core of Stanier's mission. The period until his relinquishment of direct executive responsibility in 1941 was prolific, as shown in Table 4.5. This fleet was the essence of modernity with Belpaire fireboxes and superheated, tapered boilers. Other than with the multi-cylinder locomotives, all valve motion was located outside to maximise accessibility. Given the rapid construction of so many, it was inevitable that teething troubles and broader problems should be encountered.

Stanier's first 'Pacifics', the 'Princess Royals', were notable for the number and diversity of modifications among such a small group. This was understandable as the new CME was a man in a hurry, without the time allowed to Gresley to refine not only the detail but also some critical design issues (courtesy of *Pendennis Castle*) with his own 'Pacific' family. The boilers of the 'Jubilees' proved troublesome and at one time up to fourteen variants were in use before the optimal design was worked out. This situation, at odds with the objectives of standardisation, caused Stanier considerable worry, although the general soundness of his thinking was borne out by the instant success and widespread acceptance of the two-cylinder 'Black 5'. The 3P 2-6-2T was regarded as his least successful design, having been developed from the earlier, poorly regarded Fowler-era version. Broadly comparable size-wise with the dazzling GWR Class '4575' 2-6-2T, here was an example of mediocrity requiring more thorough treatment than merely the fitting of a taper boiler.

Nevertheless, it was testimony to the quality of Stanier's overall achievements that his successors saw no need for radical change from his design and construction precepts. The only remaining gap in the fleet was filled by Ivatt's 'Mickey Mouse' 2-6-2T, a competent small 'Prairie' tank that, with its tender version and its larger 'Mogul' brother, provided overdue means of replacing the Fowler 4F 0-6-0. Stanier had acceded to requests for more of this antiquated, type, and forty-five were built between 1937 and 1941; at least they had the saving grace of being cheap to construct.

The restocking programme relied heavily upon implementation of ideas imported from Swindon, which H. A. V. Bulleid (son of O. V. S.) assessed in sixteen categories in his work *Master Builders of Steam*. H. A. V. B.'s views would have been well-informed and are valuable in coming from a neutral standpoint. His dispassionate summary of 'typical 1934 LMS comments' and ultimate fate of each category showed a balance in favour of Stanier's introductions; his succinct assessment appears in Appendix E.

The number of locomotives built to Stanier's designs during his tenure was 1,328, of which 795 were in service by the end of

Early in the 1900s the GWR had set new standards with its 2-8-0 Class '28xx', regarded by many as Britain's finest heavy freight locomotive until the arrival of the 2-10-0 BR Class 9F in 1954. Stanier continued the 'Consolidation' theme with his 8F of 1935, which he seemed to regard as a logical modernisation of the '28xx', with outside valve motion. Early in the Second World War the type was adopted as a standard for the War Department and built in large numbers by the LMS, other railway companies and commercial manufacturers. No 8413, seen here in about 1944 on the GWR at Goring, was part of a batch of eighty constructed at Swindon. This exercise proved influential in the revised design practices adopted by his old friend, F. W. Hawksworth, on the post-war GWR; it must also have been personally satisfying to Stanier to see examples of this highly successful type being produced by his old employer.

The Swindon format did not always travel as well as it had with the Class 8F 2-8-0. In 1930 the LMS had introduced a parallel-boilered 3P 2-6-2T that was a lacklustre performer, and in 1935 more of the type appeared, which were virtually the same below the running plate but with a taper boiler. If Stanier had hoped to match the brilliance of the GWR's 'Small Prairie' Class '45xx', he was to be disappointed as this was considered his least successful type. Weight was slightly down on the earlier version, but this design was still too heavy and under-boilered (or over-cylindered). No 40202 is seen on shed.

Three-cylinder 'Jubilee' Class No 5667 *Jellicoe* in the late 1930s. This locomotive had been built in February 1937 with the later domed boiler. *Lens of Sutton*

Stanier's classic – Class 5 4-6-0 No 5068 with the original domeless boiler at Kentish Town in 1936. Lens of Sutton

Progressive development with the 'Princess Royals' led to the 'Princess Coronation' or 'Duchess' Class of 'Pacifics' in 1937, a design also subject to numerous detail variations and to streamlined and non-streamlined versions. The effect of the former, which followed contemporary trends in Art Deco design, was certainly striking but apparently not much to the designer's liking. Only the first five (Nos 6220-24) appeared in the blue and silver livery displayed here on No 6229 Duchess of Hamilton at Willesden in 1938. This locomotive had appeared the previous year as class leader No 6220 Coronation; the identities were swapped so that No 6220, alias No 6229, could tour the United States in non-original maroon livery with gilt body bands. The blue livery, by then about a year old, does not appear to have worn very well and removal of the streamlined body panels to improve access to the inside motion has done nothing for the overall appearance.

No 6240 *City of Coventry* was built in 1940 in streamlined crimson and gilt livery, despite the demands of the times. This livery is still apparent in this view, thought to have been taken in 1943. Lord Stamp apparently regarded time spent on locomotive cleaning as wasted, and it must have been quite a rarity by this date. Nevertheless the image is interesting not least for the modified ladders needed to enable cleaners to reach the casing.

Table 4.6: Impact of Stanier locomotives on the LMS motive power fleet since 1931

	1923	1931	Actual reduction, 1923/31	% reduction, 1923/31	1937	Actual reduction, 1931/37	% reduction, 1931/37
Fleet total	10,289	9,797	492	4.78	7,657	2,140	27.9

1937. The impact upon the company's motive power fleet since 1931 was substantial, as seen in Table 4.6.

The exercise yielded a ratio of withdrawals to new construction of about 2.7 to 1, but efficiencies were achieved through more than just replacement of old machinery. All aspects of operating standards and methods received attention, yielding better returns at individual unit level. This is illustrated through comparison of the 'Jubilees' with the GWR 4-6-0 'Castle' Class. The three-cylinder 4-6-0s were engaged in a broad range of passenger duties (e.g. third-string power after the 'Pacifics' and 'Royal Scots' on the Western Division, but premier motive power on the Midland Division), making their work similar to that undertaken by the 'Castles'. Analysis of the two types reveals:

	'Jubilee'	'Castle'
Construction period	1934-36	1923-50
Number built	191	171
Average career annual mileage:		
Highest	64,000	c50,000 (No 4080)
Lowest	41,000	c32,000 (No 7008)

Greater annual mileages are understandably achievable with new locomotives, but it was noteworthy that twenty of the original low-superheat 'Jubilee' boilers covered between 70,000 and 77,000 miles in a single year. Even allowing a margin for error, these engines consistently achieved 15-20% higher annual mileages than their Great Western counterparts. This could have only been possible with improvements in all aspects of motive power management at works and depot level.

The comprehensive nature of Stanier's reforms was emphasised by improved utilisation of locomotive types that predated his arrival on the LMS, as exemplified by the following average annual mileages:

Class	1927-30	1936	% increase
ex-LNWR 4-6-0 'Prince of Wales'	31,830	38,210	20
4-6-0 'Royal Scot'	54,970	72,250	31
2-6-0 'Crab'	30,730	40,440	32

Here was cogent evidence of the success of Stanier's progress towards superior utilisation and thus a better investment return on capital assets. Management accounting standards among the

No 6399 *Fury* stands in the paint shop at Derby Works in September 1932. Comparison with the lower photograph on Page 49 shows that the novel features of this experimental machine were confined to the revolutionary boiler. *R. S. Carpenter*

THE LMS TURBOMOTIVE

'Big Four' were unimpressive, but the statistician in Stamp would have instantly recognised what was being achieved. Such progress validated the wisdom of poaching Stanier from the GWR, but also showed that the bar confronting any new initiative such as the Turbomotive had been raised.

Despite a few blemishes, Stanier's programme was a story of success under conditions of adversity stemming from both external and internal factors. It is intriguing therefore that a solitary experimental machine appeared in the programme, at a time when there were so many other pressing issues. (The rebuild of No 6399 *Fury* with a taper boiler can be excluded in this context as a sensible use of surplus material.) It is interesting therefore to note the decision sequence that covered the early examples of the next motive power generation.

Stanier took up his appointment on 1 January 1932, and subsequent decisions by the Locomotive Committee soon witnessed policy changes. On 27 January the 'conversion' of fifteen Claughtons to three-cylinder 'Patriots' following the process adopted for the prototypical pair was approved as an addendum to the 1932 new-build programme, although progressively fewer 'Claughton' parts were used as this project proceeded. Then in July aspects of the previously agreed 1933 new-build programme were reconsidered – specifically 'conversion' of more 'Claughtons', together with a rebuild of ten 'Prince of Wales' 4-6-0s, and construction of five of a new design of 2-8-0. The 'Claughton' programme was completed, but the other two projects were cancelled. Concurrently, Stanier's policy was initiated by approving three 7P 'Pacifics' together with forty 5P5F 2-6-0s and five 2-6-4Ts (the latter with tapered boilers and three cylinders).

These initiatives were logical modernisations of proven themes, except with regard to the 4-6-2 type, which represented new territory. The first two 'Pacifics' were completed in July and November 1933, but these milestone events were preceded by the Committee's approval of 22 February 1933 for the third (No 6202) to be built as a turbine locomotive at a cost of £13,500, compared with £8,075 each for the conventional version.

Rebuilding of ex-LNWR 'Claughton' 4-6-0s as 'Baby Scots' was a significant step in the provision of a modern, medium-power mixed-traffic locomotive that later formed a key component of Stanier's restocking programme. This remarkable photograph portrays 4-6-0 'Patriot', BR No 45516, *The Bedfordshire and Hertfordshire Regiment* departing from Southampton Docks on 16 February 1950 at the head of a troop train conveying the 1st Battalion of that regiment following 25 years' continuous service overseas. Although bearing its BR number, the locomotive is still in its pre-war LMS lined crimson livery, which appears to be in good condition. The time warp effect is increased by the LNER varnished teak coaching stock.

No 6170 *British Legion*, with its Type 2 boiler, formed the basis for a rebuilding programme of 4-6-0s with the Type 2A, which commenced in 1943, not long after Stanier had left the LMS for government service. By 1955 all seventy of the 'Royal Scots' together with eighteen 'Patriots' and two 'Jubilees' had been so treated, resulting in a particularly effective type. No 45532 *Illustrious*, seen at Euston, was one of the rebuilt 'Patriots', displaying its essential similarity with the rebuilt 'Royal Scots'. The main difference visual was found in the modern cab, whereas the 'Scots' retained their original Fowler-era design.

CHAPTER FIVE

The Turbomotive: Conception and Design

TEN years before Stanier joined the LMS, Gresley's large engine policy had initiated 'Pacifics' for the East Coast Main Line, and the non-streamlined Class 'A1'/'A3' had evolved into a competent fleet. The LNER's reputation for speed and modernity on these services was enhanced by the London-Edinburgh non-stop service, made possible with the gimmickry of the corridor tender, a measure that probably had little financial justification.

The LMS had a matching need for large express engines capable of working unassisted from London to Glasgow. The alternative of changing a 'Royal Scot'-sized engine en route was time-consuming, and would have been detrimental to optimal utilisation. High daily mileages were important to the economics of large locomotives, as was later exposed with the LNER 2-8-2 Class 'P2', whose inefficient rostering on Edinburgh-Aberdeen/Dundee workings led to long periods in steam on shed. This resulted in excessive fuel consumption that was a contributory factor to the type being considered unnecessary by Thompson, despite the prodigious loads it was hauling at this time.

In meeting the demands of through running, the importance of a wide firebox as was possible with a 'Pacific' had been long recognised. The first proposal dated from 1913 and the concept was revived by Hughes at Horwich in 1923/24. Exploratory work towards a compound 'Pacific' continued under Fowler, but was halted through the intervention of J. E. Anderson (the Motive Power Superintendent and technically subordinate to Fowler), supported by J. H. Follows, Chief General Superintendent. Anderson's conviction that a 4-6-0 would fill the need stemmed from the performance of GWR No 5000 *Launceston Castle* on loan to the LMS in 1926, and led to the 'Royal Scot' Class of the following year, conceived and constructed in a hurry. Anderson's actions have been attributed to a stubborn attachment to the ex-Midland small engine policy, but other factors supported this attitude. He was concerned that a 'Pacific' would face clearance problems (although a later survey revealed that this fear had been exaggerated), and that the cost of rebuilding turntables for larger locomotives would be prohibitive.

Despite some defects, the 'Royal Scots' in original form were generally sound engines, but they lacked the capacity to operate regularly with heavier loads between London and Glasgow. By 1931 it was widely accepted that something larger was needed, so the 'Pacific' type was high on Stanier's agenda, in addition to the need for a fleet of modern general-service machines.

Creation of a 'Pacific' by stretching a ten-wheeled design had previously proved less than ideal as witness GWR 4-6-2 No 111 *The Great Bear* which was based on the 'Star' Class, and the North Eastern 4-6-2 (LNER Class A2) that was derived from the 4-4-2 Class Z. On the other hand, Gresley largely designed his Class 'A1' from scratch, but even then this essentially satisfactory type still required refinement over succeeding years. Stanier was starting more than ten years after Gresley, and under pressure to render workable solutions quickly. This was reflected in the variety found among his first thirteen 'Pacifics', with the Turbomotive embracing the most radical differences.

Why the LMS chose to experiment with the turbine concept at the start of a major fleet renewal programme deserves consideration in view of the expense and risk. According to Stanier, the impetus came through an approach from Dr Guy of Metropolitan-Vickers, who provided information on the impressive work of the first Ljungström locomotive on the Grängesberg-Oxelösund Railway. With the approval of Sir Harold Hartley, Vice-President of the LMS, Guy and Stanier paid a visit to Sweden that led to a working cooperation between the LMS, Metropolitan-Vickers and the Swedish engineers.

Dr Guy had chosen well, as progress with the project arose in no small part from Stanier's technical background, intellect, and strategic vision. Among the GWR design practices he brought to the LMS, a few were found wanting, but he evidently had no difficulty in admitting their weaknesses, or in accepting sound counter-views from subordinates. Despite the stability and conservatism implied by his experience with the Old Company, he had a strong streak of modernism in his temperament and an enthusiasm for new technology. These traits may not have been

THE TURBOMOTIVE: CONCEPTION AND DESIGN

> LONDON MIDLAND AND SCOTTISH RAILWAY COMPANY.
>
> MECHANICAL & ELECTRICAL
> ENGINEERING COMMITTEE.
>
> Euston Station.
>
> 22nd February, 1933.
>
> Provision of Turbine Gear Driven Locomotive.
>
> Submitted memorandum (14th February 1933) from the Chief Mechanical Engineer and the Chief Operating Manager, together with covering memorandum from the Vice Presidents (Sir Harold Hartley and Mr. Lemon) recommending that one of the three four-cylinder 4-6-2 class locomotives, authorised by Mechanical & Electrical Engineering Committee Minute No.142 and Traffic Committee Minute No.3221 of the 27th July, 1932, be built as a geared turbine locomotive, in order that comparative trials may be made between this type of driving mechanism and the ordinary reciprocating gear.
>
> Turbine locomotives with condensers had been tried on the L.M.S. system on two previous occasions but had proved unreliable in service, but the locomotive it was proposed to construct would have a non-condensing turbine, developed by the Ljungstrom Company, the arrangement consisting of a main turbine driving the coupled wheels through totally enclosed gears running in oil, and the exhaust led up the chimney, an outline of the locomotive being shewn on diagram E.U.149 submitted.
>
> Messrs. Metropolitan-Vickers who have taken up the rights of manufacture in this country of the Ljungstrom turbine drive for locomotives were satisfied as to its commercial possibilities and were prepared to supply the turbine and gearing, including quill drive, for £6,000.
>
> The estimated cost of the new standard 4-6-2 engine without tender was £8,075, and the cost of the same engine fitted with a turbine and gearing, after making allowance for not having to provide cylinders, motion and other standard parts, would be approximately £13,500.
>
> The submission of the proposal had the approval of the Executive Committee, who were of the opinion that it was desirable to investigate this new type of locomotive even if it did not hold out immediate possibilities of financial savings, and whilst the increased cost of interest would be £270 per annum, it was anticipated there would be a saving of at least £150 per annum in coal consumption, with additional improvement in performance.
>
> The Chairman stated that the proposal had been recommended to the Board by the Traffic Committee, subject to reference to the Mechanical & Electrical Engineering Committee
>
> Approved.

The Executive Authority dated 22 February 1933 for construction of the Turbomotive.

Below: A preliminary drawing of the planned steam turbine locomotive prepared at Euston in 1932/33. There are several prominent differences from the locomotive that eventuated, specifically a two-stage reduction drive, final drive apparently external to the gear case, and single chimney. The arrangement for reverse drive does not seem to have been worked out. The tender appears to be as for No 9002, intended for the third 'Pacific' but actually coupled to the 'Royal Scot' 4-6-0 for its American tour.

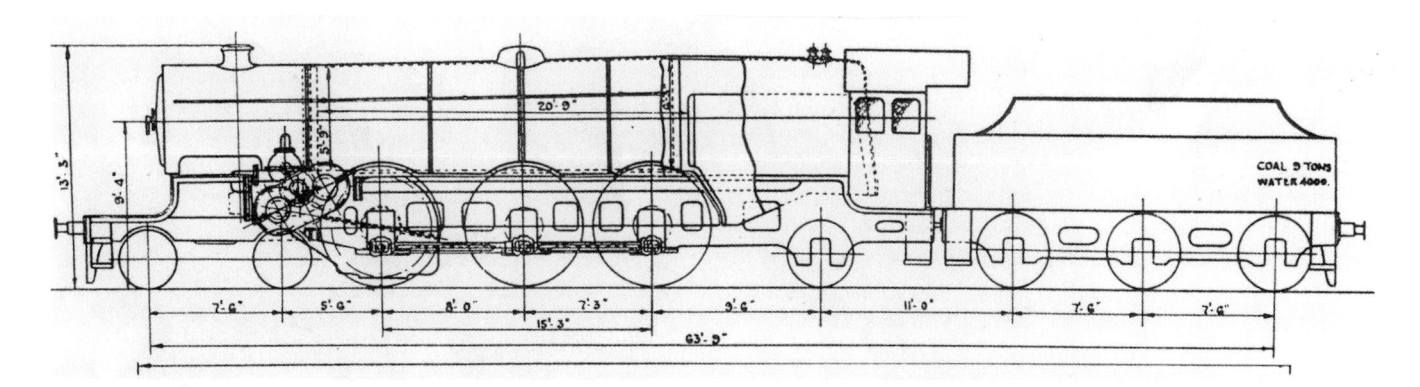

immediately apparent in 1932, but they were certainly recognised during the Second World War. Leaving railway service in 1942, he became a Scientific Advisor to the Government, was later engaged in jet aircraft development, and won the ultimate accolade of election as a Fellow of the Royal Society.

From his experience with *The Great Bear* at Swindon he was familiar with the challenges of producing an effective 'Pacific'. Apart from its design deficiencies, this engine had been confined in operational scope, highlighting constraints that a jump in size invoked – axle loadings, bridge capacity, loading gauge clearances, and turntable length. On the LMS the new 'Pacifics' might meet immediate traffic demands but, should still more powerful machines be needed in the future, a solution using alternative technology might be necessary.

One option was to investigate whether compounding could extract greater power from an existing type. Stanier had relevant experience from the GWR's three French-built 'Atlantics', and from his collaboration in 1926 with F. W. Hawksworth, Chief Draughtsman, in designing a compound 'Castle'. This seems to have been an attempt to circumvent constraints (principally bridge loadings) then thought to prohibit a locomotive larger than the standard 'Castle'. C. B. Collett, who had little design experience and was definitely no innovator, summarily vetoed the idea, but the underlying point remained that infrastructural constraints might enforce radical solutions.

The LMS was already engaged with a compound experiment of more complex form than had been considered for the 'Castle'. In 1930 the North British Locomotive Co had delivered No 6399 *Fury*, which combined a 'Royal Scot' chassis, wheelbase, bogie, cab and tender with a complex ultra-high-pressure boiler and compound expansion. The boiler was of German origin known as the Schmidt-Henschel design, and was sponsored in Britain by the Superheater Company. Firebox water tubes used distilled water in a closed circuit to generate steam at 1,400lb per sq in, whose heat in turn generated steam in a second circuit at 900lb per sq in, which supplied a single high-pressure inside cylinder. Exhaust steam was mixed with steam from a third circuit at 250lb per sq in to supply two outside lower-pressure cylinders.

The agreement with the Superheater Company was in the nature of a joint venture whose terms were heavily weighted in favour of the LMS. The railway company provided (and retained ownership of) a set of standard 'Royal Scot' mechanical components while the Superheater Company bore the cost of the boiler and directly related parts. The LMS agreed to share in the cost of the boiler up to a specified limit, but subject first to the locomotive proving satisfactory under normal service conditions. No 6399 was a troublesome machine that never undertook revenue-earning duties, but spasmodic test runs continued under Stanier's tenure until 1934, when he finally ordered abandonment of the project. The company's modest financial commitment is possibly the reason why experimental work was allowed to continue for so long.

Contemporary investigations elsewhere with ultra-high-pressure boilers also failed to achieve lasting benefits. Gresley introduced his 4-6-4 No 10000 in 1929, which employed a 450lb per sq in water-tube boiler based on marine engineering practice and manufactured by Yarrow & Co on the River Clyde. The intention had been to create a locomotive similar to the Class 'A1' 4-6-2 in terms of power but with reduced fuel consumption. An extended programme of modifications and trials together with haulage of service trains failed to sustain the hoped-for results. Also, continued refinement of the 'A1s' had resulted in improved performance that eroded the comparative advantages sought through the novel boiler; No 10000 was converted to a conventional, streamlined 4-6-4 in 1937. Attempts to produce ultra-high-pressure steam locomotives in other countries also failed to prove viable.

No 6399 was Stanier's last direct encounter with compound steam, although therein possibly lay a missed opportunity. There is a risk where innovation introduces several ideas concurrently that the benefits of one that works well might be negated or camouflaged by the malign impact of others that do not. Stanier, unsurprisingly given his background, was lukewarm about the original 'Royal Scot' boiler, but use of one on No 6399's chassis would have allowed comparative assessment of a 'normal' compound against the standard product. Perhaps he had already decided on the type 2 boiler for the reincarnated No 6399/ 6170 that led to the type 2A version used in rebuilding the 'Royal Scots', 'Patriots' and 'Jubilees'. Also, compounding was indelibly identified with the Midland cause, while elements at Crewe could recall the antics of William Webb's engines. It might simply have been prudent to call time on further essays into that field.

Financially, the risk with No 6399 had been minimised, doubtless satisfying Stamp's economic acuity, but technically the project had led nowhere. This failure highlighted the positive aspects of the Beyer-Ljungström turbine engine (No 6233). For all its complexity, cost and shortcomings, No 6233 had successfully worked ordinary trains of varying weights over different routes.

Ljungström's elimination of the condenser and associated utilities engendered crucial simplification, allowing adaptation of a standard chassis. This enabled repetition of the cautious approach adopted with *Fury* in using components that could be conveniently recycled into a reciprocating locomotive if need be. Use of a 'Princess Royal' base also facilitated objective comparison with the conventional version. Further, express locomotives spent their working hours close to their capacity limitations, thereby assisting assessment of the turbine drive's potential. However, the Turbomotive differed from *Fury* in one key respect, as the project risk rested with solely the LMS.

The first two 'Princess Royals' (Nos 6200 and 6201) were completed on 27 June and 3 November 1933 respectively, but the Turbomotive (No 6202) was not ready until 29 June 1935, two days before completion of the first 'production series' 'Princess Royal', No 6203 *Princess Margaret Rose*. Considering the host of issues that had to be tackled on other fronts, creation of a revolutionary prototype so quickly was an achievement comparable with delivery of 4-6-0 No 6100 *Royal Scot* by North British against a tight schedule in 1927.

The importance of the 'Princess Royal' project was evident in the shortage of large locomotives. Comparison of those in the 7 and 8 power classifications (as applied by British Railways in 1948) with the LNER fleet tells its own story. At the time of Stanier's appointment, the LMS had none, and at nationalisation there were only fifty locomotives rated 8P and fifty-four rated 7P. The LNER's large engine policy had yielded seventy-six (8P and 7P) by 1931, and 140 by nationalisation. Another sixty-three appeared to LNER designs under BR auspices whereas the LMS camp saw only one further 8P locomotive and thirty-seven more in the 7P category – all the latter through rebuilding. Comparative details appear in Appendix C.

Facing the dual demands for large locomotives and comprehensive fleet modernisation, experimentation with turbine drive might have seemed an unjustified digression from Stamp's objectives. Longer-term considerations apparently formed part of the equation as diesel power for rail was still in its infancy and then incapable of cost-benefit justification. It was significant that the decision to proceed was taken so early in Stanier's regime, well before delivery of the first two 'Pacific's and revelation of their initial shortcomings. The project suggested planning for a new

THE TURBOMOTIVE: CONCEPTION AND DESIGN

The initial order for Stanier 'Pacifics' was for three locomotives, two reciprocating and one non-condensing steam turbine. The first of the trio was No 6200, seen here in as-built condition. This locomotive was completed on 9 June 1933, whereas manufacture of the unique components for Turbomotive No 6202 meant that the latter was not completed until 29 June 1935.

Construction of No 6202 was documented in writing and photographically, and a comprehensive account appeared in The Railway Gazette for 29 June 1935, timed to coincide with completion of the locomotive. This and the following photographs depict various phases of the construction, commencing with this view (artistically framed by the shell of No 6202's cab) of the boiler prior to mounting on the chassis.

The chassis nearing completion with the steam valves and control rodding fitted.

The leading driving wheels being in place indicates that the gear train has been installed. The left-hand (forward) set of steam valves is receiving attention.

This is the left-hand side of the chassis, apparently slightly later than the previous view as the cab had been aligned with the running plate.

generation of steam power capable of meeting more challenging performance criteria.

Cumulative experience thus far had isolated a number of established and prospective advantages that a non-condensing steam turbine locomotive might deliver, summarised in the chart on the following page.

Construction costs

The Engine History Cards for the 'Princess Royal' series record the locomotives' costs as follows:

Locomotive Nos	Engine cost (£)	Tender cost (£)
6200	12,657	2,006
6201	11,675	1,691
6202	20,383	2,065
6203-12	8,538	1,154

These figures emphasise how absence of scale economies militated against the cost-effectiveness of a prototype or a single locomotive. Each of the production series was produced at a cost 67% of that incurred with No 6202. In that context, the Turbomotive's £7,726 premium over No 6200 was hardly excessive. Further, had the turbine design been multiplied, the unit cost of

Non-condensing Steam Turbine Locomotive Cascade Chart of Benefits

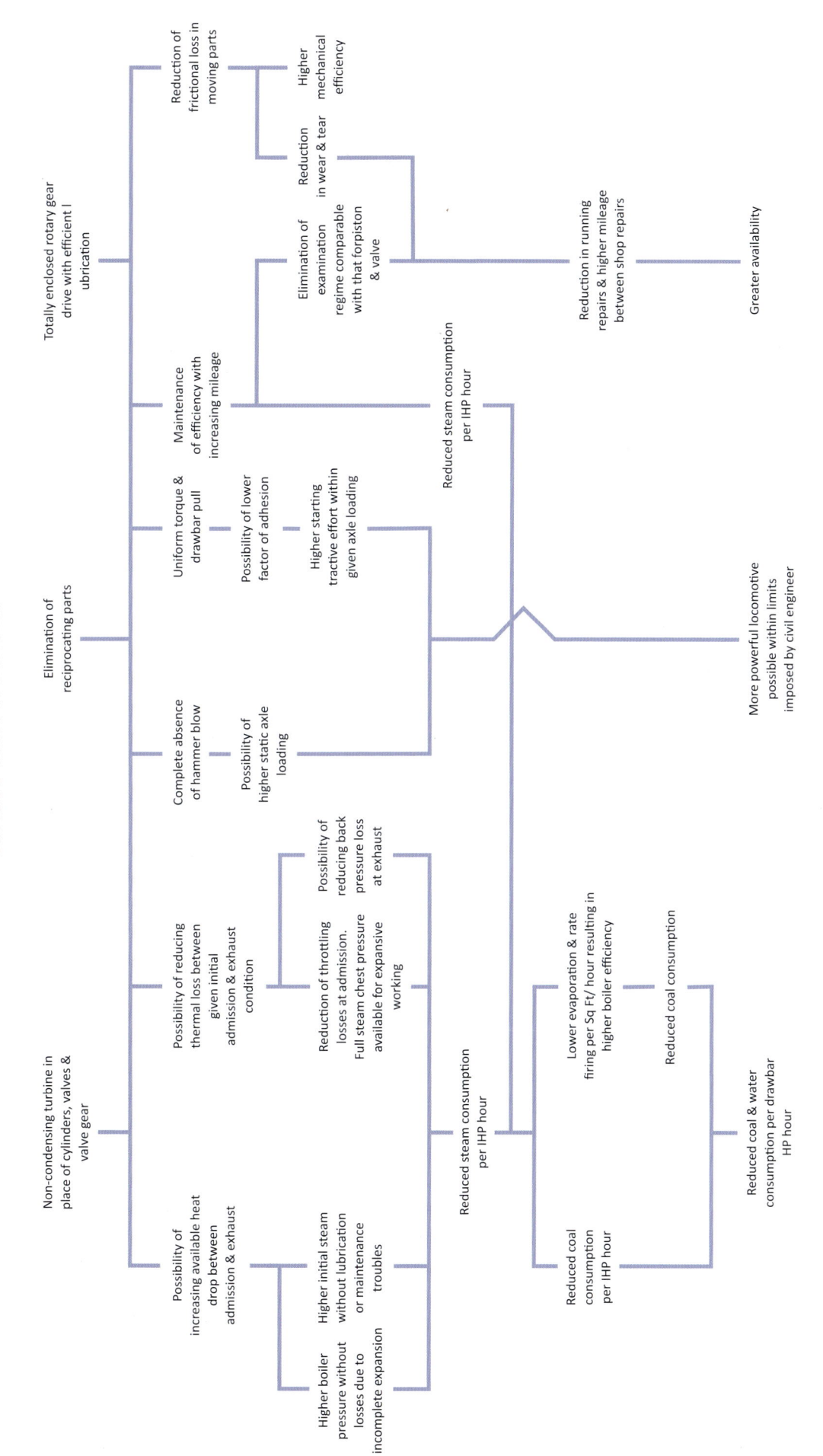

- Non-condensing turbine in place of cylinders, valves & valve gear
  - Possibility of increasing available heat drop between admission & exhaust
    - Higher boiler pressure without losses due to incomplete expansion
    - Higher initial steam without lubrication or maintenance troubles
  - Possibility of reducing thermal loss between given initial admission & exhaust condition
    - Reduction of throttling losses at admission. Full steam chest pressure available for expansive working
    - Possibility of reducing back pressure loss at exhaust
  - Complete absence of hammer blow
    - Possibility of higher static axle loading
  - Elimination of reciprocating parts
    - Uniform torque & drawbar pull
      - Possibility of lower factor of adhesion
      - Higher starting tractive effort within given axle loading
  - Totally enclosed rotary gear drive with efficient lubrication
    - Reduction of frictional loss in moving parts
      - Higher mechanical efficiency
    - Reduction in wear & tear
    - Maintenance of efficiency with increasing mileage
    - Elimination of examination regime comparable with that for piston & valve
      - Reduction in running repairs & higher mileage between shop repairs
        - Greater availability

- Reduced steam consumption per IHP hour
- Lower evaporation & rate firing per Sq Ft / hour resulting in higher boiler efficiency
- Reduced coal consumption
- Reduced coal consumption per IHP hour
- Reduced coal & water consumption per drawbar HP hour
- More powerful locomotive possible within limits imposed by civil engineer

A close-up view of the left-hand steam valves and piping leading to the forward turbine.

later examples would have reduced. Another measure concerns the Beyer-Ljungström turbine locomotive, which had cost £37,000 to build. That machine and No 6202 undertook similar types of work, and performance levels were very broadly comparable. No 6202's lower cost and greater mechanical simplicity demonstrated the progress achieved through elimination of the condenser and auxiliary systems.

Aesthetically, the Turbomotive's outward appearance was an improvement on the Beyer-Ljungström, looking much as would be expected of an express engine. The novel elements related to the transmission system with bulbous casings below the running plate and over the bogie on either side that housed the two turbines. The control mechanism was enclosed within two further casings set longitudinally on the running plate with the leading face of both located just rearward of the smokebox front. That on the left extended back to the cab while on the right it went only as far back as the rear of the smokebox. In 1939 the right-hand casing was extended back to just forward of the centre splasher. With a

The view from above, awaiting final painting.

Boiler in process of being lowered onto the frames.

The almost complete locomotive is seen in the paint shop; a section of the left-hand control casing over the forward steam valves has yet to be fitted.

The completed locomotive awaits final painting.

normal engine, these fittings would have greatly impeded access between the frames, but this need was now redundant.

Other distinctive external features were the grid set between the frames above the front running plate and the absence of cylinders and valve motion. The result was a well-proportioned and handsome locomotive, recalling the adage 'if it looks right, then it is right'.

The boiler
Three boilers (Nos 6048-6050) were constructed for use with the initial trio of 'Pacifics'. In accordance with contemporary policy that Stanier had brought from the GWR, all three were domeless and Nos 6048/49 had low-degree superheat as at the time the case for anything higher was unresolved. The logic behind the GWR's stance was that its engines, using good-quality Welsh coal, performed satisfactorily with low-degree superheat, thus reducing fuel wastage through discharge of unutilised energy up the chimney. This argument had force, especially with locomotives that might exert maximum effort only for limited periods, and there were situations where superheating in any form wasted fuel. For example, shunting duties typically included frequent intervals either coasting or stationary, when the boiler could recover without detriment to overall performance. The other key point was that higher temperatures meant drier steam and a need for more efficient lubrication.

With turbine drive, high-degree superheat was obligatory rather than discretionary as dry steam reduced the risk of condensate damaging the turbine blades. Further, the issue of lubricating oil in direct contact with steam, which could be so problematic with reciprocating locomotives, did not arise as the bearing surfaces were remote from the steam flow. Thus boiler No 6050, intended for the Turbomotive, had a significantly larger superheater surface than the preceding pair, but it lay idle for almost two years waiting for Metropolitan-Vickers to complete the manufacture of the turbine and gear train.

Stanier was disappointed with the initial performances of the conventional 'Pacifics', so he experimentally fitted boiler No 6050 to locomotive No 6200, with spectacular results. This was a turning point in his thinking, to which he made reference following the presentation of R. C. Bond's paper on the Turbomotive to the Institution of Locomotive Engineers on 30 January 1948. The minutes of the subsequent discussion noted that, 'He thought that at this stage he ought to confess that, having been brought up as a Great Western man, he thought, with his limited experience, that the Great Western were right and everyone else was wrong, and that a two-row superheater was all that was necessary for a locomotive. He soon had grounds, however, for altering his opinion.'

He continued that investigation had shown the large tubes of the Schmidt-type superheater to be inefficient in heat transmission, but that the 1-inch-diameter tubes to which he had been accustomed did this particular job better. The solution had therefore been to move from a two-row to a four-row superheater. Stanier's tone was self-deprecating, as 'limited experience' was hardly a term to be associated with his professional standing. The minutes noted that he concluded by stating: 'He had therefore learned a good deal from the work which was done on the LMS with regard to Superheaters.'

This episode highlighted the incidental benefits that can stem from experiments and had widespread repercussions.

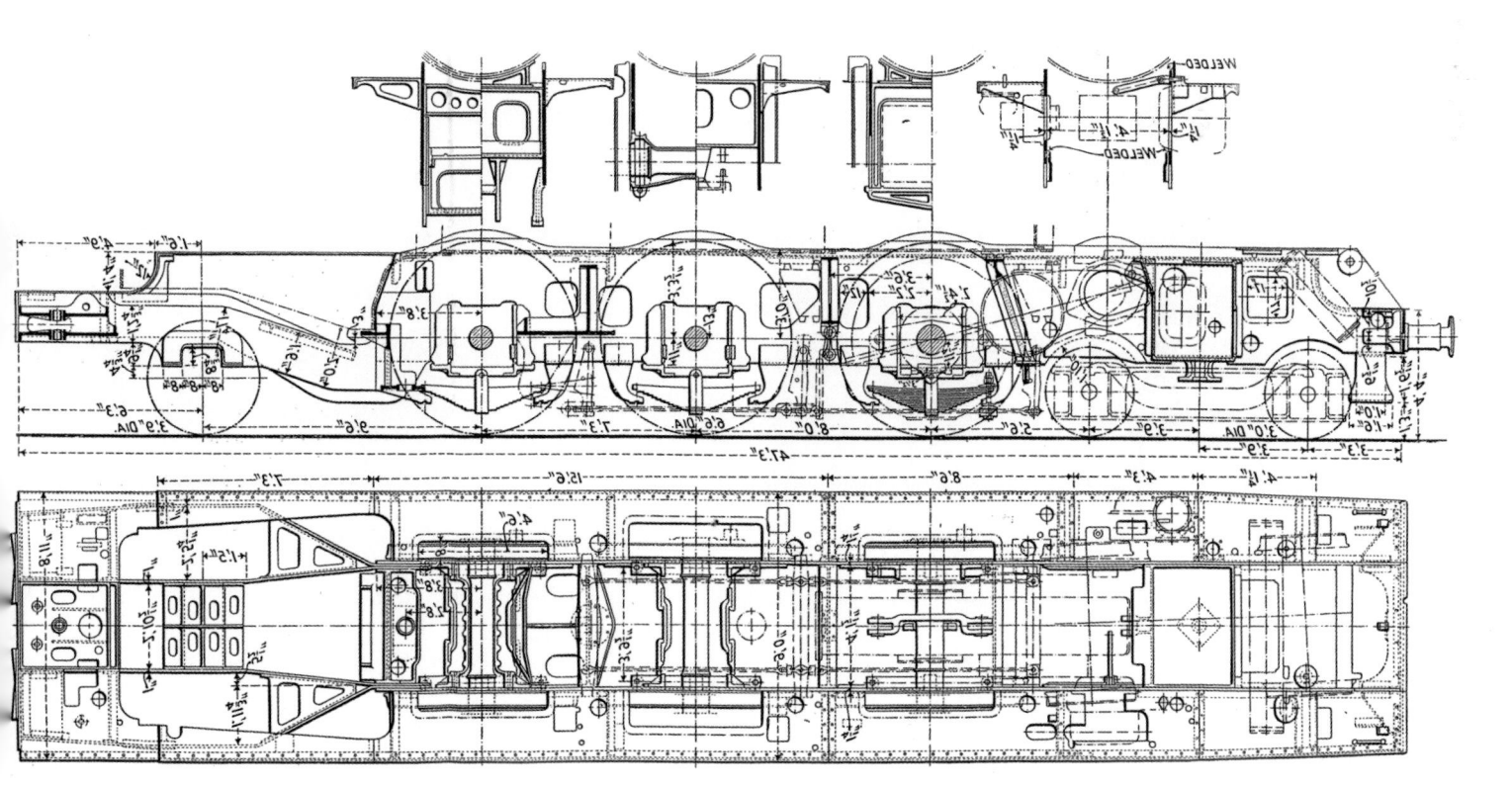

Front, side and plan drawings of the frames.

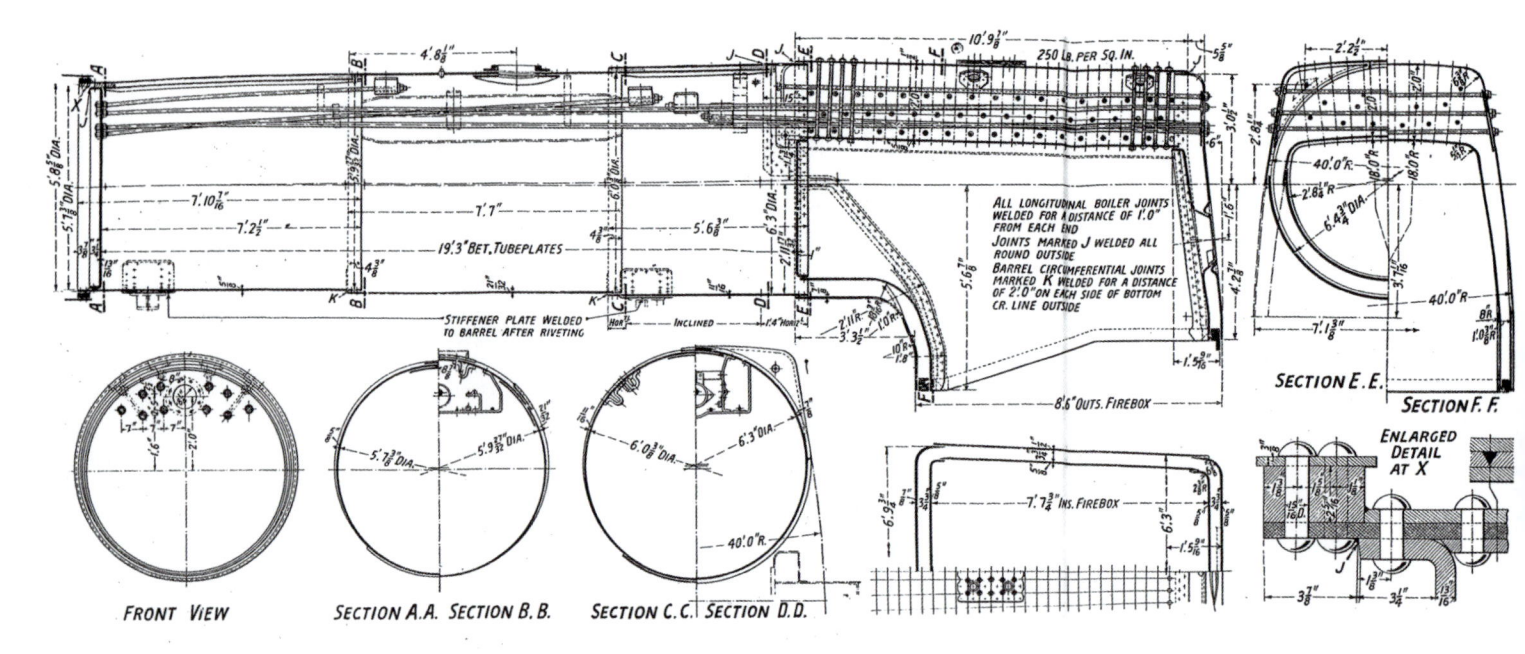

Side drawing of the original, domeless boiler

Boiler No 6050 went into the general boiler pool for the 'Princess Royals' and was never used with the Turbomotive. Design changes were made to the boilers built for the production series (Nos 6203 to 6212), and for No 6202 itself. In due course Stanier relayed his findings to his old boss at Swindon, but not for the first time Collett dismissed his progressive views. Nevertheless, these ideas found more fertile ground with Hawksworth, who applied them successfully after the war when poor-quality fuel was a serious problem.

It seems that the decision to use boiler No 6050 was taken some time before May 1935. At the time of the switch, No 6202 was not far from completion and boilers Nos 9100 to 9109 were being built for the production series 'Princess Royals' (Nos 6203 to 6212). These boilers were domeless like the original trio, but differed in having combustion chambers. The barrel tapered from a diameter of 6ft 3in at the throatplate to 5ft 8 5/8in at the smokebox tubeplate. The combustion chamber increased the firebox heating surface but necessitated reduction of the distance between the tubeplates to 19ft 3in from the 20ft 9in of the original boilers fitted to Nos 6200/01. The decision having been taken to install roller bearings on all axles, there was concern about overall weight, so reduction was sought by using 2% nickel steel for the barrel and firebox wrapper plating in boiler No 9100, which had been earmarked for the Turbomotive.

This boiler stayed with the Turbomotive until July 1936, when it was replaced by No 9236. The latter also had a combustion chamber and 2% nickel steel plating, but was constructed by seal welding, rather than the riveted assembly used previously. Like the first boiler it had a double blast-pipe and chimney, but was unique in being built new with a dome. (Domeless boiler No 9235 was constructed concurrently as a spare for the reciprocating engines.) A feature of the 'Princess Royal' Class was the variety of boilers used and their subsequent rotation, which led to changes in heating surfaces through differing tube and superheater dimensions. Externally the varieties were domeless and domed, with or without combustion chamber. Boilers Nos 6048/49 received domes in 1935-36, while Nos 9100-09 and 9235 were so treated between 1952 and 1956. It was important that locomotive No 6202 should always carry a boiler with the optimal level of superheat needed for turbine drive. After July 1936 the only boiler used by the Turbomotive was No 9236 and, without a suitable spare available, repairs necessitated longer periods out of service.

The key differences in the dimensions of the boilers fitted initially to the first three 'Pacifics' are shown in Table 5.1. Boiler No 9236 was twice used with reciprocating engines while the Turbomotive was out of service. The Engine History Card for No 6210 *Lady Patricia* shows it fitted to that locomotive during a Heavy General repair (4.9.43 to 21.10.43), and that it was replaced

Table 5.1: Boiler dimensions of the first three 'Pacifics'

Boiler No(s)	Tubes (2.25in)	Superheater	Heating surface – tubes (sq ft)	Heating surface – superheater (sq ft)	Heating surface – grate (sq ft)	First fitted to loco No
6048/49	170	16-element 11 swg	2,523	170	190	6200/01 from new
6050	110	32-element 11 swg	2,240	623	190	6200 from 9.5.1935
9100	112	32-element 13 swg	2,097	653	217	6202 from new
9236	81	40-element 11 swg	1,951	577	217	6202 from 22.7.1936

Front, side and plan drawings of the smokebox.

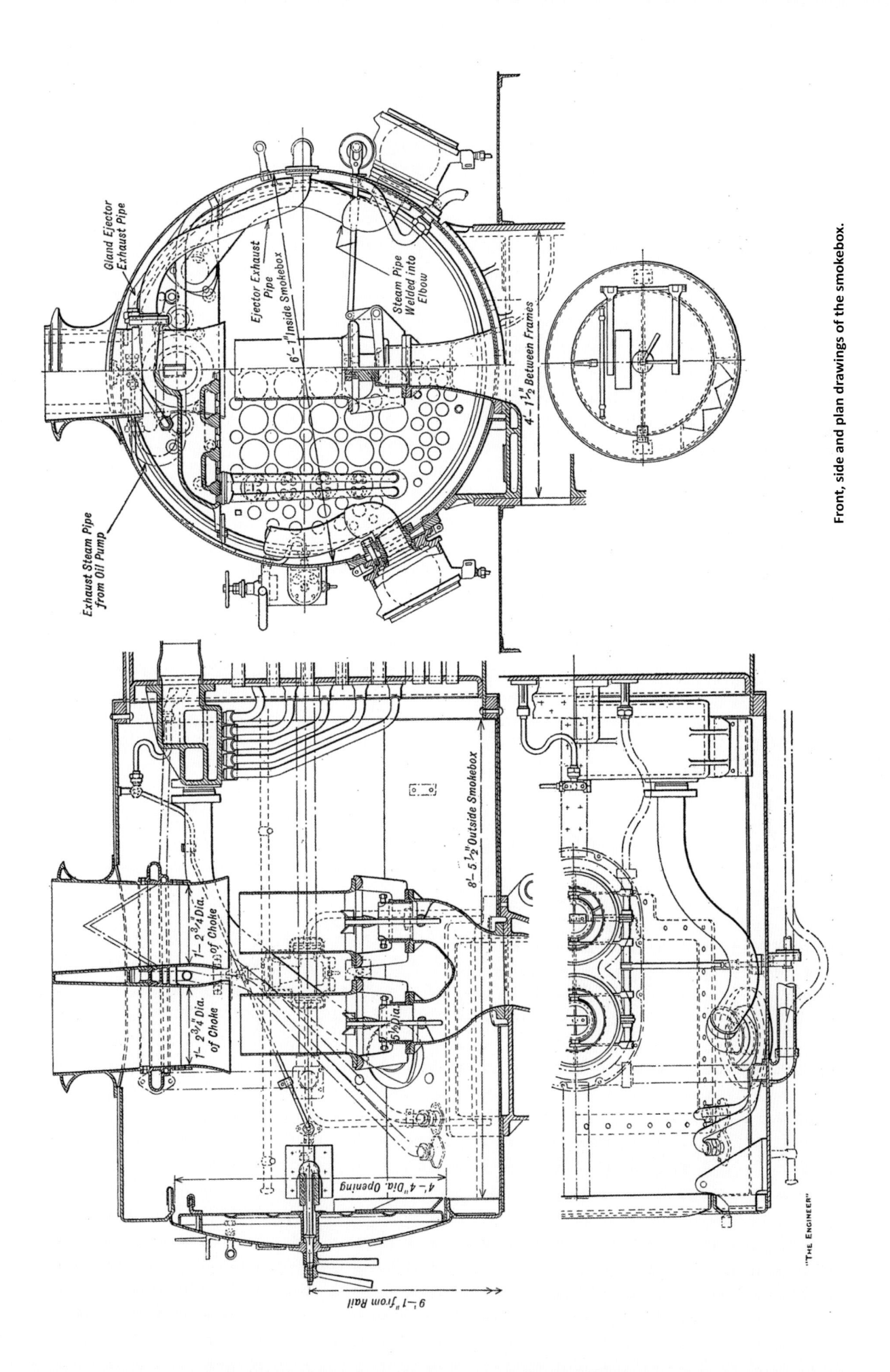

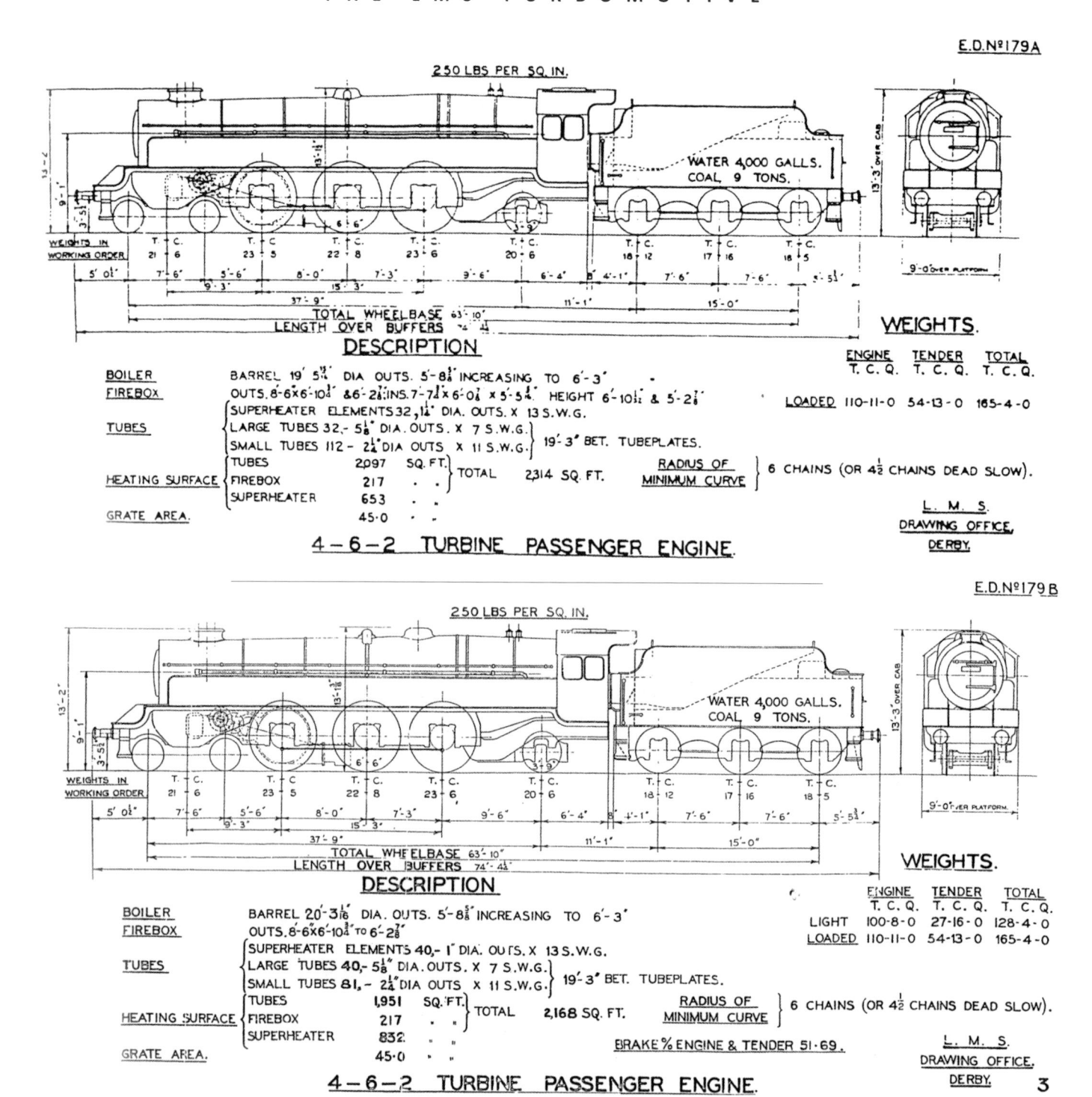

Weight diagrams for the locomotive as built with the domeless boiler, and following the fitting of the second domed boiler (No 9236) in July 1936.

on No 6210 by boiler No 9106 during a Light Service repair (15.8.44 to 9.9.44). The boiler was then restored to the Turbomotive, which returned to service on 22 September 1944 after its 402-day Heavy General. It would seem therefore that as a temporary arrangement No 6210 ran with a double chimney between October 1943 and August 1944.

Following the Turbomotive's withdrawal for rebuilding on 6 May 1950, boiler No 9236 appears to have been placed in the 'Princess Royal' pool. It re-entered service on 13 September 1950 with No 46204 *Princess Louise*, following that locomotive's Heavy Intermediate repair. No 46204 underwent a Heavy General repair between 28 February and 26 June 1952, during which boiler No 6048 was fitted in replacement. No 46202 *Princess Anne* entered service on 15 August 1952 carrying boiler No 9236.

Except for the surmised temporary use with No 6210 and the experimental short-term modification of boiler No 6049 while in low-superheat condition with No 6201 *Princess Elizabeth*, there was no apparent circumstance in which a 'Princess Royal' should

Table 5.2: Key dimensions of the two boilers carried by the Turbomotive

Boiler No:	9100	9236: as built	from 1938 §	from 1946 *	from 1952 §
Tubes	112 x 2.25"	81 x 2.25"	81 x 2.25"	81 x 2.25"	101 x 2.25"
Superheater (sq ft)	32 element	40 element	40 element	40 element	40 element
	13 swg	11 swg	11 swg	11 swg	9 swg
Tubes sq ft)	2097	1951	1951	1951	2232
Superheater (sq ft)	653	577	832	540	720

§ Trifurcated s/ heater elements   * Modified s/ heater elements   Firebox heating surface - 217 sq ft throughout

carry a double chimney. The sequence of events after 6 May 1950 therefore suggests that boiler No 9236 was converted to a single blast-pipe and chimney between then and September 1950. There seems to have been no particular reason why No 46202 *Princess Anne* should carry boiler No 9236, unless to explore the new design's potential, making use of the high superheat. Although No 46202 was officially withdrawn in May 1954 as a consequence of the Harrow disaster, the boiler was repaired and returned to the 'Princess Royal' pool. It saw further service with No 46212 *Duchess of Kent* (25.2.1954-1.9.1958), and with No 46208 *Princess Helena Victoria* from 13 January 1960 until that locomotive was withdrawn on 20 October 1962.

The key dimensions of the two boilers carried by the Turbomotive are shown in Table 5.2.

Steam feed

While the leading firebox and boiler dimensions conformed with prevailing practice for the 'Princess Royals', other than regarding superheat, there were ancillary features unique to No 6202. Deriving directly from established turbine practice, advantage was sought in the installation of feedwater heating. Partially expanded steam was bled from the forward turbine and passed through a transversely located tubular feedwater heater, placed immediately behind the oil cooler (described below). The feedwater heater worked in series with the Davis & Metcalfe (Type 12) exhaust steam injector, located in its normal position on the fireman's side. This injector could supply water up to 3,600 gallons per hour at a temperature of 60°F, and operate with an exhaust steam pressure as low as 1lb per sq in above atmosphere. It could supply water against a pressure of 40lb per sq in above the boiler's normal operating maximum, which provided an ample margin to overcome the additional frictional resistance incurred in the passage of the feedwater heater.

Water from the exhaust steam injector was delivered direct to the boiler at a temperature of 190-200°F; inclusion of the feedwater heater increased the temperature to 275°F, and this was calculated to render a 3-4% reduction in fuel consumption.

Steam passed from a conventional superheater header through a strainer mounted on the outside of the smokebox to a steam chest placed immediately above the turbine spindle between the frames. The turbines were fed direct from the steam chest, emission from which was through valves whose operation was hand-controlled in the cab. Thus the number of valves open determined the speed of the turbine – the valves were opened progressively as the locomotive started and gathered speed.

There was one flexible pipe for each valve and steam entered at the high-pressure end of the turbine cylinder. There were six nozzles to each of these pipes to ensure constant and balanced delivery of steam.

Double blast-pipe and chimney

By the 1930s it had been established that in a reciprocating locomotive the character of the exhaust had no significant effect on the production of draught. Further, use of long-travel valves, improved design of steam ports and passages, and better-proportioned blast-pipes had greatly improved steaming efficiency through elimination of throttling and minimisation of exhaust backpressure. Weight of steam discharged, and its velocity, had proven to be key, and these factors were more easily satisfied in the Turbomotive given the simplicity of its steam circuit as compared with a conventional engine.

Nevertheless, while recognising the advantages of a generously proportioned blast-pipe area, the LMS had no prior experience in the design of double-exhaust arrangements, nor was there any relevant experience to be drawn from previous turbine experiments. Despite the non-pulsating nature of the exhaust, it was deemed wise to install a mechanism to allow for adjustment of the blast-pipe area. This was achieved through sliding sleeves in the blast-pipe caps that were operated by a cam on the forward steam turbine valve spindle. The blast-pipe area was automatically increased or decreased dependent upon the number of steam supply valves open. Practice showed this feature to be unnecessarily complicated, and the position was set at minimum, with an overall beneficial effect on steaming. The aggregate area of the twin blast-pipes was 31sq in and the exhaust steam pressure varied from 1lb per sq in with two valves open to 3-4lb per sq in with four valves open.

There remained a residual feeling that the blast arrangements deserved further consideration. Following the fixing of the jumper blast-pipe, the only variable driving control was the six steam valves that governed the volume of steam directed at the forward turbine. Circumstances could make it hard to restore boiler pressure while on the move, and to redress this shortcoming a sand gun was fitted to clean the tubes made dirty by virtue of the soft, continuous draught. There are conflicting reports about the date this equipment was fitted. One authority states that it was installed during the Light Ordinary repair that commenced in September 1941, but it is clear from the account of a journey made in 1939 (Chapter 7) that it was useful in helping correct a difficult set of circumstances. On that occasion a means of sharpening the exhaust, if only temporarily, would have been helpful.

Turbines and transmission system

Superheated steam was directly admitted from the steam chest to

Side view of the steam valves, gear train and transmission for the forward turbine.

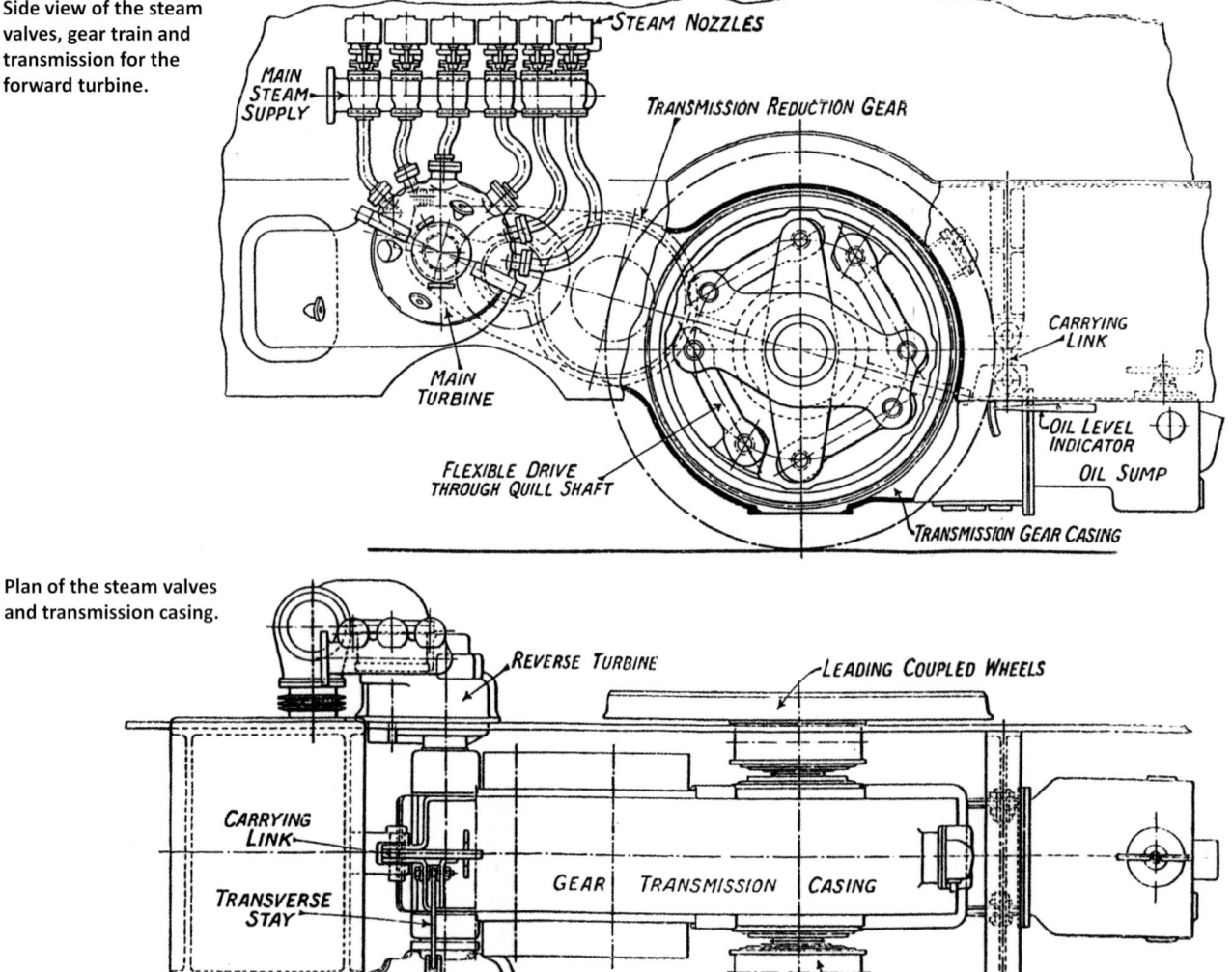

Plan of the steam valves and transmission casing.

the totally encased forward (left-hand) turbine, which was a combined impulse and reaction type, as had been developed by Ljungström. Passage through the turbine was governed by two separate stages that exploited different laws of physics. The first admission valve directed steam through a jet at impulse blades mounted on the turbine spindle. The force upon the blades was solely kinetic, resulting from the velocity of the steam rather than its pressure, as in the earliest forms of turbine. This force was in accordance with Newton's Second Law, which states that the sum of external forces upon an object is equal to its mass multiplied by the accelerative vector sum (i.e. the external force). Impulse turbines have been in use since antiquity, and are recognised as having limited efficiency. In this case, its principal task appears to have been to impel the turbine spindle to start turning.

Torque was mainly created by the action of the larger, sixteen-blade axial flow reaction turbine mounted adjacently to the impulse blades. The reactive section was operated by steam pressure rather than velocity and comprised a series of rotating blades mounted on the spindle, set in stages of progressively greater diameter towards the centre-line of the locomotive. This volume expansion was necessary to accommodate the falling pressure as steam approached the exhaust jet at the end of the casing, rather as in a compound reciprocating locomotive the diameter of the low-pressure cylinder(s) must be greater than that of the high-pressure cylinder(s). At this stage Newton's Third Law was at work, which states that all forces between two objects exist in equal magnitude and opposite direction.

On completion of its cycle, steam was discharged to the atmosphere by means of the blast-pipe, thereby creating the necessary draught. The pattern of pressure drop, assuming a full boiler working pressure of 250lb per sq in was approximately 225lb per sq in at admission of the superheated steam to the turbine and approximately 10lb per sq in on discharge through the blast-pipe. Thus each blade accounted for a pressure drop of roughly 14-15lb per sq in. The shape and proportion of the turbine blades was critical in optimising power over a wide speed range, as turbine

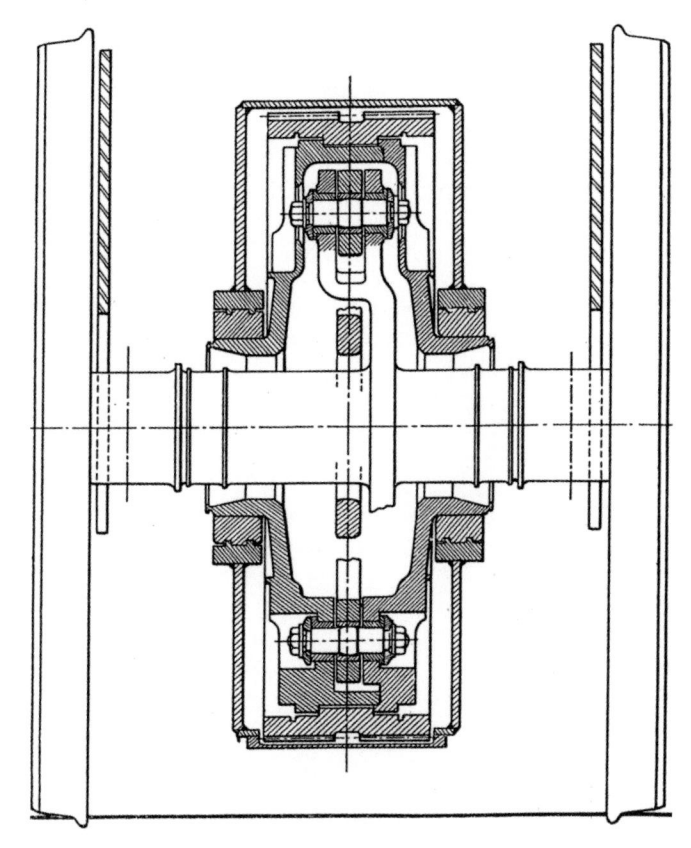

Cross-section of the quill drive mounted on the leading driving axle.

efficiency is severely reduced at very low or high speeds. It can be surmised therefore that particular care was necessary in the design of this aspect, which would have been more technically complex than that for a power station turbine, which typically operates at a constant 3,000rpm.

The right-hand reverse turbine was simpler, comprising a four-blade impulse turbine, with no reaction element. This was naturally significantly less powerful than its companion as it was anticipated that it would only be required for light engine movements. Figures advising the power rating of this turbine do not seem to have been released. and it was notable that R. C. Bond in 1946 seemingly chose to ignore a direct question on this subject.

Boiler, frames, wheels and tender were manufactured in the normal manner at Crewe, with turbines and associated reduction gears supplied by Metropolitan-Vickers. Early in the assembly process, the frames were despatched to Manchester for installation of the transmission set. The two turbines were mounted outside the frames on a single turbine spindle, forward of the leading driving axle and enclosed within bulbous casings below the footplate, approximately in the position of the outside cylinders of a conventional locomotive.

The turbine spindle was mounted transversely at right angles to the frames, and the left-hand turbine had a nominal maximum capacity of 2,600hp at 62mph. The arrangement of the blades, set in sixteen stages, ensured maintenance of high efficiency over a wide speed range. This turbine was permanently coupled through double-helical triple-reduction gearing to the leading coupled axle (the driving axle) through a 34.4:1 ratio that equated a turbine speed of 13,500rpm with a road speed of 90mph. The final drive gear wheel surrounded the driving axle and was connected to two arms, forged solid with the axle, by means of four pivoted links and a yoke, which also surrounded the axle, in such a way as to permit relative motion between the gear wheel and axle due to rise and fall of the axleboxes within the guides. The gear wheels ran in white metal bearings rigidly attached to the gearbox casing and were permanently engaged with the leading driving axle, as was also the forward turbine.

This connection was by means of an intermediate hollow quill shaft fitted with flexible diaphragm couplings, linked to the high-speed pinion. This was the first stage in a set of double-helical, triple-reduction gears, which were enclosed within a sealed gearbox mounted between the frames and were restrained from sideways movement relative to the spindle. The first and second reduction pinions were made slightly flexible to ensure equal pressure on the teeth. The final (slow-speed) pinion encircled the leading coupled axle and was connected to it by a series of floating links, thereby providing flexible linkage that absorbed any movement in the axle relative to the frame. A further precaution took the form of leaf springs between the rim and the boss of the slow-speed pinion to reduce transmission of shocks back to the high-speed pinion. This arrangement meant that, with steam supply cut off, the forward turbine idled during any movement of the locomotive either forward or reverse.

The reverse turbine, mounted on the right-hand side, drove through an additional single-reduction gear that gave an overall ratio of 77:1 (theoretically 45% of the forward maximum) and in normal forward running it remained stationary, being out of mesh with the gear train. The centre-line of the single reverse reduction gear was co-axial with the high-speed pinion and the main gear transmission. It was engaged by means of a sliding splined shaft and a dog clutch operated by a control in the cab, which included a protective device to prevent accidental engagement while moving forward. Originally, engagement of the clutch was effected by a small steam-driven motor that proved troublesome and an unnecessary complication. This was replaced with hand-operated gear that included a ratchet-inching mechanism to adjust the alignment of the gear cogs to ensure smooth engagement, and it was essential for the locomotive to be stationary prior to engagement of reverse. Reportedly this modified arrangement worked satisfactorily although it was the cause of failures (discussed in the next chapter), which might have been due to incorrect use by untrained personnel.

The assembly process at Crewe was well documented, but search of the Metropolitan-Vickers archives and other records has failed to elicit drawings or photographs of the internal layout of the turbines, or their dimensions. By the time of construction, the Ljungström brothers were apparently operating solely through AB Ljungström Ångturbin (ALÅ). This was a research and development company that generated its revenue from the sale of R&D to manufacturers, while undertaking no direct commercial production. The key to maximisation of torque lay in each individually crafted turbine blade, the dimensions for which were the result of years of study. While the LMS is unlikely to have had the expertise to manufacture copies, sale of the information to a commercial manufacturer would have been conditional upon it not being shared with third parties.

Thus the manufacturing rights for turbines and reduction gears were confined to Metropolitan-Vickers, which had repercussions for the Turbomotive's availability as failures imposed delays pending production of replacement components. In a prototype with so many novel features, provision of spares in advance was impracticable, as it could not be prejudged which parts were most likely to fail, and at what frequency. Further, the economics would have been distorted by the obligation to pay royalties on those parts, regardless of whether they were actually used. (It should be noted that mechanical engineers were not above purloining new ideas; Churchward and Robinson developed their own superheaters to avoid royalties, and at the time of his death in 1921 Schmidt was pursuing legal action for breach of intellectual property rights.)

As a concluding note, study of the frame plan shows the space efficiency of the two turbines, each occupying a volume roughly equivalent to a pair of outside cylinders and piston valves. This contrasted with the significant amount of room between the frames occupied by the triple-reduction helical gear chain.

Lubrication and cooling

With saturated reciprocating locomotives, traditional lubrication methods had been essentially administered by hand. Superheating brought the need for mechanical systems to ensure constant protection against the ravages of hot dry steam. The high rotational speed of the turbine and primary pinion introduced an entirely fresh dimension to the issue. Considerable care was thus taken to ensure adequate protection of bearings, not only for each individual component but also to prevent the risk of consequential damage to other parts of the transmission chain, and to the turbine blades themselves.

All turbine and gear bearings were lubricated by a closed circulating system that drew from an oil well located centrally between the frames and integrated with the rear of the gearbox casing. Circulation was effected by three pumps, one of which was reversible and submerged in the oil well. This reversible pump was mechanically driven by the main (slow-speed) pinion to which it was connected by means of an increasing gear. Thus it only worked when the locomotive was moving forward or backward and the volume delivered was directly proportionate to the speed.

The other two pumps were steam-driven Worthington-Simpson reciprocating pumps controlled from the cab, and were particularly important in maintaining adequate circulation on starting or when moving slowly. They were kept working after the locomotive had come to rest so that the oil would act as a coolant in removing heat that would otherwise be conducted along the turbine spindle to the journals.

On leaving the mechanical pump and the left-hand steam pump, oil passed through a radiator-style cooler centrally located below the smokebox. The cooler was covered by a hinged fall plate and it was normal for the locomotive to work with this plate set at about 45° to the horizontal so as to capture more airflow. On emission from the cooler, oil was distributed to the turbine bearings, and the gear train bearings. Additionally, oil was passed to a series of sprayers that directed lubricant at the cogs of the double-helical reduction gear sets. This system operated constantly in motion and when stationary.

While moving forward, a plunger valve allowed a small oil flow to reach the reverse turbine bearings but, on engagement of reverse gear, this valve opened to admit a full flow to the reverse turbine bearings. The feed from the second steam pump supplied the reverse turbine bearings only.

The pressure developed by each of the steam pumps was about 7lb per sq in, as monitored by gauges in the cab, and while in motion the gear-driven pump raised the main circuit pressure to about 16lb per sq in at 60mph. Oil temperatures on entry to the cooler varied between 120 and 180°F and on exit between 80 and 140°F. The differential remained constant at about 40°F regardless of operating conditions.

Despite the sealed nature of the turbines and transmission, contamination did occur. An auto-clean strainer with magnetic elements was fitted adjacent to the oil well, and was cleaned daily. Also, despite its dry nature on entering the turbines, a limited amount of condensed steam that was not discharged through turbine gland ejectors had to be drained off as part of the daily service regime, and typically this amounted to about a gallon. Oil was changed every 6,000 miles and could be reused after purification.

The system was well planned although difficulties did necessitate modifications mainly stemming from the reverse turbine transmission chain and associated controls, and from occasional leakages, as discussed in Chapter 6. With hindsight it was concluded that efficiency would have been improved with two separate circulating systems, one for the turbine bearings and the other for the transmission. However, lubrication was generally reliable in daily use, contributing significantly to performance levels. The accompanying schematic summarises the configuration: (see following page).

Roller bearings

With initial concerns about weight containment, it had been intended to fit roller bearings only to the bogie and trailer truck axles, but during construction it was concluded that in the absence of hammer blow there was sufficient margin to allow installation on all axles, including the tender. Timken tapered roller bearings were fitted and they proved very successful. On inspection after 158,000 miles of running, it was found that the outer races of the leading coupled wheel bearings had been rotating in the housings, causing local wear measured at a maximum of 0.014in. A repair using a proprietary process called 'fescolising' was instituted and no more problems were incurred.

Examination of the bogie bearings at 249,000 miles in 1944 revealed that due to expansion and contraction of air inside the boxes, steam had been drawn in that had then condensed on the cooler parts of the axles. This condensate contaminated the oil, causing slight pitting of the bearing races and rollers. A modified steam vent pipe was installed to eliminate this problem.

In retirement Stanier remarked that the collaboration with Timken had led to satisfactory results and that it seemed to have been largely overlooked by the engineering community that the Turbomotive was then the only British locomotive equipped with roller bearings throughout.

Driving controls

The main control box was placed in the cab in the position normally occupied by the reversing screw. A single handle turned clockwise

The Turbomotive lubrication diagram

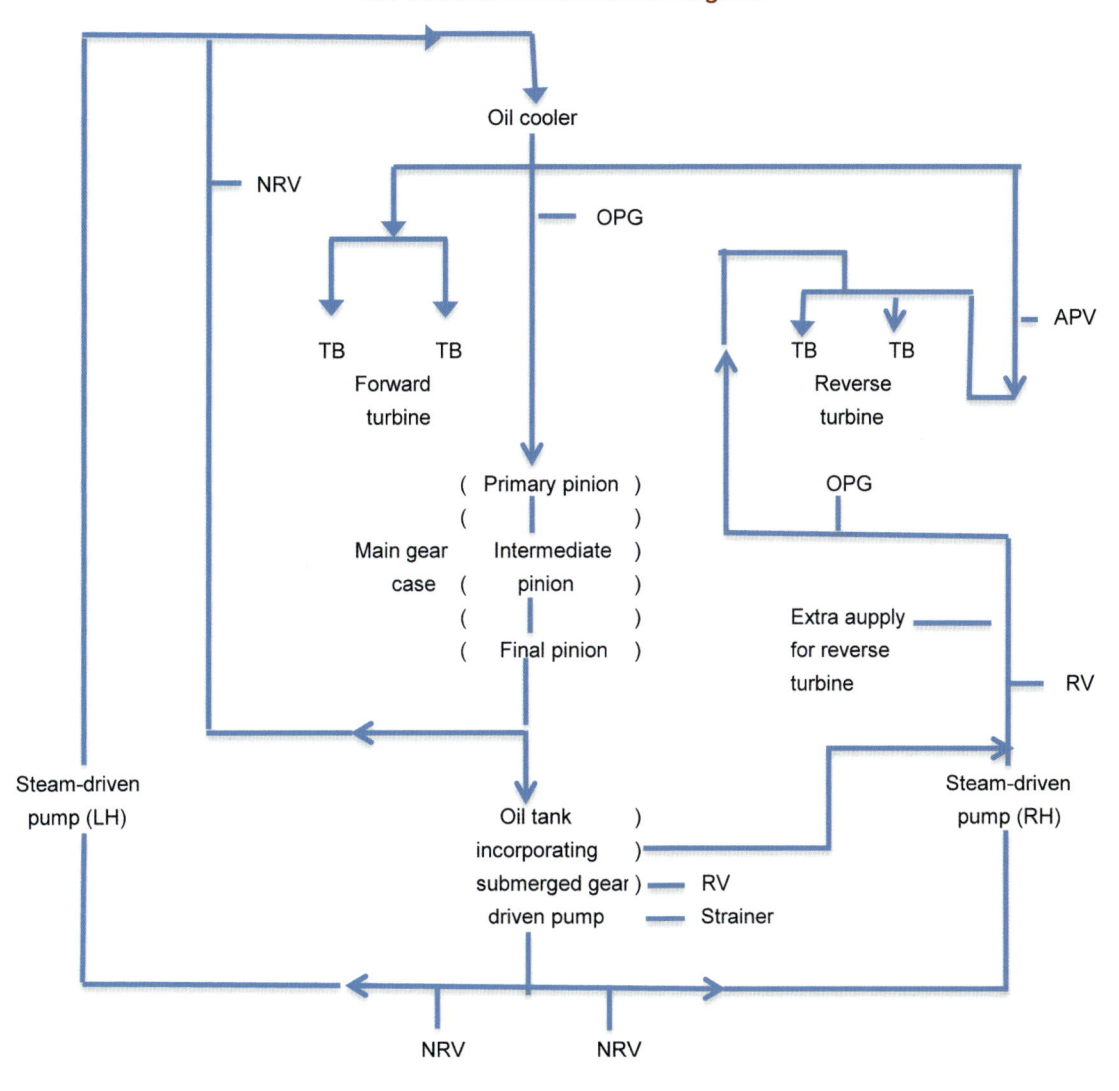

APV = Automatic plunger valve: open in reverse gear/ small feed in forward gear
NRV = Non-return valve
OPG = Oil pressure gauge
RV = Relief valve
TB = Turbine bearing

Right: The performance of the roller bearings was considered particularly successful, warranting these photographs in *The Railway Gazette* for 22 September 1944 showing their condition after 250,000 miles. In the accompanying article, E. S. Cox remarked, 'There is little first-hand information applicable to British practice. The experience gained in the further operation of this turbine-drive locomotive will go far towards providing information for British railway locomotive designers.'

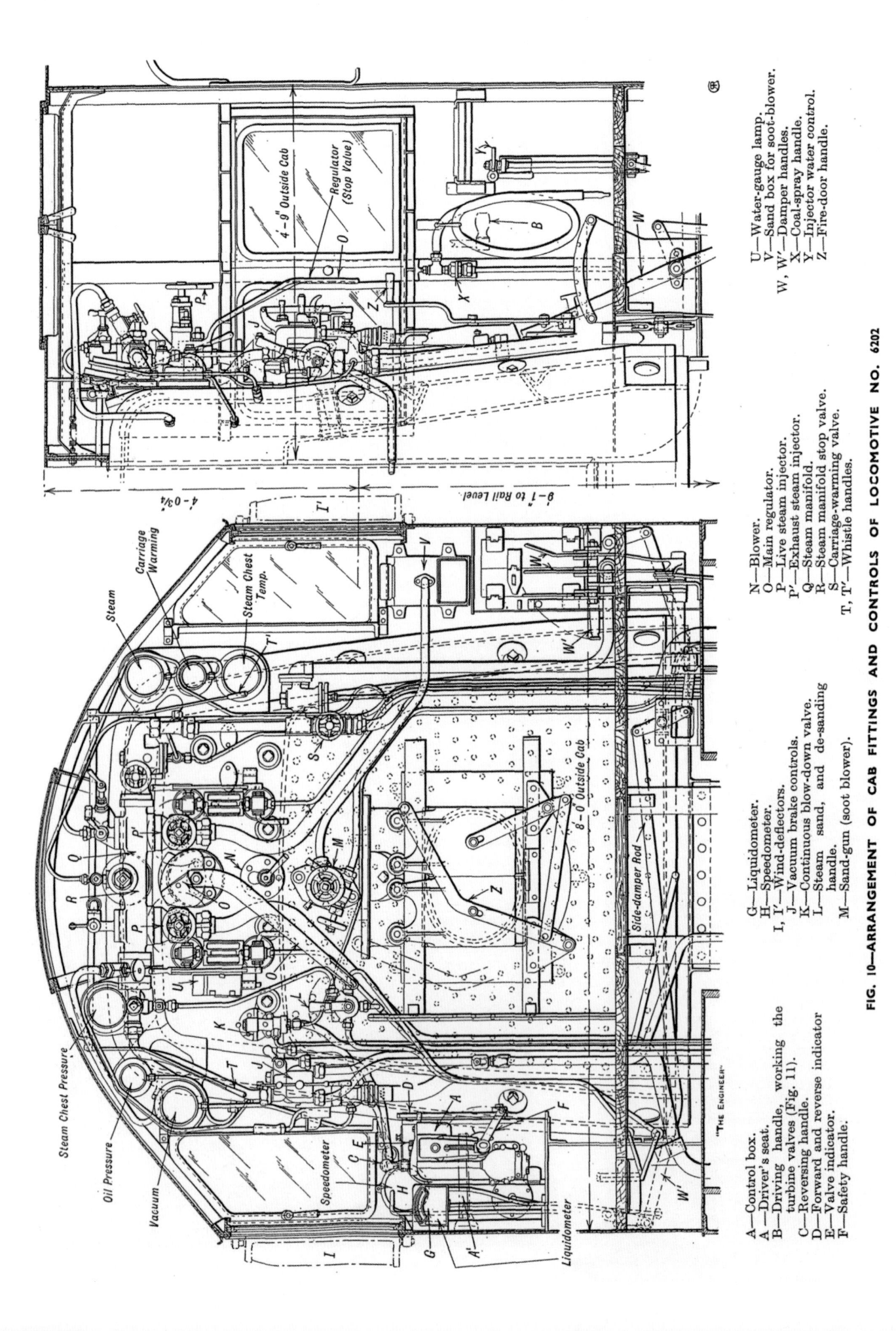

A—Control box.
A'—Driver's seat.
B—Driving handle, working the turbine valves (Fig. 11).
C—Reversing handle.
D—Forward and reverse indicator
E—Valve indicator.
F—Safety handle.
G—Liquidometer.
H—Speedometer.
I, I'—Wind-deflectors.
J—Vacuum brake controls.
K—Continuous blow-down valve.
L—Steam sand, and de-sanding handle.
M—Sand-gun (soot blower).
N—Blower.
O—Main regulator.
P—Live steam injector.
P'—Exhaust steam injector.
Q—Steam manifold.
R—Steam manifold stop valve.
S—Carriage-warming valve.
T, T'—Whistle handles.
U—Water-gauge lamp.
V—Sand box for soot-blower.
W, W'—Damper handles.
X—Coal-spray handle.
Y—Injector water control.
Z—Fire-door handle.

FIG. 10—ARRANGEMENT OF CAB FITTINGS AND CONTROLS OF LOCOMOTIVE NO. 6202

from the neutral position opened in succession the steam admission valves to the forward turbine. The same handle when turned anti-clockwise from neutral opened the reverse turbine admission valves in succession, but this was protected by an interlocking mechanism that prevented engagement of the dog clutch before the handle was placed in neutral with all forward steam valves closed. Further, the reverse turbine valves could not be opened before the dog clutch was properly engaged and, in similar fashion, the forward steam valves were inoperable while the reverse turbine was connected to the transmission chain. A further precaution lay in another interlocking mechanism that prevented engagement of reverse before the locomotive had come to a halt.

A steam manifold was installed above the firebox door plate in the cab with valves for the injectors, ejector, engine and tender steam brakes, carriage warming, gear case oil circulating pump, sight feed lubricator to the regulator, and whistle. Steam supply could be cut off by means of a single valve that controlled admission to the manifold.

There were more gauges fitted in the cab than would be found in a conventional locomotive:

Steam-chest pressure
Oil temperature (before entry to cooler)
Oil pressure
Oil temperature (following emission from cooler)
Liquidometer, to show oil-level in the sump
Speed indicator
Back-pressure in the turbine exhaust

The tender
Three enlarged tenders of Midland style numbered 9000-9002 were built for locomotives Nos 6200-6202. The wheelbase was stretched to 7ft 6in + 7ft 6in with Timken roller bearings; carrying capacities were 8 tons and 4,000 gallons. Although originally earmarked for the Turbomotive, tender No 9002 was coupled to No 6100 *Royal Scot* (alias No 6152) for its tour of the United States. The coal capacity of these tenders was inadequate for London-Glasgow duties, and their poor self-trimming characteristics meant that packing in extra fuel over the prescribed limit led to safety issues.

As a result, the familiar Stanier curve-sided tender was introduced, still of riveted construction but with improved self-trimming and a 9-ton capacity. No 9003 was the prototype for this type, entering service on 29 June 1935 coupled to the Turbomotive. The recorded cost of £2,065 included patterns and other one-off expenses that totalled £329; as a further indication of economy of scale, the tenders built for 'Pacifics' Nos 6203-12 cost £1,154 each.

This type was visually more in keeping with these large engines, and the increased capacity was welcome but still inadequate. In 1936-37, shortly after the final 'Princess Royal' (No 6212) started work, all the reciprocating locomotives received replacement tenders of welded construction with the coal capacity increased to 10 tons. (In the 1950s consideration was apparently given to provision of new tenders with even greater capacities, but this idea did not proceed.) However, No 6202 retained its original 9-ton riveted tender No 9003 throughout its career, including its short life as a reciprocating engine. The smaller capacity was adequate for the shorter London-Liverpool services with which it was associated throughout its career in normal service.

Livery
The standard 1928 LMS crimson lake livery, which has been fully described in other publications, was applied when new, but with minor differences related to the control casings. The forward section on the left beside the smokebox was unlined black, with the remainder adjacent to the boiler and firebox in crimson lake. The colours were segregated by vertical lining that corresponded to the smokebox/boiler join; this lining, edged black, continued at just above running plate level back to the cab, where it was completed with another vertical strip at the casing's rear. The shorter right-hand casing was all black, but when this was extended rearwards that section to the rear of the smokebox was painted in similarly segregated crimson lake. There is uncertainty about the lining shade, as that for Nos 6200/01 when built was 'pale straw' (similar to that used by the Midland Railway). However, by 1935 a darker shade described as 'mid chrome yellow' had become official and it is not definite which was carried by No 6202. This livery continued until after the war, except that in 1937 the shading of letters and numbers was changed from black to vermilion.

In 1946 the LMS adopted a new livery of glossy black with lining in maroon (a darker shade than crimson lake) and straw (lighter than previously). No 6202 emerged on 8 April 1947 in this livery following its lengthy Heavy General repair. After another extended absence for repair, it appeared in March 1949 in the neo-LNWR lined black that had been formally adopted by British Railways, and renumbered 46202 with the first BR emblem (the 'cycling lion') on the tender. This styling saw out its career as a steam turbine.

Stepping ahead to the short interlude as a reciprocating machine, No 46202 *Princess Anne* entered service in the fully lined BR green that was then replacing both the blue and black on express locomotives. All the LMS 'Pacifics' were in course of being so treated, and it must have been a source of some satisfaction to Stanier to see them dressed in a livery so close to that of the old Great Western.

Sources of components
Several outside contractors were suppliers to the project:

Alfol Insulation Co Ltd: insulating material for boiler, firebox, control valves and piping
British Timken Ltd: axlebox roller bearings (engine and tender)
Colvilles Ltd: 'Ducol' high-tensile steel for the mainframes; boiler barrel and firebox wrapper plates
Davies & Metcalfe Ltd: exhaust steam injector
Geo. Turton, Platts & Co Ltd: buffers
Gresham & Craven Ltd: live steam injector
Henry Wiggin Ltd: monel metal firebox stays
Metropolitan-Vickers Electrical Co Ltd: turbines, transmission gear, control valves, feedwater heater
The Superheater Company Ltd: superheater
Worthington-Simpson Ltd: steam pump for oil-cooling circulation

A three-quarter official photograph of the completed locomotive.

CHAPTER SIX

Maintenance and Modifications

KEY to a novel design's effectiveness is the relationship between its complexity, running expenses, and resultant improvement in performance over the norm. Compared with preceding turbine machines, simplicity eased the Turbomotive's maintenance regime, contributing when in operable condition to respectable annual mileages. Nevertheless, its availability was constrained for several reasons:

1. As the first of its kind in Britain, its transmission remained unique throughout its career.

2. Design and construction of the turbines and the gear train was 'hi-tech' compared with equipment used in conventional locomotives. It could reasonably be expected that normal service conditions would reveal features requiring modification or refinement.

3. It was uneconomic to hold spares of specially manufactured parts as, without prior experience, it was impossible to prejudge the probability of individual component failure, or the likely cause. Thus periods out of service were lengthened by delays pending manufacture of replacement parts.

4. Increased traffic demands necessitated the locomotive's removal from store in 1941, but repair periods thereafter were lengthened due to wartime pressures on the manufacturers. This was especially relevant to the final drive failure and damage to the high-speed pinion sustained in July 1943.

5. The locomotive's novelty and lack of relevant experience induced greater caution during inspections.

On the other hand, significant advantage lay in the absence of unbalanced horizontal forces and the total enclosure of the gearbox with lubrication at constant pressurisation. These elements rendered efficiencies that were impossible in a normal locomotive where some mechanical parts are exposed to dry superheated steam, and others to atmospheric contamination. It was estimated that the turbine transmission improved mechanical efficiency by 6 to 8%, and was less prone to deterioration as mileage increased. In a conventional locomotive, wear to gland packings, pistons and valves increased the incidence of steam leakage to the detriment of operating economics. Dynamometer trials with a 'Royal Scot' confirmed an 8% increase in fuel consumption over 28,000 miles, necessitating valve and piston examination every six months or on reaching around 30,000 miles since the last works visit.

Improved availability and shorter periods out of service formed an important part of Stanier's modernisation programme. The Turbomotive's record was counter to these objectives and the following absences were excessively long:

Repair type	Commenced	Duration (days)
Light Service	02.06.1938	124
Light Ordinary	08.02.1939	148
Light Ordinary	17.09.1941	257
Heavy General	11.06.1943	402
Heavy General	09.03.1946	337
Light Casual	16.04.1948	280

NB Period 1939-41, when locomotive was formally stored out of traffic. is excluded.

Details entered on the Engine History Card and an explanation of the repair classification system appear in Appendix D-1. No 6202's stoppages were mainly occasioned by equipment failure rather than through a scheduled repair programme. Mechanical repairs were not possible at depot level, making works visits more frequent than might otherwise have been necessary. Although categorised under the repair classification system, their unscheduled nature contributed to delays awaiting a suitable 'slot' for dismantling and fault diagnosis. In several instances, reference to Metropolitan-Vickers was necessary for replacement parts. A further complication arose with the unique high-superheat boiler No 9236, for which there was no spare (there was a pool of fourteen boilers for twelve 'Princess Royals').

Periods out of service were recorded as the dates of entering and leaving the works, and the resultant number of weekdays (including Saturdays). Compared with No 6205 (completed one month after the Turbomotive), the annual days spent in the works show that the conventional locomotive required substantially less attention:

Year	Days under repair	
	6202	6205
1935	77	-
1936	69	50
1937	86	25
1938	124	100
1939	148	55
1940	-	30
1941	92	55
1942	213	67
1943	173	15
1944	241	62
1945	71	88
1946	253	78

Year	Days under repair	
	6202	6205
1947	148	100
1948	223	112
1949	91	57
Total weekdays	2,009	894
Average p.a. 1936-49	134	60
Average p.a. excluding 1939-41	154	69

Source: LMS Engine History Cards

(No 6205 was the most interesting of the 'Princess Royals', following removal in 1938 of its inside valve motion to be replaced by rocking levers actuated by the outside Walschaerts valve gear. The need to absorb the resultant frame stresses was apparent in the massive outside bracing. This method of valve actuation was the reverse of the classic GWR 'Star' Class arrangement; the only other example in these islands was the Great Southern & Western four-cylinder 4-6-0 Class '400' in its original, unsatisfactory form.)

There is a disproportionate aspect to these statistics. The Turbomotive's annual mileages from 1936, excluding the years 1939-41, were 69% of those for No 6205, whereas its days in works averaged more than double those of No 6205. This implies that the Turbomotive incurred a lower rate of depot-level stoppages (light maintenance, boiler washouts, etc).

Visible evidence of the stresses imparted by reciprocation was found in the 1938 modification to No 6205 *Princess Victoria*. The inside valve motion was replaced by rocking levers actuated by the outside Walschaerts valve gear, necessitating additional slide bar bracing as shown in this close-up view..

MAINTENANCE AND MODIFICATIONS

REPAIR HISTORY

Date to works	Weekdays out of traffic	Mileage rom new	Reason for stoppage	Summary of work
6.8.35	26	6,100	Oil leakage from turbine bearings and presence of water in roller bearing axleboxes	Modification to oil seals; examination of main gears
24.9.35	76	9,164	Failure of reversing mechanism at reverse turbine	Overhaul of reverse turbine and reversing mechanism; forward turbine and gears examined
15.1.36	17	12,644	Failure of reverse turbine	Repairs to reverse turbine and clutch; forward turbine and gears examined
15.5.36	34	40,653	Failure of reverse turbine	Overhaul of reverse turbine; forward turbine and main gears examined; control gear examined
14.7.36	15	45,688	Oil leakage from turbine bearings	Reverse turbine opened up for examination; main gear wheels examined; new boiler with 40-element superheater fitted
28.1.37	64	78,812	Failure of forward turbine	Overhaul of forward turbine; reverse turbine examined; main gear train examined; sludge removal cover fitted to oil tank; oil system thoroughly examined; all wheels removed for turning; spring and brake gear, and coupling rods repaired
18.10.37	21	122,127	Routine repairs and attention	Complete overhaul of reverse turbine
2.6.38	123	158,502	Routine repairs & attention	Service repair; both turbines overhauled; larger oil drain pipes fitted to forward turbine thrust bearings; distant reading indicator fitted to main oil tank; all engine and tender wheels turned; forty small tubes changed; all superheater flue tubes re-expanded and beaded; 523 stay nuts changed; firebox seams fullered
8.2.39	147	177,413	Failure of forward turbine	Forward turbine completely repaired; main gears examined; reverse turbine bearings renewed; new control box of improved design fitted and control rods overhauled; new top frame bars fitted to leading bogie and springs changed; wind plates fitted alongside smokebox
21.9.39 to 24.7.41			Withdrawn for storage	
17.9.41	257	195,370	Failure of reverse turbine	Reverse turbine completely overhauled; additional Worthington pump fitted to augment oil supply to reverse turbine unit
21.11.42	42	219,243	Oil leakage from both turbines	Both turbines opened up for examination
10.7.43	378	249,261	Failure to flexible drive between slow-speed gear wheel and driving axle	Heavy General repair including overhaul to both turbines, and repairs to gears and flexible drive
18.12.44	27	252,573	Failure of reverse turbine bearing	Attention to reverse turbine bearings as a result of oil passage obstructed during previous repair
12.4.45	43	273,545	Oil leakage from turbine bearings	Both turbines removed from frames for examination

The Turbomotive is under repair in Crewe Works on 18 August 1935, following the first stoppage on the 6th of that month. The reason was a sudden loss of oil and the presence of water in the roller bearing axleboxes. The locomotive had only covered 6,100 miles by that stage, but an examination of the main gears was also undertaken. Repairs took the form of modifications to the oil seals, the Turbomotive being out of service for twenty-six days. To improve access, the bogie has been removed and placed to the right of the cab. *W. L. Good*

MAINTENANCE AND MODIFICATIONS

Two further views of No 6202 in the works on that same day. *Both W. L. Good*

While shunting at Willesden on 28 January 1937, the forward turbine suffered its first failure at 78,812 miles. Although more reliable than its companion, this was considered a major failure that raised questions about the concept's viability. The forward turbine was returned to Metropolitan-Vickers for overhaul while Crewe thoroughly examined the reverse turbine, main gear train and lubrication system. Also, the wheels were removed for turning, and the coupling rods, brake gear and springs were inspected and repaired where necessary. The extent of the work is apparent in the number of important components that have been removed when this picture was taken on 14 February 1937. Only the boiler, then only a few months old, appears to have been left undisturbed. These repairs kept the Turbomotive out of service for sixty-four days. *L. Hanson*

special design to cope with temperature differences, being in close proximity to the feedwater heater and turbine cylinder. The diaphragm had move inwards by one-eighth of an inch, which was sufficient to foul the tips of the first-stage turbine blades. These had stripped completely, and fragments had damaged the other blades. During repairs, a locking mechanism was introduced to ensure that the diaphragms stayed in placed, and radial clearances for the moving blades were increased. The reported cumulative mileage at which this failure occurred does not reconcile with the Engine History Card, which shows a stoppage (Light Ordinary) for sixty-four days from 28 January 1937 when the cumulative mileage was 84,760

The second incident with the forward turbine was apparently the only failure to occur at speed, near Leighton Buzzard on an up working from Liverpool. Nothing amiss had been noted thus far when at more than 60mph the turbine spindle broke at the point where a retaining nut held a thrust collar in place. This breakage allowed the turbine rotor to move laterally, causing severe damage and necessitating the return of the unit to the manufacturer for complete overhaul. The mileage run to this incident was 177,413; the locomotive was stopped for 147 days from 8 February 1939 under a Light Ordinary classification. During these repairs the opportunity was taken to modify the right-hand control box by extending the casing rearwards for about 2 feet.

Despite the forward turbine's comparative reliability, these two failures were costly to rectify, raising doubts about the project's long-term viability. A counter-argument held that the spares situation had exacerbated the length of the stoppages and that both were roughly the equivalent of a big-end failure in a conventional locomotive, which often caused extensive damage (to cylinders, motion and crank axle). With No 6202, damage was limited to the forward turbine only.

Slow-speed gear flexible drive failure

A serious failure occurred in June 1943 during shunting at Camden following arrival from Liverpool. The coupled wheels locked solid without warning and examination revealed several broken teeth on the high-speed pinion. It was unclear whether this was the cause or the effect of another component failure in the transmission chain. The locomotive was hauled dead to Crewe for investigation with the coupling rods removed and the driving axle jacked up off the rails. At this stage the recorded mileage was 249,261 from new and 71,848 since return to work following its extended period in store from the commencement of the war.

It was established that the fault had originated in the flexible drive between the slow-speed pinion and the driving axle, as a result of wear sustained in normal use. The cumulative effect of slackness in the pins and bushes that connected the slow-speed pinion to the floating link and driving axle had led to a string of damaged components in the transmission chain. A full commentary on the nature of the damage appears in Appendix D-4.

The extensive nature of the failure meant that repairs were costly and time-consuming. Classified as a Heavy General repair, the locomotive was out of service for 402 days – its longest absence from duty, excluding the period in storage. The timing was unfortunate as Metropolitan-Vickers was extremely busy with a heavy order book of war-related work. The cause was judged to have been due to an inadequate inspection and maintenance regime rather than any design shortcoming, and a thorough inspection of the flexible drive every 100,000 miles was instituted. Also, bearing in mind that the forward turbine had not been opened up since 1939, a Heavy General repair was considered timely.

Oil leakages from forward and reverse turbine bearings
After about 10,000 miles from new, an intermittent oil leakage from the turbine bearings occurred, and with greater frequency as mileage increased. The turbines were undamaged by these events, and the oil loss was relatively modest, but a number of modifications were tried to eliminate this annoying problem.

An associated problem, characteristic of turbines generally, was leakage of condensed steam through the bearings leading to oil emulsification over time. Aeration at all bearings and gear teeth was inevitable and this was intensified by oil contaminated with water and solid particles, which accentuated leakages. With a stationary turbine, it was usual for the oil reservoir to hold about 5 to 8 minutes' of pump supply, but the constricted space below the running plate limited the capacity to less than 1 minute's supply. This acknowledged design shortcoming meant that oil had little or no time to settle within the cycle and was delivered to the bearings and gear sprays in a frothy state.

The aeration theory was supported by an increase in oil leakage following the fitting of the second Worthington pump without any increase in the reservoir capacity. Oil in a frothy mixture moved more slowly than as pure liquid, filling the oil passages and eventually overflowing into cavities around the bearings. These cavities were needed to help keep the bearings cool and to allow escape of any steam that might have passed the glands, which otherwise would have condensed and contaminated the oil.

To reduce leakage, the drainage passages, already of greater diameter than the supply passages, were increased further, but to no positive effect. There was also a fear of emulsified and aerated oil reaching boiling point, but careful monitoring showed that the cooler did its job well with temperatures never rising above about 180°F. While working it was normal for the footplate in front of the smokebox and above the oil cooler's protective grid to be set open at about 45° to the horizontal to improve the flow of cooling air.

Redesign of the lubrication system
It was recognised that separate, independent oil circuits for gears and bearings would have been preferable in slowing the lubrication cycle, and in reduction, if not elimination, of the cross-contamination risk. With recognition of the reservoir's inadequate capacity must have come realisation that the transmission's safe operating margins were not as wide as might have been desirable.

This was arguably the design's most unsatisfactory aspect and one that could not be corrected because of limited space – a penalty incurred through using the 'Princess Royal' chassis layout. As the Beyer-Ljungström locomotive had proved that 'mixed-traffic' driving wheels were no inhibition to high speeds, it was evident that the 6ft 6in driving wheels were unnecessarily large. A second turbine locomotive using, say, 5-foot-diameter driving wheels below a boiler of similar dimensions and pitch to that used with No 6202 would have yielded a valuable extra 9 inches of free depth between the line of the axles and the running plate.

Smoke deflectors
The most prominent change in appearance arose from drifting smoke and exhaust steam, a problem that never affected the 'Princess Royals'. With No 6202, forward visibility could be impeded by the continuous uninterrupted draught without sufficient blast to lift exhaust clear of the smokebox. In February 1939, during the Light Ordinary repair, smoke deflectors were fitted, which solved the problem. Their style was similar to the large type first fitted to the original 'Royal Scots', with the upper section canted inwards.

Post-1946 failures
The paper presented by R. C. Bond in 1946 concluded on a generally optimistic note with expectations that design shortcomings had been resolved and that a promising future might be anticipated. This was supported by the Turbomotive's impressive contribution in 1945 when its second highest annual mileage was recorded. Further, there was acknowledgement that teething and operational problems were inevitable in such a revolutionary concept, however carefully it had been designed. Against the feeling that the key shortcomings had been 'engineered out', it must have been acutely disappointing that roughly the same number of stoppages occurred after 1946 as had afflicted No 6202 prior to the war. Apart from the lengthy absence for the 1946/47 Heavy General service, the other stoppages were of comparatively short duration and six were officially 'Not classified', suggesting a propensity to relatively minor component failures not previously encountered.

Also, the period of post-war reconstruction continued to exert pressure on human and material resources. In an era when rugged simplicity and easy access to mechanical moving parts were prerequisites for high availability levels, the fully enclosed transmission and the unique aspects of No 6202 were hardly conducive to making the most of difficult conditions. It would be useful to know more about the causes of failures in this period. The only information traced is a report that on 21 November 1949, while hauling the 8.30am to Liverpool, time was lost all the way to Rugby, where No 46202 was replaced by a Class 5 4-6-0. The train was an hour late at Stafford and the Turbomotive was later seen being towed north by an ex-LNWR 0-8-0. This sequence of events seems more typical of a conventional locomotive in difficulties than failure of the turbine drive.

Routine maintenance

The unique features necessitated special procedures on shed to maintain an optimum operating condition. These measures were covered partly by the special instructions to drivers and fitters (Appendices D-2 and D-3). A further issue concerned tubes, especially the accumulation of dirt in the large tubes at the firebox tubeplate. The cause does not seem to have been recorded, but presumably resulted from the continuous draught without any cleansing effect imparted by blast. The result was a need to clean the tubes with far greater frequency than was needed with reciprocating engines.

This obligation militated against economic acceptance of No 6202. A legacy of the Stamp/Stanier revolution was a continuing commitment to improvement of availability, and the post-war LMS was seeking to achieve annual mileages of 100,000 with its ordinary 'Pacific' fleet, a level markedly above what had proved possible so far.

In the discussion following presentation of the R. C. Bond paper, E. S. Cox revealed that plans were in hand to install extra inspection covers in the gear case to enable routine inspections on shed rather than at the works. These modifications do not appear to have been made, but this statement suggests that by 1946 there was a feeling that problems had been sufficiently corrected to enable more of the service regime to devolve to depot level.

Reliability assessment

At least one account has described the Turbomotive's performance and reliability history in somewhat derogatory terms, drawn in part from comparison with the record of the 'Princess Royals'. However, No 6202's frequency of works visits was not significantly higher than members of that class, and it could be argued that the rate at which repairs were administered was actually lower. Beyond the special instructions to fitters (Appendix D-3), all other maintenance was carried out at Crewe, whereas it was normal for light repairs to conventional locomotives to be administered at depot level, without details appearing on the Engine Record Card.

Financial stringencies had much to do with the periods out of service. Constraints on capital expenditure meant adherence to the basic 'Princess Royal' format, whereas a more radical departure from convention would have yielded better results – as discussed above in the context of lubrication. Also, it was sensible to rely on the manufacturer for replacement parts in view of the project's prototypical nature. Periods out of service were thus inevitably longer, a situation made worse by conditions during the war and in the immediate years thereafter.

Within another peer group, the Turbomotive unquestionably outshone its rivals. The first half of the 20th century saw several attempts at fundamental revision of the traditional British steam locomotive, and these efforts form an objective basis for comparison. Among other experiments with steam turbines, only the Beyer-Ljungström locomotive undertook revenue-earning service, but suffered reliability issues and came at an unacceptably high capital cost. Other radical departures (the Kitson-Still locomotive / 4-6-0 No 6399 *Fury*/ Southern Class 'N' No A816 / Bulleid's 'Leader') failed to advance beyond preliminary road trials.

The only other unusual machine to see extended revenue-earning service was Gresley's water-tube-boilered compound Class 'W1' 4-6-4 No 10000, between November 1929 and August 1935. This locomotive encountered problems with superheater design, draughting arrangements, compound expansion ratio and reversing gear, necessitating a continuing programme of modifications, including more than twelve months out of service in 1933/34. At the time of its withdrawal for rebuild as a conventional locomotive, No 10000 had accumulated 90,000 miles during six years in express service; the Turbomotive clocked up more than 128,000 miles on similar duties in its first thirty months.

Economic assessment

The war had clearly interrupted the pattern of testing and modification, and it is reasonable to assume that a conclusive view on financial viability would otherwise have been formed some three or four years earlier. R. C. Bond opined at the 1946 meeting that an increase in both pressure and degree of superheat would improve efficiency. In this context one of the audience remarked on the high number of experimental fitments to other locomotives that were worth neither removal nor perpetuation. The hope was expressed that the Turbomotive should be spared such adornments in any modification programme, the implication being that simplicity in design had yielded technical and financial advantages.

Bond's closing remarks following presentation of his paper provide an informative insight on how the LMS hierarchy had come to regard the Turbomotive. These comments are quoted direct from the minutes of the meeting:

'He had been asked by a number of speakers whether the locomotive was a commercial success. Sufficient time had not elapsed to give a complete answer to that question, and he could not go further than say that, in his opinion, experience up to that date had been extremely encouraging. No other engine, so fundamentally different from ordinary types, had run 300,000 miles or more in revenue-earning service. At that very moment it was hauling a special train from Liverpool; no objection had been raised to the turbine locomotive being used to work that special train, reliable time-keeping on which was most important. The locomotive was doing its work well, and he felt that in the next five years the results obtained from it would be much more consistent than those obtained during the first ten years, while the minor troubles were being overcome.'

CHAPTER SEVEN

Operating Performance

THE Turbomotive was subjected to three series of dynamometer trials, in May and October 1936, and June 1937, between Euston, Carlisle and Glasgow on the 'Royal Scot' and similar services. Two of the production series 'Princess Royals' also participated, and comparisons of consumption levels are shown in Table 7.1. No difficulties were faced by any locomotive in keeping time over their complete journeys, or in recovering from out-of-course delays. The best sectional timings achieved by No 6202 during the trials, together with relative trainloads, are shown in Table 7.2, while Table 7.3 shows the best sectional timings achieved by conventional 'Pacifics' Nos 6210 and 6212 during the trials, again with their respective trainloads.

It was evident that the Turbomotive was a competent machine, capable of matching the performance of the 'Princess Royals'. Its abilities were far in advance of earlier British turbine locomotives, and it was free of the teething problems that affected its immediate predecessor, the Beyer-Ljungström engine, thus validating the non-condensing steam turbine configuration.

It had originally been hoped that in service between London and Glasgow fuel consumption would be 10-15% lower than with 'Princess Royals' Nos 6200-01, but the trial results show no sign that this objective was achieved. Although no clear pattern can be certain, later experience indicated some improvement, although there were reports of fuel consumption sometimes being significantly higher. However, crews generally considered that the locomotive's steaming was very good under normal conditions, and one driver estimated that on one particular duty 7,500 gallons of water were consumed whereas a 'Princess Royal' would have used 8,000-8,500 gallons.

Given its express locomotive status, assigned crews would have been competent and experienced, and fuel would usually have been of good quality, which suggests that fluctuating performance rested on the driver's ability to adjust to the unique characteristics. It is not known how many different drivers were employed in the tests, but the short allocation to Liverpool Edge Hill (February to May 1936) had confirmed the importance of using a limited number of crews who could acquire adequate working familiarity. In this respect, the number of failures involving the reverse turbine and shunting movements might have been significant, i.e. unsympathetic treatment by untrained shed personnel.

In a conventional locomotive, the rate of steam consumption is determined by steam chest pressure, the degree of valve cut-off and the rate of piston stroke. Thus if the first two factors remain constant, consumption varies in accordance with changes in speed. With a turbine, consumption on starting under load is high as more valves must be opened to induce the blades to turn; consumption thus considerably exceeds that of a reciprocating engine and boiler pressure drops rapidly. On the other hand, the greater volume of steam expended to get the locomotive moving helped stimulate the draught and thus the rate of combustion, encouraging swift restoration. This fluctuation was considered irrelevant provided usage was confined to main-line express duties, but it would be unacceptable on duties requiring frequent stops.

Another difficulty for the driver was the absence of those factors that in a reciprocating machine helped him subconsciously gauge how well the locomotive was working – varying levels of vibration, exhaust beat, etc – thus indicating the need for perhaps quite subtle changes in settings. Further, smooth running and absence of the usual noises made determination of speed difficult, and monitoring of the speedometer essential. During the war the Turbomotive was the only LMS locomotive to retain this instrument.

There was a nominal correlation between a reciprocating locomotive's cut-off settings and the number of valves open with the Turbomotive, and the settings noted in the dynamometer tests are shown in Table 7.4.

During the later tests, the tendency to work with fewer steam supply valves open might have indicated that drivers were becoming skilled in their control. Nonetheless, the locomotive lacked the infinite variability provided by a reciprocating engine fitted with a screw reverse, where miniscule adjustments in the

THE LMS TURBOMOTIVE

No 6210 *Lady Patricia* was one the 'Princess Royals' assigned in 1936 to dynamometer trials for comparison with the Turbomotive. Seen at Polmadie and renumbered 46210 using an LMS-style font but retaining the previous owner's tender insignia, it is in one of the hybrid liveries quite common in the early post-nationalisation period.

The other 'Princess Royal' engaged in the trials was No 6212 *Duchess of Kent*, seen in 1938. The last of the production series, this locomotive uniquely carried from new for several years a smokebox door secured by ten circumference lugs rather than the more modern central screw lock or dart. *J. F. Hull*

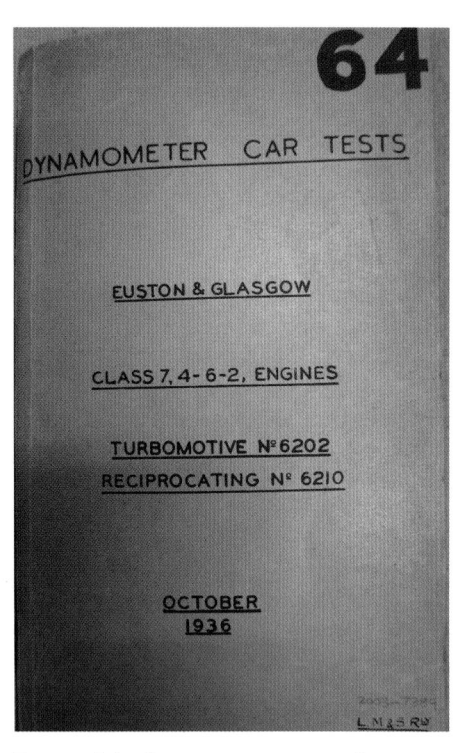

Report of the dynamometer tests against 'Princess Royal' No 6210.

Views of the front, left-hand side and right-hand side of the Turbomotive before the fitting of the domed boiler.

Table 7.1: Comparisons of consumption levels between Nos 6202/10/12 during trials, 1936-37

	May 36	May 36	Oct 36*	Oct 36*	June 37
Engine No	6212	6210	6202	6202	6202
Aggregate pre-trial mileage	19,511 §	1,778 §	32,371	63,812	102,915
Total miles	1,608	1,608	1,608	1,207	1,608
Coal consumption:					
- lbs per mile	42.9	44.98	42.4	45.15	41.6
- lbs per drawbar horsepower/hour	3.2	3	3	2.9	2.8
Water consumption:					
- gallons per mile	36.1	37.26	34.2	35	37.1
Coal consumption					
- lbs per sq ft grate/hour	50.4	52.2	50.4	54.6	50.7
Water consumption:					
- lbs/ lbs coal	8.4	8.3	8.1	7.7	8.9

§ Since last works visit
* Results affected by adverse winds

Table 7.2: Best sectional timings achieved by No 6202 during trials, 1936-37

	May 36 Distance (miles)	May 36 Booked (min-sec)	Oct 36 Actual (min-sec)	Oct 36 Tons	June 37 Actual (min-sec)	June 37 Tons	Actual (mins)	Tons
DOWN								
Euston-Tring	31.8	38	36-00	536	38-20	553	37-05	489
Stafford-Whitmore	14.0	16	15-50	536	13-50	553	14-35	484
Carnforth-Carnholme	12.8	14	12-55	474	14-05	475	12-10	489
Oxenholme-Tebay	13.0	16	16-20	470	14-55	486	16-00	484
Tebay-Shap Summit	5.8	10	8-50	470	7-10	486	7-35	484
Beattock-Summit	10.0	18	16-50	474	15-15	486	16-10	489
UP								
Uddington-Law Junc	9.75	14	14-05	327	15-10	319	13-20	489
Symington-Beattock Summit	17.00	18	21-50	497	23-15	486	16-20	483
Carlisle-Plumpton	13.00	20	20-15	499	18-30	486	18-35	483
Penrith-Shap Summit	13.50	19	20-00	499	15-05	486	16-30	489
Crewe-Whitmore	10.50	14	14-00	497	14-35	486	13-15	483
Bletchley-Tring	15.00	16	13-45	497	13-50	486	12-30	489

Table 7.3: Best sectional timings achieved by conventional 'Pacifics' Nos 6210 and 6212 during trials, 1936-37

	Distance (miles)	Booked (mins)	6210 Actual (mins)	6210 Tons	6212 Actual (mins)	6212 Tons
DOWN						
Euston-Tring	31.8	38	45-15	480	38-45	569
Stafford-Whitmore	14	16	14-55	480	15-20	569
Carnforth-Carnholme	12.8	14	13-30	512	13-35	477
Oxenholme-Tebay	13	16	14-10	482	17-20	507
Tebay-Shap Summit	5.8	10	8-40	512	9-30	507
Beattock-Summit	10	18	18-40	486	18-20	477
UP						
Uddington-Law Junc	9.75	14	15-15	319	16-20	305
Symington-Beattock Summit	17	18	23-40	486	23-15	472
Carlisle-Plumpton	13	20	20-00	486	21-15	472
Penrith-Shap Summit	13.5	19	20-40	486	19-55	472
Crewe-Whitmore	10.5	14	14-45	486	14-40	475
Bletchley-Tring	15	16	14-45	486	14-35	472

OPERATING PERFORMANCE

Table 7.4: Correlation between reciprocating locomotive's cut-off settings and number of valves open on Turbomotive

	6212 00% % cut-off	6210 00 % % cut-off	6202, May 1936, No. of valves open	6202, Oct 1936, No. of valves open
DOWN				
Euston-Camden	55 00%	45-25	6 00%	5 00%
Willesden-Tring	25 00%	20-25	4-5	4 00%
Stafford-Whitmore	25-23	25-20	4-5	4-5
Carnforth-Grayrigg	18-35	20-35	4-5	4-5
Tebay-Shap Summit	20-45	20-43	4-5	4-6
Beattock-Summit	25-50	25-56	6 00%	5-6
UP				
Uddington-Craigenhill	20-25	20-35	4 00%	4 00%
Symington-Beattock Summit	25-45	25-35	5 00%	4-5
Carlisle-Plumpton	30-20	35-20	5-4	3-5
Penrith-Shap Summit	20-30	20-35	3-5	4-5
Crewe-Whitmore	25-20	38-20	5 00%	3-5
Bletchley-Tring	18 00%	20 00%	3-4	3-4

regulator and the cut-off permitted 'fine-tuning'. This lack of flexibility in the Turbomotive's controls was probably the main reason for failure to achieve significant, sustained savings in fuel consumption.

Performance was also carefully monitored in a return working of the 'Royal Scot' on 24/25 June (the year is not recorded, but is believed to have been 1936), and the results are tabulated in Table 7.5.

Table 7.5: 'Royal Scot', 24/25 June 1936(?)

Date	24 June	25 June
Route	Euston-Glasgow	Glasgow-Euston
Engine weight (full)	152 tons	152 tons
Train weight		493 tons (throughout)
From Euston	489 tons	
From Symington	320 tons	
Train miles	402	402
Ton miles:		
- excluding engine	190,702	194,316
- including engine	251,838	255,452
Time		
- actual running (minutes)	436	433
- including stops (minutes)	445	436
Speed		
- average mph	55.3	55.7
- maximum mph	85	81
Work done:		
- horsepower minutes	374,593	357,455
- horsepower hours	6,243	5,958
Horsepower minutes per ton mile (excluding engine)	1.97	1.84
Coal:		
- total weight lbs	17,084	16,156
- lbs per mile	42.4	40.2
- lbs per ton mile excluding engine	0.0895	0.083

Date	24 June	25 June
Route	Euston-Glasgow	Glasgow-Euston
- lbs per ton mile including engine	0.0678	0.063
- lbs per drawbar horsepower hour	2.735	2.71
- lbs per sq ft of gate area per hour	52.2	49.8
Water:		
- total gallons	15,155	14,420
- gallons per mile	37.7	35.9
- lbs per ton mile including engine	0.602	0.565
- lbs per drawbar horsepower hour	24.3	24.2
Evaporation:		
- lbs of water per lbs of coal	8.87	8.92

Mileages

Later concentration on London-Liverpool return services meant that daily mileages virtually matched those of the 'Princess Royals' on Anglo-Scottish services. The latter engines made a single daily journey between London and Glasgow (401 miles), whereas the Turbomotive went out and back each 24 hours – a return journey of 395 miles. The lower mileages attributed to No 6202 resulted from longer periods out of service for maintenance and repairs.

No 6202's record was distorted by storage from September 1939 to July 1941, and by three prolonged absences, from September 1941 to July 1942, June 1943 to September 1944, and March 1946 to April 1947. Discounting those intervals, which were caused or exacerbated by external factors, Table 7.7 (next page) shows the adjusted mileage comparisons for the 'full' years (1936-38, 1945, 1948 and 1949).

The Turbomotive achieved some impressive annual totals, during the years 1936 and 1945 in particular. No 6202's mileage

At work on the main line (reported as Basford Sand Siding) on 15 August 1936.

Table 7.6: **Annual average mileages of 'Princess Royals' and Turbomotive up to 31 December 1949**

Locomotive No	6200	6202	6205	6208	6212
1933	26,781				
1934	78,158				
1935	47,687	9,815	37,826	35,330	21,295
1936	67,464	73,268	82,451	96,158	99,018
1937	61,712	45,441	85,168	66,060	69,453
1938	72,873	44,176	67,657	85,613	79,001
1939	50,076	12,998	67,174	66,181	62,008
1940	71,140		44,395	68,138	69,577
1941	53,758	6,314	57,343	53,996	62,202
1942	59,373	33,702	49,048	46,848	59,272
1943	49,191	30,618	65,184	54,710	57,750
1944	53,876	3,521	64,346	35,058	52,171
1945	60,244	61,524	57,332	37,509	44,815
1946	58,403	12,358	44,659	56,711	48,544
1947	52,483	39,230	43,125	49,233	37,553
1948	55,942	23,101	41,872	55,381	46,321
1949	38,404	45,563	62,096	60,780	35,410
Accumulated total	957,565	441,629	869,676	867,706	844,390
Average p.a. 1936-1949	57,496	30,844	59,418	59,455	58,793

Source: LMS Engine History Cards

Table 7.7: **Adjusted annual average mileages of 'Princess Royals' and Turbomotive excluding periods out of service**

Locomotive No	6200	6202	6205	6208	6212
Total	356,639	293,073	396,576	401,501	374,018
6202 as percentage	82%	-	74%	73%	78%

Allocation and usage

No 6202 was allocated to Camden throughout its career except between 22 February and 19 April 1936, when it was shedded at Liverpool Edge Hill. In its later manifestation as BR 46202, it remained on Camden's roster until 27 June 1953, when it was transferred to Crewe North, sadly then only a book entry.

Apart from the dynamometer trials and some 'Royal Scot' workings, the Turbomotive was almost exclusively associated with the London-Liverpool route, although there were instances of it working between Euston and Crewe on North Wales services, and of appearances at Shrewsbury, presumably while running in after works attention. The decision to concentrate on the London-Liverpool route appears to have been for practical reasons rather than as a reflection of its haulage capacity north of Crewe. In event of failure, the locomotive would not be too remote from the specialised assistance available at the works. Also, regular employment on specific duties meant that only a small group of enginemen needed to be familiar with the locomotive.

This working pattern allowed convenient monitoring of performance from the trackside. For example, the passing times of No 6202 on the down 'Merseyside' (6.05pm ex-Euston) at Stafford and Crewe were recorded on forty occasions, as described in Table 7.8.

for the latter period (61,524) was higher than any of the 'Princess Royals', whose totals varied between 37,509 (No 6208) and 60,244 (No 6200).

OPERATING PERFORMANCE

Table 7.8: Passing times of No 6202 on down 'Merseyside' at Stafford and Crewe:

Passing	Stafford	Crewe
	Late (average 5½ minutes)	Late (average 4 minutes)
	– previous service running late 4	– previous service running late 5
	– bad steaming/poor coal 2	– bad steaming/poor coal 2
	– fog, Stafford-Crewe 1	
	– cause not known 3	– cause not known 2
	On time 11	On time 1
Early (average 3 minutes) 20	Early (average 3 minutes)	29

In steam at Liverpool Edge Hill shed.

This view of the right-hand side of the locomotive following fitting of the domed boiler was taken at Shrewsbury, a favourite destination for return running-in workings from Crewe.

Haulage capacity and duties

The turbine drive seems to have shown up most to advantage in haulage characteristics. On starting the turbine was at its most inefficient, but thereafter the steady, even torque yielded acceleration equal, if not superior, to that of a reciprocating engine, but with less propensity to slip. No 6202 had no difficulty in lifting seventeen coaches up to Camden, whereas other 'Pacifics' usually took banking assistance for fourteen or more. On the other hand, the small reverse turbine was of little help in banking empty stock trains out of the terminus after arrival at Euston.

The first published report of No 6202's road performance concerned the haulage of 380 tons over 152.7 miles between Crewe and Willesden Junction in just over 138 minutes, including an average of 75.6mph over the 67-mile Welton-Wembley section. Before the war, the highest authenticated speed recorded was 98mph.

An interesting test of the engine's capacities was noted in September 1942 in wet weather with greasy rail conditions on the 8.30am Euston-Liverpool service. The load comprised seventeen vehicles weighing 515 tons as far as Crewe, where the Blackpool

At work near Crewe, with the smoke deflectors fitted.

No 6202, in the 1946 LMS livery, awaits a Light Casual repair at Crewe Works on 2 May 1948. The engine is seen in its final (turbine) form following modification to the right-hand control casing and installation of smoke deflectors. The Light Casual repair kept the Turbomotive out of service from 16 April 1948 to 10 March 1949, a total of 280 days, calculated on a six-day week. This was the last of its long absences before withdrawal for rebuilding on 6 May 1950. In the period between March 1949 and May 1950 there were five other visits to the works for Light Casual or Unclassified repairs that varied between four and twenty-two days. *P. Fox, Transport Treasury*

OPERATING PERFORMANCE

In British Railways lined black livery at Crewe.

Below: The Turbomotive's limited power in reverse was quickly recognised when trying to bank trains following arrival at Euston. It is therefore unclear what was intended in this well-known photograph at the head of a nine-coach empty stock working at Bushey in 1935. The authors speculate that with the locomotive not long in service, this was a test working to establish the reverse turbine's maximum capacity, perhaps on a Sunday when traffic was less busy. *E. R. Wethersett*

No 6202 working light engine, apparently also at Bushey on the same date as the previous photograph, page xx bottom..

The Turbomotive on arrival at Euston.

portion (nine coaches) was detached, leaving 280 tons for Liverpool. Signal delays had been incurred in the Watford area, but Stafford was passed on time and Crewe was reached 1 minute early. Following a fast run with the reduced load, Liverpool was reached 3 minutes early.

The Turbomotive was mostly associated with the 8.30am Euston-Liverpool, returning the same day with the 5.25pm Liverpool-Euston, which on a Monday-Saturday basis equated approximately 2,330 miles per week. It started to appear on these workings before the war at a time when the up service (at an average of 64mph) was the fastest scheduled on the LMS. During and after the war it appears to have been engaged almost exclusively on these turns, although from 1940 onwards and for the rest of its career as a turbine engine, the schedules were significantly eased. Following the war, while remaining on Camden's roster, it was crewed alternately by men from there and Edge Hill shed under the continuing discipline of always having a specially trained fitter aboard.

Impressions from the footplate

A six-part article in *The Engineer* for April/May 1940 described the Turbomotive and earlier initiatives with steam turbines, and included an account by E. H. Livesay of two footplate journeys. The precise dates are not given but they both appear to have been in the short window between 31 July 1939 (completion of Light Ordinary repair) and 21 September 1939 (placement in store). The account of the up journey refers to 'a perfect autumn evening'.

Euston-Liverpool down

On this occasion, the on-board fitter's skills were needed even before leaving Camden as difficulty was experienced in engaging reverse gear. The engine would not move without his use of the inching gear but, once this was effected, in backing down towards Euston the smooth and seemingly effortless thrust of the turbine was immediately felt.

No 6202 departed punctually on the 10.40am to Liverpool, with a trainload of approximately 400 tons. Acceleration was smooth and reasonably rapid; sand was not needed and there was no hint of slipping. Indeed, sand from the trickle-type feed was not applied throughout the observer's two journeys. Two steam valves were opened to get the train under way and as speed built up the absence of the traditional staccato-type exhaust was striking, with the continuous flow of spent steam being almost noiseless. The turbine pinion emitted a rising, singing note up to about 15mph at which point the pitch moved beyond the aural register. It was this feature that gave rise to the nickname 'Gracie Fields' because 'she sings as she goes'.

On the 1 in 70 Camden Bank, a third steam valve was opened and smooth acceleration continued. Speed had risen to 35mph at the top of the bank, which was reached in 3½ minutes (1¼ miles) from the start. The enthusiastic driver proudly pointed out the

Departing Euston in 1938.
H. N. Twells collection

At work on what appears to be a train of fifteen or sixteen coaches.

quality of the acceleration, although the observer privately opined that this was not particularly special. He felt it could have been easily matched or surpassed by a 'Princess Royal' or 'Duchess', but the impression of smoothly flowing power was extraordinary. Willesden was passed at 60mph, 9½ minutes from the start, at which point another noise emerged – a deep, unobtrusive musical hum from the gear train.

On the continuous rise to Tring, speed (according to the speedometer) varied between 55 and 60mph with two valves open. Kings Langley (21½ miles) was passed at 26 minutes from start and Tring (32 miles) at 37½ minutes. Once over the summit at Tring, a steam valve was closed and speed increased to 75mph with just one valve open on the gentle descent to Cheddington (36½ miles in 41½ minutes). The draught was modest but in drifting steam mode the smoke deflectors kept forward visibility clear. The single-bore Linslade Tunnel was traversed in the normal fashion with dampers and firedoor closed, and Bletchley (47 miles) was passed after 50½ minutes at 72mph with two valves open. Steaming and boiler pressure remained steady to a degree unequalled in the observer's experience, and the soft, even draught kept the fire bed undisturbed. It was noted that the arrangement whereby the blast-pipe area was automatically adjusted in relation to the number of steam valves open had by then been abandoned.

The journey continued in similar fashion, passing Wolverton in 55 minutes, Roade in 1hr 2½min, and Weedon in 1hr 11½min, with speed fluctuating continuously around 60-65mph. Steam was shut off on leaving Kilsby Tunnel and the locomotive drifted to Rugby (1hr 26½min), which was passed at the regulation maximum of 35mph. No 6202 had run slightly ahead of schedule since Willesden, with 85 miles covered at an average of 58mph, and by now was 1½ minutes early. This surprised the observer as the engine's actual speed had been deceptive, aided by the consistently quiet and uneventful footplate conditions.

After Rugby, with time in hand, running was further moderated and boiler pressure remained constant at 245lb per sq in, the driver remarking that it was easier to hold the pressure steady than with a reciprocating locomotive. With one steam valve open, the 14½ miles to Nuneaton were covered in 15½ minutes. After taking water on Hademore troughs, the second valve was opened for the rise to Lichfield, even time having been recorded from Tamworth to there. Stafford was passed with steam shut off 2 minutes ahead of schedule. The 14 miles of gentle rise to Whitmore troughs brought no change to the calm cab routine. The riding was very good but not in the observer's experience significantly better than either the 'Princess Royal' or 'Duchess' classes. The constant torque and lack of cylinder thrust heightened the awareness of track variations.

A side view prior to the control casing modification and fitting of the smoke deflectors.

Arrival at Crewe was 2 minutes early at 1.30pm, having covered the 24½ miles from Stafford in 33 minutes with one steam valve open for most of that stretch. The 158 miles from London had taken 170 minutes at an average of 55.8mph. The schedule was undemanding and the Turbomotive had performed comfortably with plenty in reserve, and no sign of the crew's abilities being taxed in any way.

A local colleague replaced the Camden fitter at Crewe. A trouble-free start was made and two valves were used as far as Weaver Junction, passed 1 minute early. From there to Sutton Weaver three valves were engaged for the 1 in 100 climb. Ditton Junction being passed 2 minutes early, speed was then moderated, but nevertheless arrival at Liverpool Lime Street was 2½ minutes ahead of the scheduled 2.18pm. The average for the 35½ miles from Crewe had been 46.8mph, and that for the 193½ miles from London 53.9mph.

The engine reversed back to the shed at a maximum of about 20mph. The observer was especially keen to stay aboard as the depot access was notoriously difficult, requiring several fore-and-aft shunting movements, and he wanted to see how the reverse gear mechanism behaved. It proved that the inching gear had to be employed twice, but without any difficulty.

Liverpool-Euston up

The observer's second footplate experience started when he climbed aboard at Liverpool following the train's 2.18pm arrival from Euston. Release from the buffer stops was delayed by 45 minutes due to extra train movements connected with the outbreak of war. During the wait, an onlooker enquired whether the Westinghouse brake was fitted, and the observer advised that it was actually the Worthington oil-circulation pump, whose 'pant' was similar.

Shed access was again difficult, requiring two applications of the inching gear for reverse shunting movements. Apart from coaling and watering the engine, it was necessary to clean the fire as inferior fuel had been used on the down run. Coupled with the delay in release from Lime Street, time was short to complete the turnaround. No 6202 returned to Lime Street with the same crew of three that had come down, its fire not properly restored, and boiler pressure low. Coupling up to the 425-ton train was swiftly completed and departure was 3 minutes late at 5.28pm, with pressure at 210lb per sq in. The 1 in 93 climb to Edge Hill was tackled with four valves open and no sign of slipping. After a signal stop at Edge Hill, the train restarted at 5.34pm and accelerated rapidly over the level half-mile to Edge Hill Junction, followed by another climb of 1 in 93 to Wavertree. From there speed rapidly rose to 60mph down to Mossley Hill, followed by an adverse signal at Allerton, which was passed at dead slow.

Speed was back to 60mph by Halebank troughs, 9½ miles from Lime Street, and the observer noted how little spray was generated in picking up water, as a result of the 'economiser' fitted to the tender. This gadget took the form of an inverted metal 'U' fitted in front of the pick-up scoop, and lowered concurrently into the trough. The economiser forced water away from the trough sides to created a hump along the centre-line, directly in the path of the scoop, thus maximising the volume gathered and minimising waste.

Ditton Junction, just after the troughs, is at the foot of a 4-mile climb at 1 in 100-115, for which four steam valves were opened. The summit was passed at 55mph but the fire was still inadequate, with pressure down to 175. The fireman was skilfully building up the fire but pressure continued to fall, and at Sutton Weaver was down to 160lb per sq in and falling. The observer remarked on the novelty of an express locomotive going full chat with a heavy load and a boiler pressure 90lb short of the blowing-off point. The crew by then were showing concern at the state of affairs; the sand gun was employed and pressure stabilised during a 50mph speed restriction at Sutton Weaver.

By Weaver Junction speed was back to 60mph but the driver was concerned about the soft exhaust blast. He apparently wished, as did also the observer, for a means of sharpening it – a case where the erstwhile adjustable blast-pipe jumper ring might have been helpful. At least the smoke deflectors were working well in lifting the exhaust clear of the boiler.

Pressure was up to 185lb per sq in at Hartford, passed at 60mph, and continued to climb at Winsford where adverse signals brought speed down to 25mph; by then the train was 11 minutes down on schedule. Three steam valves were open for the 4½ level miles from Minshull Vernon, and this mode continued to Crewe, reached 10½ minutes late. The 35½ miles from Crewe had taken more than 50 minutes, caused by the out-of-course stop and sundry adverse signal restrictions, at an average speed of 42mph. The fireman's difficult time had resulted largely from deficiency in draught. The Camden fitter, who had ridden on the down journey described earlier, joined the footplate at Crewe and together with his local colleague set about trying to improve matters, including attention to the oil cooler. The running plate above the cooler was raised to the customary 45° angle as this had apparently been overlooked in the rush at Edge Hill.

Departure from Crewe was 12 minutes late, by which time pressure had risen to 225lb per sq in. Two valves were open for the long rise to Whitmore troughs, which were passed at 60mph. Steam was shut off for most of the 12-mile descent to Stafford and speed rose to 75mph. Close to Great Bridgeford, with 250lb per sq in showing, the safety valves lifted for the first time. Stafford (24½ miles from Crewe) was passed in 27 minutes at an average of 54.5mph, and the 9½ miles from there to Rugeley took 8½ minutes at an average of 67mph.

Hopes of a significant recovery were dashed by two signal checks near Armitage, the first almost bringing the train to a halt and the second reducing speed to 20mph. No 6202 had caught up with a slower service, but this was overtaken at Lichfield by which time the train was 18 minutes late. The pace then rapidly increased with Tamworth passed at 75mph, the 25 miles from Lichfield being covered at an approximate average of 70mph. Down the falling gradient to Brinklow almost 80mph was reached before steam was shut off for the 25mph restriction on the switch to the through line at Rugby, passed 17 minutes down.

The 4½-mile climb to Kilsby Tunnel was made on three valves, with speed rising to 55mph. Speed continued to rise on the 7-mile descent from the tunnel, and Weedon was passed at 80mph. The 19½ miles from Rugby to Blisworth were covered at an average of 63mph and the succeeding 8½ miles to Castlethorpe at an average of 68mph, peaking at 83mph before easing back to 60mph for the troughs. Wolverton was passed with three valves open at 75mph, with the driver making every effort to recover lost time.

Linslade Tunnel was taken fast, still on three valves, and the sand gun was applied on the ascent to Tring, by which point the deficit had been reduced to 15 minutes. Opportunities for further recovery were few over the remaining 32 miles, and there were several signal checks close to London, including being almost halted at Camden. Arrival at Euston was at 8.55pm, 15 minutes late. The total journey time from Liverpool had been 207 minutes and, allowing for the two out-of-course stops and numerous signal checks, the observer rated the average speed of 56mph as very good. In particular the 67mph average between Lichfield and London compared well with the best performance previously noted by him when No 6229 *Duchess of Hamilton* on the 'Coronation Scot' had covered this stretch in 3 minutes less but with a load lighter by 125 tons. The elapsed time from Wolverton to London was actually superior to that of the 'Duchess'.

The speeds over these two journeys were recorded by reference to the Turbomotive's speedometer, rather than by the usual methods of measurement. This instrument was electrical rather than mechanical and had been manufactured by Thomson-Houston. It comprised an AC generator driven from the left rear coupling rod pin, a DC voltmeter scaled in miles per hour on the speedometer dial, and the necessary rectifier. Flexible armoured cabling connected the generator to the speed indicator, which was conveniently positioned immediately in front of the driving position. This system was considered more reliable than the traditional Haslar and Flaman devices, with proneness to inaccuracy limited to 5% variation, and only at low speeds.

Impressions from the lineside

Brief reports serve to illustrate the impression that No 6202 gave to onlookers and admirers. Known to observers as the 'Turbo', many were surprised by the unchanging, strange whoosh of the exhaust. On the other hand, a young trainspotter wondered in 1938 why the Turbomotive on the down 'Merseyside' (6.05pm ex-Euston) was the only engine that always passed Acton Bridge with the steam shut off. Another came from a group of gangers whose warning cry was always 'Here comes the Ghost Train!'

Summary

The out-and-back Liverpool journey reports reflect two very different sets of circumstances. On the down service the Turbomotive displayed excess capacity on a relaxed schedule that hardly tested its abilities. The up train's problems were largely caused by outside circumstances, although dirty tubes and the need to use the sand gun appeared to be directly associated with the soft exhaust. Certainly the inability to restore full boiler pressure over the Liverpool-Crewe section added to the delays and contributed to the loss of path before Lichfield, suggesting that a mechanism to sharpen the exhaust in adversity might have been warranted. Also, while problems with the reverse gear mechanism had by then been resolved, it was evident that it could still be difficult to operate.

CHAPTER EIGHT

Rebuild and Tragedy

THE Turbomotive was probably most effective from the mid-1940s onwards, following the Heavy General repair of 1943/44 and resolution of the problems that had emerged during the previous decade. During another lengthy Heavy General in 1946/47 it was repainted in the final LMS livery, and commenced work with British Railways on 3 January 1948, following a Light Ordinary repair. It was renumbered as No 46202 in the week-ended 13 March 1949 and repainted in BR black, with lining that could be considered as quasi-LNWR. Use of this livery on large passenger locomotives was generally unpopular and short-lived, but this treatment suited No 46202 well. The authors believe it looked its finest in this guise.

Regardless of its potential then evident, the Turbomotive's future could only be regarded as uncertain, pending formulation of a new motive power policy. The new BR administration, headquartered in the old Great Central Hotel at 222 Marylebone Road, confronted a task even greater than that which faced the railways after the First World War. This time around, the system had sustained far more wear and tear through over-exploitation of physical resources, and through being an important target for aerial bombing.

BR's difficulties were compounded in the immediate post-war period by a crisis in coal supply as the mining industry strove to meet burgeoning demand. There were several causes, but a long-term consideration was that, under the stress of two world wars, coal had been taken from the larger, more conveniently placed seams, which meant that in future it would be more difficult and thus more expensive to extract. In 1946/47 oil had been pursued as a viable alternative fuel source for steam engines due to competitive pricing of the heavier crudes. However, the promising conversion programme was halted abruptly when devaluation of the pound sterling saw an overnight 30% increase in all import prices. Setting aside the understandable preference to use UK manufacturers, any re-equipment programme employing diesel or electric locomotives that required overseas-sourced specialised components or technical know-how would have been burdened with a similar cost escalation.

However desirable the long-term goal of modernisation, R. A. Riddles and his team faced the reality that coal-fired steam would remain the main energy source for the foreseeable future. It followed that any measure that might improve performance and/or reduce fuel consumption deserved investigation. Before and following the war innovation by the 'Big Four' had embraced diesel, electric and gas turbine traction, but exploratory initiatives into next-generation steam locomotives were few. Despite pre-war progress with three-cylinder conjugated valve gear and some use of rotary cam valve gear, the LNER had since opted for more conventional solutions employing one reciprocating motion set per cylinder in three-cylinder designs. The GWR had a single poppet valve locomotive that had operated rather in the shadows for some years; it was briefly assessed, then discarded.

Since early in the war the Southern had been especially creative with four new steam types that reflected Oliver Bulleid's iconoclastic and highly creative temperament. The 0-6-0 Class 'Q1' was the simplest and the best, whereas the good points of the 'Merchant Navy' and smaller 'West Country' 'Pacifics' were confounded by their bad, generating endless controversy. Bulleid, never one for half measures, went further by reviving Britain's fleeting acquaintance with articulated steam. His last design was a maximum-adhesion 0-6-0+0-6-0 Meyer with cabs at both ends, and another for the unfortunate fireman amidships. Setting aside the awkward internal layout, offset boiler and complex gadgetry including sleeve valves, one aspect might have been relevant to a new generation of large express locomotives.

The 'Leader' project had been envisaged and approved, surprisingly, as a potential replacement for the venerable London & South Western 0-4-4T Class 'M7', which weighed about 60 tons, but it evolved into a 130-ton main-line express locomotive. Apart from the lost opportunity of the Beyer Peacock/LMS Garratt, the 'Leader' was the most tangible evidence of the notion that articulation could form part of a new steam generation. This concept had also been briefly considered in the context of

THE LMS TURBOMOTIVE

No 46202 in its final style as the Turbomotive in the lined black livery that it acquired in 1949. *Real Photographs, National Railway Museum*

This publicity photograph of the recently rebuilt 'Princess Anne' Class 4-6-2 No 46202 *Princess Anne* was taken at Crewe Works on 14 August 1952. The following day was HRH Princess Anne's second birthday, when the locomotive was officially named.

The rebuilt locomotive's nameplate.

110

Dimensional variations between LMS 'Pacifics'

	'Princess Royal'	Turbomotive
Numbers	6203-12	6202
Wheelbase	7ft 6in + 5ft 6in + 8ft 0in + 7ft 3in + 9ft 6in	7ft 6in + 5ft 6in + 8ft 0in + 7ft 3in + 9ft 6in
Driving wheels	6ft 6in	6ft 6in
Loco length	49ft 2in	49ft 2in

	'Princess Anne'	Non-streamlined 'Duchess'
Numbers	46202	6230-34/6249-55
Wheelbase	7ft 6in + 5ft 6in + 7ft 3in + 7ft 3in + 9ft 6in	7ft 6in + 5ft 6in + 7ft 3 + 7ft 3in + 9ft 6in
Driving wheels	6ft 6in	6ft 9in
Loco length	48ft 10in	48ft 8in

Garratts for the GWR (4-6-0+0-6-4 and 2-8-0+0-8-2 wheel arrangements) and the Southern (4-6-2+2-6-4).

Other than limited application of rotary cam poppet valves, British Railways had little time for innovations with steam, although considerable patience was extended regarding the Southern Region's doomed attempts to make something of the 'Leader'. In this scenario the Turbomotive, as a unique experiment, was on borrowed time despite its operational effectiveness. Withdrawal from service on 6 May 1950 might have been widely regretted at operating level but, in the prevailing circumstances, must have caused little surprise. However, the official LM Region Locomotive Allocation List dated 4 November 1950 recorded No 46202 as still based at Camden (together with six 'Patriots', six 'Jubilees', twelve 'Royal Scots', twelve 'Duchesses', but no 'Princess Royals'), and it was apparent that further service was contemplated.

The Midland Railway legacy inherited by BR meant that there was a continuing dearth of large locomotives on the West Coast route. This was redressed in small part by the return of No 46202 as a conventional 'Pacific' on 15 August 1952 on which day (HRH Princess Anne's second birthday) it was formally named *Princess Anne*. It was fitted with plates stating 'Rebuilt Crewe 1952'.

Rather than create another example of the 'Princess Royal' Class, the rebuilt No 46202 benefited from experience gained with the later 'Pacifics'. 'Duchess'-style cylinders (inside of cast steel, outside of cast iron) were installed, together with new sets of valve motion. Replacement frames were provided, modified at the front end to accommodate the domed Type 1 boiler (No 9236) carried since July 1936, but now fitted with a single blast-pipe and chimney. Other new components comprised the crank axle, smokebox, superheater and elements. The original cab was retained but modified to accept the reversing gear. The 6ft 6in driving wheels were re-machined and re-balanced.

It was originally intended to install open platforms at the front end in the style adopted with the de-streamlined 'Duchesses', but this feature was changed to traditional curved drop ends, as used on the 'Princess Royals'. However, the drop-end profile differed as the running plate from the smokebox to just forward of the trailing driving wheel axle was set higher, then stepped down with the remainder at the normal height rearwards to the cab front. The original riveted tender (No 9003) was retained and the result was an attractive locomotive that looked exactly what it was, a 'Princess Royal'-'Duchess' hybrid. The differences from the earlier 'Pacific's were sufficient for it to be designated as the 'Princess Anne' type, and the dimensional variations are outlined in the Table above. The other leading dimensions of No 46202 *Princess Anne* itself are shown in the Table below.

Other leading dimensions of No 46202 Princess Anne

Cylinders (four)	16½in x 28in
Boiler:	
Maximum diameter	6ft 3in
Tube length	19ft 3in
Centre-line above rail	9ft 1in
Heating surfaces:	
Firebox	217sq ft
Tubes and flues	1,951sq ft
Superheater (40 elements)	752sq ft
Grate	45sq ft
Boiler pressure	250lb per sq in
Weight (loco only)	105 tons 4 cwt
Adhesive weight	66 tons 8 cwt
Maximum axle load	22 tons 4 cwt

The combination of 'Princess Royal' driving wheels and 'Duchess' cylinders resulted in a tractive effort of 41,538lb. By this criterion it was the second most powerful British steam locomotive, 101lb greater than ex-LNER 4-6-4 No 60700 and exceeded only by 2-8-0+0-8-2 Beyer Garratt No 69999.

Now distinguished by GWR-style lined green livery, the rebuilt No 46202 returned to Camden for use on the London-Liverpool services it had previously worked as the Turbomotive. No trials were undertaken to assess its theoretically enhanced capabilities, but perhaps these were intended (the first dynamometer tests with the Turbomotive had been conducted after 30,000 miles). Performance records of its short career in this form have not been traced, but there is no evidence of any adverse impressions. The rebuilding had cost £8,875 (construction of a BR 'Britannia' 'Pacific' was priced at £22,573) and was a viable means of extending an express engine's working life. In the normal course, No 46202 should have worked until the early 1960s.

* * *

No 46202, Britain's second most powerful steam locomotive.

No 46202 on shed at Liverpool Edge Hill in GWR-style lined green with its long-term partner, tender No 9003. *Rev Eric Treacy*

No 46202 is seen from a slightly different angle, also at Liverpool Edge Hill.

Before environmental legislation took effect, fog caused by the smoke of millions of chimneys often afflicted the London area during the winter months. The year 1952 was particularly bad for air pollution, epitomised by the Great Smog of 5-9 December. However, the hazards of poor visibility had already come to universal attention two months earlier through the events of 8 October.

As ever, traffic congestion on the West Coast Main Line in the London area was intense that morning. To help relieve pressure, it was normal practice to switch local services to the up fast line to utilise gaps in paths caused by late-running expresses from the north. Thus the on-time 7.31am Tring to Euston stopping train comprising nine coaches conveying 800 passengers hauled by 2-6-4T No 42389 working bunker-first was switched from the up slow to the up fast line on the approach to Harrow & Wealdstone station. At 8.19am, 1½ minutes after drawing up at the platform, this train was struck in the rear by the Perth-Euston sleeping car express travelling at around 55mph hauled by 'Duchess' Class No 46242 *City of Glasgow*. There was patchy fog, but not considered severe enough to call out fogmen. It was later concluded that visibility had been sufficiently impaired on the approach to Harrow for a colour light signal and two semaphores set at danger to have been missed.

'Duchess' 'Pacific' No 46242 *City of Glasgow* was hauling the Perth-Euston sleeping car express when it collided with the rear of a commuter train at Harrow & Wealdstone on 8 October 1952. It was subsequently repaired for further service and is seen heading the 'Royal Scot' at Symington in later years.

114

REBUILD AND TRAGEDY

'Jubilee' Class No 45637 *Windward Islands* was pilot locomotive to No 46202 on the 8.00am Euston-Liverpool express on that fateful day. It was also withdrawn as a result of damage sustained in the accident. This view was taken as No 5637 in LMS days.

The Euston-bound express ploughed into the rear of the local train causing substantial damage. The shocked Harrow signalman, on witnessing the disaster, instantly set all his signals to danger, threw his detonator levers and sent 'obstruction danger' over the telegraph. These precautions were in vain as he had already accepted the northbound 8.00am Euston-Liverpool/Manchester express hauled by No 46202 *Princess Anne* and piloted by No 45637 *Windward Islands* (which was working back to its home shed). On hearing the detonators explode, the drivers made emergency brake applications but too late to stop more disaster as the down fast line was fouled by damage from the first collision, into which the northbound train ploughed. The Liverpool express was heavy, comprising fifteen coaches plus four vans, but was making good progress at around 60mph with super-power haulage provided by the two engines.

The damage was extensive and it was not until early the next day that services were restored over the slow line, restricted to 5mph while passing the accident site. Line clearance was continuous until late the following Sunday night. In this process the two locomotives of the northbound train, the most severely damaged of those involved, were lifted clear and placed in a siding beside the up electric line. On 9 November, final removal of damaged material was completed with evacuation of the remains of No 45637, No 46202's boiler and both tenders in wagons to Crewe. During preparatory work the preceding week, it had been decided that the chassis of the 'Pacific' chassis could be moved by rail. A temporary bogie and trailer truck was installed and tender No 10624 (in shop grey and borrowed from 'Duchess' No 46257) was attached to facilitate removal. The first move was to Willesden, then on 13 November 1952 the sad entourage was hauled to Crewe by a Stanier 8F 2-8-0.

No 46202 had covered 11,443 miles since rebuilding. When in service the Turbomotive and its reciprocating successor had been allocated to Camden, apart from the short spell at Liverpool Edge Hill in 1936. While in store (16 September 1939 to 9 August 1941) it had been allocated to Crewe North, and on 27 June 1953 it was officially re-transferred to this depot, although the remains were actually lying nearby at the works. The purpose of this book

The sad end to a fine locomotive. No 46202 stands adjacent to the main line at Harrow following the accident.

BR Standard Class 8P No 71000 *Duke of Gloucester* on public display at Crewe when newly completed in May 1954.

entry is uncertain, as repair would have seemed improbable, judging by the photographic evidence. Components unique to this engine would have needed replacement (frames and smokebox), making the exercise uneconomic. It has been suggested that the reallocation formed part of Riddles's manoeuvrings to create a 'slot' into which his replacement three-cylinder express 'Pacific' would fit. No 46202 was formally withdrawn for scrapping on 22 May 1954, although the boiler was repaired for further service. The ex-Turbomotive's faithful companion, tender No 9003, was restored to operable condition and coupled to 2-8-0 Class 8F No 48134.

The Harrow accident is most remembered for the number of casualties. Nevertheless, there was a positive outcome from that dreadful day in galvanising British Railways into the application of its Automatic Warning System, an advanced version of Automatic Train Control that the GWR, of its own volition, had installed over all its major routes before the war. ATC was costly to install and maintain, but the system had served the GWR well, as reflected in that company's exemplary safety record. Stanier had been about to introduce ATC to the LMS, but the project was suspended on the outbreak of war. Harrow was precisely the sort of busy location where risk arising from conflicting traffic movements, especially under adverse weather conditions, would have been largely eliminated by ATC. The Enquiring Officer noted that most loss of life had been through destruction of the timber-bodied coaches of the local train, but that the steel-bodied vehicles of the expresses had stood up to the double impact very well – a reminder that the inside of a modern railway carriage is one of the safest places in the world.

To make up for the loss of No 46202, R. A. Riddles by sleight of hand provided another 'Pacific' in replacement. No 71000 *Duke of Gloucester* appeared in 1954 as the only true express steam engine built under the BR standardisation programme. It was a three-cylinder machine that paid homage to the advantages of rotational motion by using Caprotti valve gear, but proved something of a disappointment as a mediocre steamer. In preservation, judicious modifications have rectified faults in the original design and construction, and the 'Duke' has proved a formidable performer, demonstrating just what is possible with a modern steam locomotive.

However, Stanier and the LMS had shown almost twenty years earlier that by stepping beyond the bounds of convention there was even more to be exploited. *Princess Anne* and *Duke of Gloucester* were impressive machines, but neither quite matched the style and potential of the Turbomotive.

The 'Duke' in service on shed at Polmadie in the same year.

CHAPTER NINE

The Philadelphia Connection

DESPITE the incursions of diesel-electric manufacturers, development of next-generation large steam locomotives continued in the USA into the 1940s, and forms of steam turbine into the 1950s. Although essentially independent of British-based pre-war experiments, these exercises identified the opportunities and limitations presented by very large locomotives. Non-condensing steam turbine drive played a role in these efforts, but its potential was under-exploited, coming too late to leave any lasting mark on steam power.

There were certain reasons why this interest in steam persisted. Even in the 1940s there was concern in the USA about the finite nature of domestic oil reserves, which it was feared might eventually enforce reversion to coal-based energy sources. Further, there was commercial incentive in high-speed, super-powerful steam engines prior to the ascendancy of domestic passenger air travel. An added stimulus lay with those Class 1 railroads that moved vast quantities of indigenous coal for industrial consumption. Finally, the low-cost reliability and simplicity of the steam locomotive underpinned its perceived role as an immutable element in a large motive power fleet.

Contrary to prevailing industry trends, the Philadelphia-based Baldwin Locomotive Works retained belief in steam's continuing viability. Established in 1825, this was the world's largest manufacturer, having built over 70,000 (mainly steam) locomotives in the period up to the Second World War. Samuel M. Vauclain, a widely admired industrialist (and inventor of the compound system that bore his name), as Chairman of the Board, had pronounced in 1930 that steam would remain the dominant motive power source for another fifty years or so.

Corporate culture is often resistant to change and, despite the progress of others in validating diesel power, this optimism was resilient. Ralph P. Johnson, Baldwin's chief engineer, published a paper in November 1945 titled 'Railroad Motive Power Trends', which stated that 'the ruggedness of the steam locomotive cannot be overlooked'. After reviewing attempts to improve thermal efficiency, he continued: 'The steam locomotive will never make any dramatic increases in thermal efficiency but I am sure that its steady improvement will continue. And I am sure that the qualities that have made it popular heretofore will ensure it a large place in future locomotive inventories.'

Events soon proved this view a profound error of judgment, and a failure to appreciate the impact of new technology. Nevertheless, the company had produced its first diesel 'switcher' (shunter) in 1939, when competitors were already building road locomotives. During and after the war production diversified into transfer locomotives, graduating to modest numbers of main-line passenger and freight designs. Unfortunately the initiative had been irretrievably lost, and Baldwin built its last conventional steam locomotive for domestic use in 1949, and for export the following year. The last diesel locomotive appeared in 1956, and the company ceased all manufacturing and filed for bankruptcy in 1965.

The Pennsylvania duplex family

Also headquartered in Philadelphia, the Pennsylvania Railroad (PRR) was the largest US railroad for much of the 20th century, as measured in traffic volume and gross revenue. Its 10,500 route miles extended across twelve north-eastern states and Washington DC, with a business around 30% greater than its neighbour and arch-rival, the New York Central Railroad, and roughly three times that of other railroads with similar lengths of route (e.g. Union Pacific and the Atchison, Topeka & Santa Fe). Unlike most American railroads, PRR built most of its locomotives, resorting to contractors only when its works at Altoona were at full capacity. The most favoured contractor was Baldwin, with whom the PRR maintained a relationship somewhat akin to that between the Great Central Railway and Beyer Peacock at Gorton, Manchester.

The PRR's principal express passenger type was the well-regarded 4-6-2 Class 'K4', of which 425 were built between 1914 and 1928. However, by the late 1920s, increasing loads were testing the capacity of the 'K4s', frequently necessitating the anachronistic practice of double-heading. The most pressing

Pennsylvania Railroad duplex-type 6-4-4-6 Class 'S1' No 6100 seen at Englewood, Illinois. *Image within the public domain*

A diagram of the duplex-type 6-4-4-6 Class 'S1' No 6100.

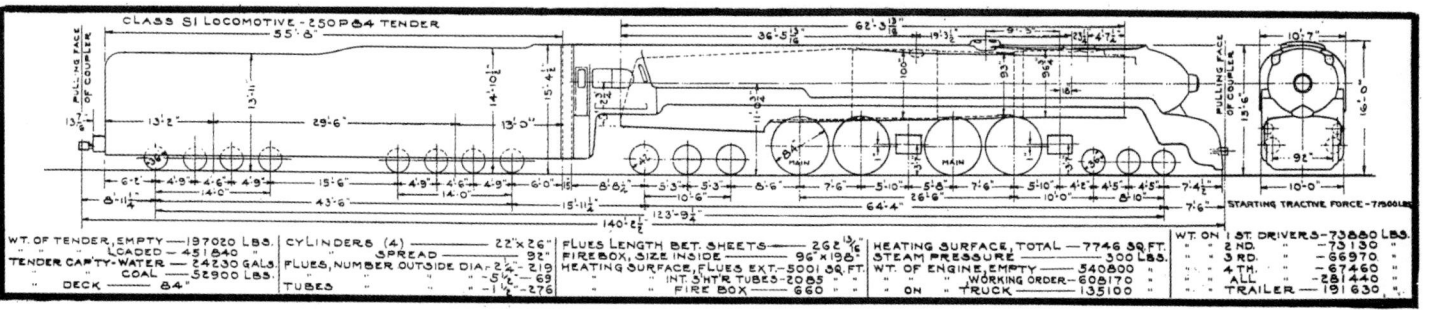

demands were on the non-electrified western section of the New York-Chicago route, where there was demand for steam engines that could perform on a par with the PRR's electric fleet. Most challenging was the need to work 800-ton passenger trains over the 713 miles between Harrisburg, Pennsylvania and Chicago, Illinois, at speeds up to 100mph.

Despite the success of the 4-6-6-4 'Challenger' Class on the Union Pacific, the Mallet type was regarded as best suited to heavy freight work. Thus a rigid-frame locomotive was regarded as essential to operate express schedules, but an eight-coupled locomotive of the size necessary induced problems of hammer blow and intense stresses when moving at high speed.

Balancing could have been improved by using three or four cylinders, but there was a long-standing antipathy towards inside cylinders, with the associated inconvenience of inside motion and costly crank axles. To circumvent these difficulties, the Vauclain compound system had been invented whereby the high- and low-pressure cylinders were mounted adjacently and a single, complex piston valve drove a common crosshead. Introduced in 1889, the system was widely applied, but valve troubles and uneven wear of other moving parts led to a general loss of interest by the 1900s, even before the significance of hammer blow had been fully recognised.

The solution adopted for enlarged passenger (and also freight) locomotives used a single frame to support two separate driving wheelsets and associated cylinders. This arrangement, known as the 'duplex' type, resulted in reduced reciprocating mass and gentler piston thrust compared with a conventional 4-8-4. The concept had been tried unsuccessfully in the 1860s in France, and Baldwin revived the idea in the 1920s. The Baltimore & Ohio Railroad, having rejected that manufacturer's overtures, built its own 4-4-4-4 Class 'N-1' No 5600 *George H. Emerson* in 1937 as America's first duplex. The length over the driving wheels was similar to the coupled wheelbase of the B&O's largest 4-8-2s, achieved by reversing the second driving wheel set with cylinders and motion to the rear, adjacent to the firebox. This experiment was terminated in 1943 as a consequence of difficulties with long steam passages and overheating of the rear cylinders.

The first duplex built by Baldwin was experimental Class 'S1' No 6100 in 1939 for service with the PRR. This engine differed from the B&O machine in having all cylinders mounted forward of their respective driving wheel sets, which necessitated a greater length. The operational objective was to haul 1,070-ton passenger trains at speeds up to 100mph on level track, and the engine's leading dimensions were extraordinary. The wheel arrangement was 6-4-4-6, the overall length (locomotive and tender) was 140 feet, and the aggregate nominal weight exceeded 474 tons. Great care was taken in the design and layout of the cylinders and motion, resulting in effective balancing of about 52% of the reciprocating mass. As the longest rigid-frame reciprocating steam engine ever built, it was expected that there would be shortcomings in so radical an experiment, but these were accepted as inevitable teething troubles.

Through display at the 1939 New York World's Trade Fair, No 6100 attracted much attention and later proved popular with crews. It was fast, powerful and rode smoothly, doubtless aided by the forward momentum of the enormous weight, and there were unauthenticated claims of speeds up to 120mph. On the other hand, the 'teething trouble' factor diverted attention from the locomotive's weight distribution, of which 46% was adhesive. The centre of gravity lay towards the rear and, with so much weight carried by the six-wheeled bogies, the load borne by the forward driving wheels was disproportionately light. There was a propensity to slip on starting, while on uneven track the forward

THE LMS TURBOMOTIVE

No 6110, the first of the pair of prototype duplex 4-4-4-4 Class 'T1s' as built with full driving wheel valances. *Image within the public domain*

A diagram of the 'T1' 4-4-4-4 following removal of the deep valances over the driving wheels.

A T1 'undressed'. The production series had much shallower driving wheel valances, and part of these were cut away in connection with the experimental fitting of Walschaerts valve gear to No 5547, as shown here. This locomotive was reclassified 'T1a' following this unsuccessful modification. *Image within the public domain*

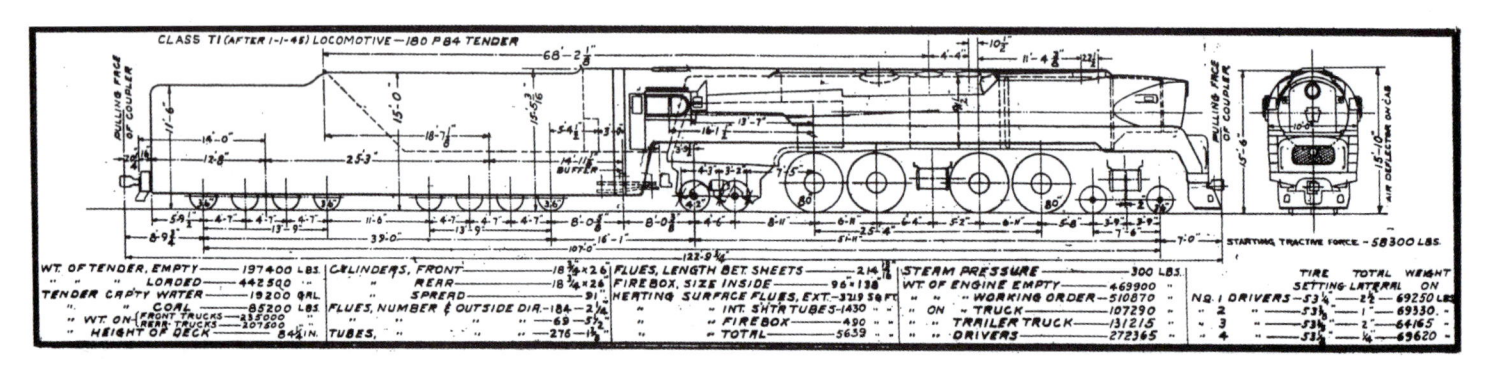

Right: This is duplex-type 4-6-4-4 Class 'Q1' No 6130 as built and before the removal of the driving wheel valances. This locomotive followed the pattern initiated with the Baltimore & Ohio Railroad 4-4-4-4 Class 'N-1' No 5600 *George H. Emerson* whereby the rear engine unit was reversed with the cylinders adjacent to the firebox. Both types were unsuccessful for the same reasons – overheating of the rear cylinders and tortuous steam passages. *Image within the public domain*

A diagram of the 'Q1' 4-6-4-4.

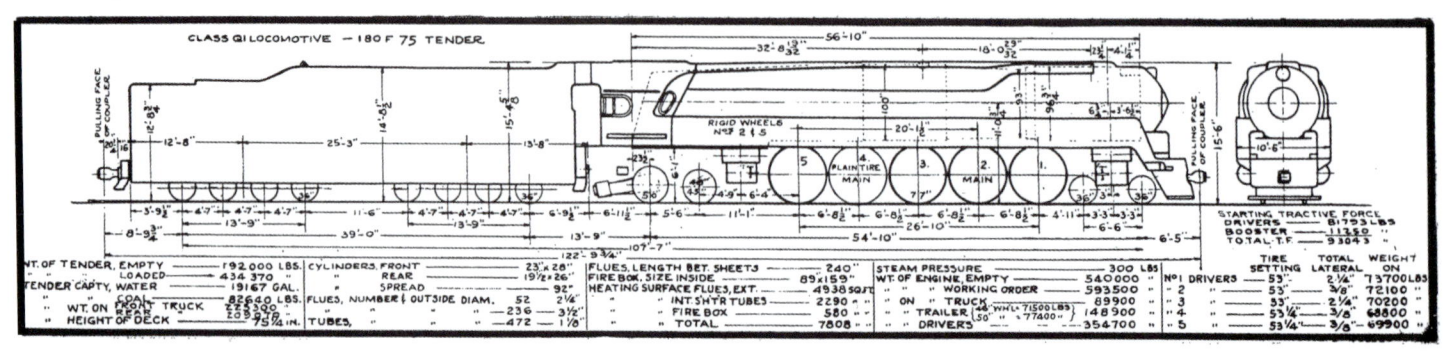

unit could also lose adhesion while on the move. With both engine units discharging through the single chimney, the noise could camouflage the sound of something amiss. If not corrected quickly there was a risk of the valve motion sustaining extensive damage.

No 6100's size anticipated substantial investment in bridges to permit a wide sphere of operations, but this did not occur. As a result, it was confined to the PRR's 283-mile section between Chicago and Crestline, Ohio (just north of the junction with the PRR's route northwards to Toledo and Detroit). No 6100 continued intermittently in service throughout the war and its last recorded work was on a train to Chicago in May 1946.

Despite the adhesion issue, the PRR persisted with the duplex system. In 1942 two prototypes of 4-4-4-4 Class 'T1' (Nos 6110-11) were built, followed by another fifty (Nos 5500-49) in 1945/46 to work the company's heaviest passenger trains. They were smaller than the experimental 'S1' and did not ride as well, but they could perform impressively in the hands of skilled drivers. Unfortunately, they were costly to run, difficult to maintain, and shared the proneness to slip. There were unsubstantiated speed claims but it seems likely that they regularly exceeded 100mph in ordinary service. Nevertheless they were generally regarded as unsuccessful and all had been withdrawn by 1952.

Despite being a major freight hauler, the PRR only ever owned thirteen Mallets, three of which were experimental while the remainder were confined to helper, switching and transfer duties. For heavy main-line freight work, reliance was placed on a ten-coupled fleet comprising around 900 locomotives with wheel arrangements of 2-10-0, 2-10-2 and 2-10-4. It was thus logical to try the duplex system with five driving axles, and the first was the experimental 4-6-4-4 Class 'Q1' No 6130 of 1942. This engine repeated the idea attempted with the Baltimore & Ohio 'N-1' in reversing the second cylinder set, valve motion and driving wheels, but problems similar to those that afflicted the B&O engine arose.

Nevertheless, the PRR persisted with duplex freight locomotives with the twenty-six-strong 4-4-6-4 Class 'Q2' in 1944/45, which reverted to the 'T1'-type layout in having leading cylinders on both driving wheel sets. A key improvement was wheel slip protection in the form of rollers that bore against the tyres of the second and fourth driving axles; on detecting a differential in speeds, these activated an electrical control that by means of a butterfly valve cut off steam and admitted air to the engine unit that was slipping. The result was considered generally satisfactory, yielding an ability to haul 125 freight cars at 50mph, but their complexity made them early candidates for withdrawal, and all had gone by 1951.

The duplex family were extraordinary machines that pushed rigid-framed steam design to the limit, but they were expensive to build and maintain. Performance could be impressive and better than contemporary single-unit diesel-electric locomotives, but they required careful driving (especially the 'T1s'). Despite the threat of poor adhesion, they were charismatic creations that attracted worldwide attention. This recognition was enhanced by the streamlining applied to the 'S1', 'T1' and 'Q1' types, which was the work of Raymond Loewy, a leading industrial designer who had a long-term association with the PRR. He went so far as to patent the treatment given to the 'S1', but the styling best remembered was the shark-nose of the 'T1s'. This feature also appeared on the early Baldwin diesel-electric locomotives and was copied by the (successful and otherwise conventional) South Australian Railways 4-8-4 Class '520' of 1943. (Although no 'T1s' survive, the styling impact can be appreciated with No 520 *Sir Malcolm Barclay-Harvey*, and in slightly different form with No 523 *Essington Lewis*, both of which are preserved in Adelaide.)

A duplex-type 4-4-6-4 Class 'Q2' at Crestwood, Ohio, on 10 April 1948. This freight design was perhaps the most successful of this locomotive family, helped by special equipment to detect and correct wheel spin on either engine unit. *Image within the public domain*

A diagram of the 'Q2' 4-4-6-4.

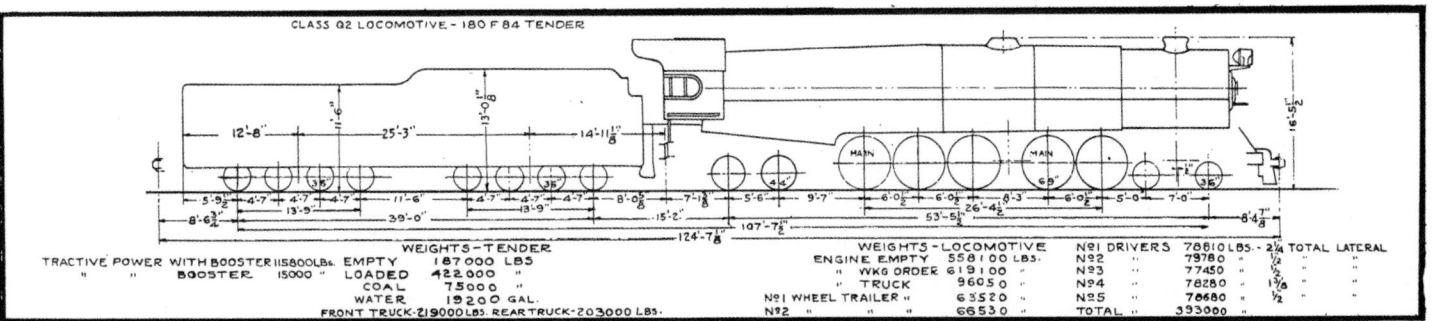

THE LMS TURBOMOTIVE

The influence of Raymond Loewy was more than just stylistic. He must have appreciated that the combined factors of size, weight and metallurgical limitations restricted practical enlargement of reciprocating steam engines. A clue to the circumvention of the problem of reciprocating mass was evident in the use of rotary cam valves on the 'T1s', but the greater conflict between hammer blow and the need for adequate adhesion remained.

The Pennsylvania steam turbine
In 1937 Loewy had recognised the qualities of Stanier's Turbomotive in his book *The Locomotive*. He described it as 'one of the most beautiful pieces of machinery ever designed by man' and went on to say that 'it has the poise, the rhythm and the balance of some magnificent ship. The engine probably represents the apex of the pre-streamlined age.' His enthusiasm apparently influenced Baldwin, and after the war Stanier confirmed that the LMS had provided technical data to that company for consideration in the construction of what became Pennsylvania Railroad 6-8-6 Class 'S2' No 6200.

This engine appeared in 1944, forming part of the Baldwin/PRR search for a new generation of steam locomotives for fast, heavy passenger duties. Although exploiting many design features of the Turbomotive, a key difference was the objective of maximum power output, unconstrained by any concern for fuel economy. Coal was significantly cheaper than in Britain, and the vast tender stood testimony to the munificence of local supplies.

Like the Turbomotive, No 6200 was a direct-drive steam turbine with the larger (forward) turbine mounted on the right above the gap between the second and third coupled axles, delivering a maximum horsepower of 6,900. The turbine shaft was connected through reduction gears to both these axles. The main turbine worked at a slower speed – 9,000rpm at 100mph compared with 15,600rpm for the Turbomotive.

The smaller turbine was mounted on the left, connected to the third axle for reverse running up to a maximum of 22mph. The power rating of the reverse turbine on the LMS Turbomotive does not appear to have been recorded, whereas that for the Baldwin giant was reported as being 25% of that for the forward turbine. Another source quotes the reverse tractive effort as 65,000lb compared with 70,000lb in forward mode. The bases for these ratings appear to conflict, but it seems that specific measures were taken to avoid the Turbomotive's mediocrity in this regard.

The enormous boiler was fitted with a Belpaire firebox that incorporated a combustion chamber. The total heating surface was 7,040sq ft, compared with 2,745sq ft for the Turbomotive when fitted with its 1936 boiler. The working pressure was 310lb per sq in, falling to 295lb per sq in at the nozzles of the steam supply valves. Multiple nozzles were installed in four groups, set in such a fashion as to allow a gradual and continuous increase in steam supply, thereby allowing more flexibility than was possible with the Turbomotive's six-nozzle arrangement. The driver controlled the opening of the nozzles by means of a single lever that crossed a gate between forward and reverse, with a complex series of protective interlocks operated by compressed air. With balanced driving wheels and no hammer blow, the flexibility of turbine drive was reiterated in the ability to exceed 100mph hauling heavy loads, notwithstanding 5ft 8in driving wheels. Intended only as a passenger locomotive, it was apparently never tried on freight work.

The locomotive's weight in working order – 263 tons (engine only) – was a contentious issue, although through circumstance rather than design deficiency. Wartime restrictions prevented use of lightweight alloys for what had been intended as a 4-8-4, enforcing the use of six-wheeled bogies. As with LMS No 6202, the engine steamed well at speed with an even draught, aided by a unique four-nozzle smoke stack, and a Worthington feedwater heater. Twin air pumps were mounted below the running plate beside the smokebox to feed the braking system, and a large radiator was fitted above the buffer beam to cool the intake of compressed air. Timken roller bearings were fitted throughout, including the two eight-wheel tender bogies, and roller bearing

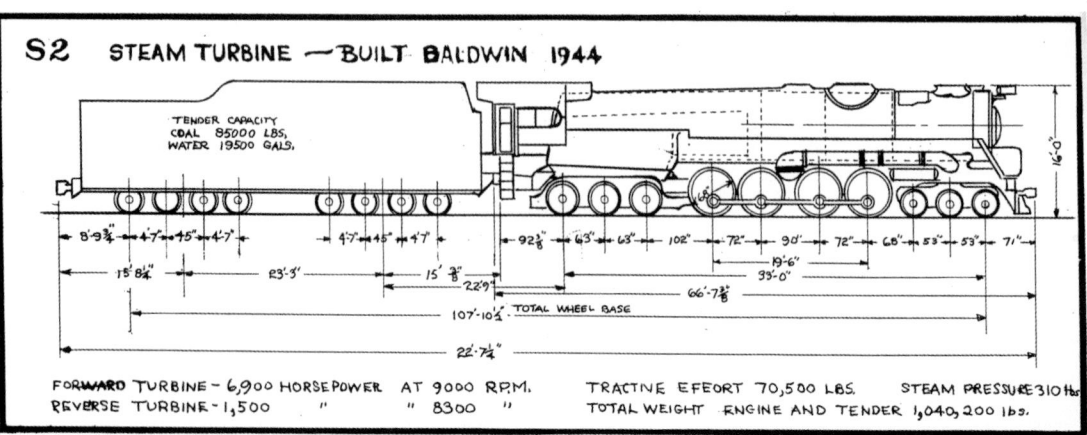

The right-hand side of turbine locomotive No 6200 following installation of small smoke deflectors. *Image within the public domain*

A diagram of 'S2' No 6200.

Super 'Iron Horse' Shows Its Secrets

Turbine-Driven Locomotive Undergoes Inspection

Capable of 120 miles per hour and a cruising speed of 100 miles per hour for passenger trains, the Pennsylvania Railroad's newest power unit is shown here in Philadelphia. Generating 6,900 horsepower, it underwent a trial run with the group of engineers and others who are listening to engineer Edward Weber, left of group, explain how the steam, fired by coal, presses against turbine blades for geared transmission to the wheels. The conventional cylinders, pistons, and driving rods are absent, although the hub links look something like the familiar driving rods.

Above and following page:
Newspaper cuttings recording the introduction into service of No 6200. The advantage of the size of the American 'railroads' compared with their European counterparts is immediately apparent.

assemblies were also fitted to the coupling rod pins. Discounting the enormous size, the massive construction of coupling rods and crank pins, and the vast tender, the locomotive looked reasonably conventional.

No 6200 worked between Chicago and Crestline every 24 hours, covering 580 miles on each round trip. E. S. Cox rode aboard the locomotive from Chicago to Fort Wayne, Indiana, a distance of 148 miles with start-to-stop sections requiring average speeds in excess of 60mph. The locomotive was worked almost continuously around 85 to 95% of its maximum capacity, i.e. with 90% of the steam nozzles open at full regulator. The 64-mile section from Plymouth, Indiana, to Fort Wayne was covered in 51 minutes, an average of 75mph that included 12 miles at 100mph or more. On this occasion the trainload was rather less than normal at 930 tons. This performance was an impressive demonstration of what turbine power could deliver, showing the irrelevance of driving

THE LMS TURBOMOTIVE

This Newest Locomotive *is Powered Like a Battleship*

EVER SINCE Matthias Baldwin built "Old Ironsides" over a century ago, railroads of this country have been constantly improving the steam locomotive to make it more powerful and more smooth.

NOW A WAY has been found to harness the *steam turbine* to a locomotive. Long ago successfully developed by Westinghouse for ocean vessels, the steam turbine is a brand new drive for railroads.

THE WESTINGHOUSE steam turbine in the Pennsylvania Railroad's direct-drive locomotive, is no bigger than your electric refrigerator, yet it will haul long passenger trains over the mountains with ease.

THE POWER-PACKED locomotive turbine is a descendant of giant Westinghouse turbines which generate much of the electricity you use. The great expansion of electric power began with these turbines.

A TURBINE is essentially a kind of steam windmill. A central revolving shaft with many blades is driven smoothly and powerfully by jets of steam, just as a boy's pinwheel is driven by the wind.

THE VELVETY FLOW of power from this 6,900 horsepower steam turbine locomotive will make trains run with extra smoothness and is a major contribution to finer transportation for you in the future.

THE RAILROADS, now carrying on one of the most spectacular research programs of any industry, are developing a dazzling new kind of transportation for you in the future. The familiar steam locomotive has been going through a remarkable series of improvements. The latest and most dramatic is *steam turbine* power, which gives the Iron Horse "new lungs."

To help produce this new locomotive, the Pennsylvania Railroad, a long-time pioneer in transportation improvements, turned to the Westinghouse Electric & Manufacturing Company and the Baldwin Locomotive Works. Working as a team, these companies have produced this latest in a great line of steam locomotives descended from "Old Ironsides." Westinghouse Electric & Manufacturing Company, Pittsburgh 30, Pennsylvania.

Westinghouse
PLANTS IN 25 CITIES OFFICES EVERYWHERE

Tune in: JOHN CHARLES THOMAS—Sunday 2:30 pm, EWT, NBC ••• TED MALONE—Monday; Tuesday; Wednesday Evening, Blue Network

wheel size. It was also a cogent reflection on the futility of streamlining, as No 6200's profile was hardly aerodynamic.

Operating experience revealed problems associated with draughting. No 6200 was consistently worked closer to its maximum output than was the Turbomotive, leading to thermal efficiency comparisons. The backpressure was estimated at 15-20% (substantially higher than was the average in the UK), the total free area through the tubes was 9% of the grate area (12% with the Turbomotive), and placement of the turbine between the second and third driving axles increased the length of the exhaust passages. These factors combined to remove an advantage of the turbine system in the ability to expand steam down to a very low pressure before exhaust. At speeds below 30mph, No 6200's draught was inadequate and boiler pressure often dropped as low as 85lb per sq in. To compensate, fuel consumption at low speeds was very heavy, and the firebox tended to overheat leading to failure of the stays. Drifting smoke necessitated the fitting of small smoke deflectors; when these proved inadequate, a larger style was used.

As mileage accumulated, a further issue arose over excessive wear in the turbine gear, which contrasted with the LMS Turbomotive's reliability in this regard. This defect might have related to wartime shortages and non-availability of preferred metals. Ostensibly these problems could have been surmounted, but the appetite for further experimentation and modification of steam locomotives was evidently waning.

The PRR's duplex and turbine fleet in summary

The PRR's investment in duplex locomotives was a fascinating exercise, especially regarding the passenger types (Classes 'S1' and 'T1'). Their size and power was a considerable step up from the trusty Class 'K4' 4-6-2 (with a locomotive working weight of about 140 tons), and probed the very limits of passenger speed and haulage capacity with reciprocating steam. The case for the heavy freight types (Classes 'Q1' and 'Q2') looked distinctly marginal with unclear objectives. For example, between 1942 and 1944 the PRR built 125 Class 'J1' 'Texas' 2-10-4s, a simple two-cylinder design of Lima origin with 5ft 10in driving wheels. Eighteen tons lighter and with a tractive effort only 5% less than that of the 'Q2', the 'J1' was cheaper to build, much simpler to maintain, and enjoyed a wide route availability.

With hindsight, the PRR's enthusiasm for the duplex system seems hard to comprehend, with more than a suspicion that both the 'T1' and 'Q2' Classes, built in quantity, were subject to the Law of Diminishing Returns, i.e. that the incremental cost of the added complexity outweighed the economic gains of the resultant operating advantages. In this context it appears that a greater measure of untapped potential resided in 6-8-6 non-condensing steam turbine No 6200.

None of the shortcomings described above seemed to preclude further development, provided that a careful LMS-style diagnostic and corrective approach was adopted. Had the intended specialised alloys been available for construction, a lighter 4-8-4 with similar power output would have been feasible, giving a lower axle loading. Combined with zero hammer blow, there appeared to be ample margins for either improved weight and power characteristics with a duly modified No 6200, or for an even larger and more powerful turbine locomotive. Further, in freight working over long distances and without the frequent stops en route that were typical in the UK, the turbine drive would seem to have considerable potential, aided if need be with a booster on the rear bogie as fitted to the 'Q2' and 'J1' heavy freight classes. In summary, whereas the duplex fleet had reached the limits, the lone 6-8-6 turbine locomotive contained significant unexploited potential.

It was a pity therefore that the Pennsylvania faction did not study the work of Ljungström and Stanier some eight or ten years earlier. By the time No 6200 entered service, delivery of the duplex fleet was in full swing with considerable money and effort already committed. However superior the concept appeared, a change of course in favour of a turbine class was probably not viable by that stage, making its marginalisation inevitable. Regrettably, the working career of steam turbine No 6200 was severely truncated, as this impressive machine was withdrawn in 1946.

The duplex fleet was also short-lived. The solitary members of Classes 'S1' and 'Q1' did not long survive the war, while the freight 'Q2' type lasted until 1951, and Class 'T1' a little longer. These amazing machines were outlived by the 'K4s', the type the 'T1' had been intended to replace. Examples of those venerable 'Pacifics' soldiered on until 1958 on lesser duties, rather as Stanier's 'Duchesses' were to be found on parcels trains in their final years.

Chesapeake & Ohio Railway Class 'M-1'

Baldwin's second attempt with a steam turbine echoed the UK experiments prior to the Beyer-Ljungström turbine locomotive by reverting to the 'power-station-on-wheels' idea. The company collaborated with Westinghouse in the creation of a 4-8-0+4-8-4 steam-turbine-electric design for use on the Chesapeake & Ohio Railway, another system that moved considerable tonnages of coal. A single Westinghouse steam turbine powered four direct current generators to deliver up to 6,000hp to eight traction motors. The electrical equipment was at the front of the locomotive with the cab immediately behind and in front of the coal bunker (capacity 26 tons), with the boiler at the rear, carried by 40-inch-diameter wheels throughout. Water was contained in a separate tender (capacity 21,000 gallons). In working order, the locomotive weighed 383 long tons and the tender 168 long tons.

Chesapeake & Ohio Railway No 500 was the first of the three prototypical steam-turbine-electric locomotives of Class 'M-1'.
Image within the public domain

THE LMS TURBOMOTIVE

Three were built specifically to work the 'Chessie', the prestige daylight passenger service between Washington and Cincinnati, at speeds up to 100mph. They were delivered in 1947/48, but the 'Chessie' was withdrawn in the latter year. It had been hoped that the return journey could be completed without the need for interim servicing but these engines proved unreliable, requiring much additional maintenance. They were usually restricted to 75mph, and their full speed and haulage potential was never really tested. The total construction cost for the trio was US$1.6 million, excluding research & development expenditure. Such a cost could only be justified with a significant advance in performance combined with exemplary reliability and availability. The trio had short careers, mainly confined to lesser duties between Clifton Forge, Virginia, and Charlottesville, Virginia; they were scrapped in 1950.

Norfolk & Western Railway No 2300 'Jawn Henry'

Based in Roanoke, Virginia, the principal activity of the Norfolk & Western Railway (NWR) was the movement of bituminous coal

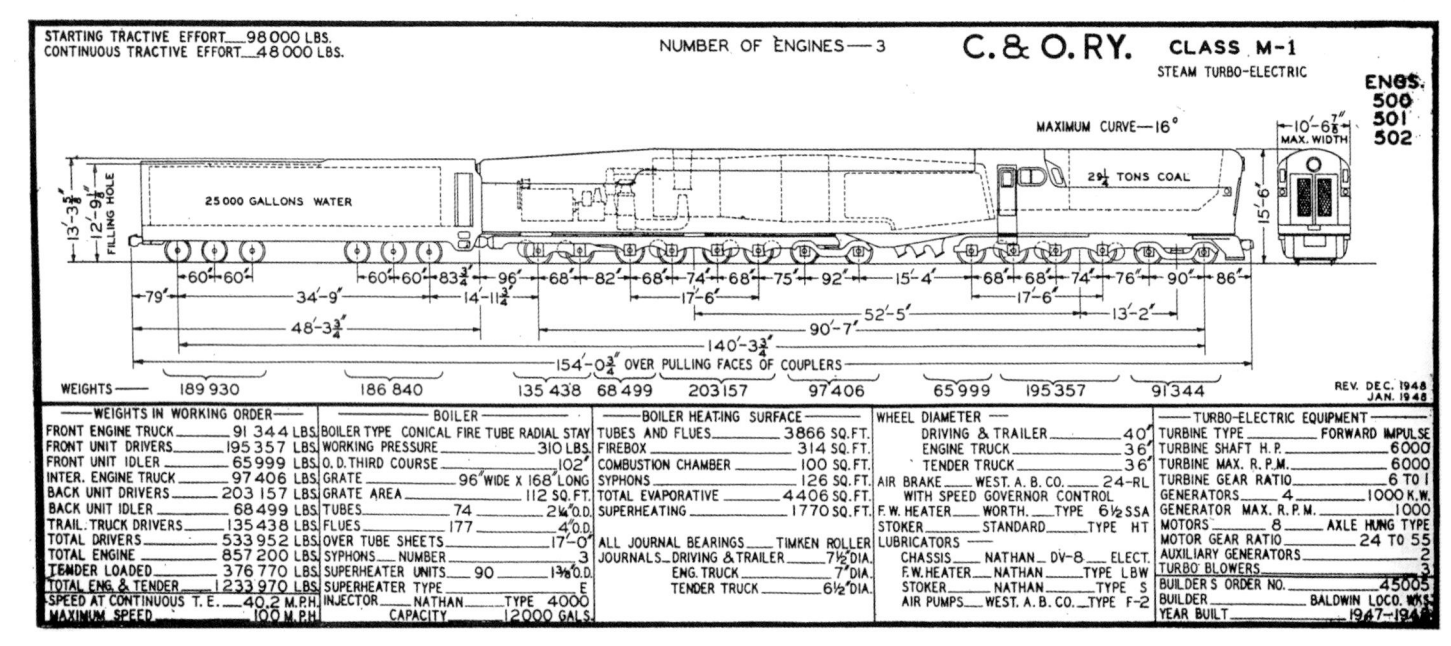

A diagram of Class 'M-1' steam-turbine-electric locomotive No 500.

Maintenance at the front of No 500. *Image within the public domain*

The driver's position in the cab of C&O No 500. *The Railway Gazette*

The engineer and fireman at the controls of Norfolk & Western Railway steam-turbine-electric locomotive No 2300, quoted in contemporary American journals as 'Simple, especially when compared with a standard reciprocating engine.'

from mines in western Virginia eastwards through the Allegheny Mountains to the port of Norfolk on Chesapeake Bay. The NWR was famously the last bastion of steam power among the Class 1 US railroads, with significant dieselisation not commencing until the late 1950s. In that regard the railway was considered a time warp, immortalised through the atmospheric photography of O. Winston Link, which recorded scenes of a rapidly disappearing America.

It was thus almost inevitable that the NWR should be the last company to experiment with a steam-turbine-electric locomotive built by Baldwin, the last major manufacturer to believe in a possible future for steam. This project commenced in 1947, about the time the Chesapeake & Ohio started operations with its unsuccessful 'M-1' type. However, the NWR proceeded in more measured fashion and it was not until May 1954 that No 2300 was ready for road trials.

The locomotive was the product of collaboration between the NWR, Baldwin-Lima-Hamilton (successor to the Baldwin Locomotive Works), Westinghouse Electric, and Babcock & Wilcox (builders of the boiler). The result was an external profile broadly similar to the Chesapeake & Ohio steam-turbine-electrics. The combined length of engine and tender was even longer at 161

No 2300 shortly after delivery in May 1954, coupled to its auxiliary water tender.
N&WR, TLC collection

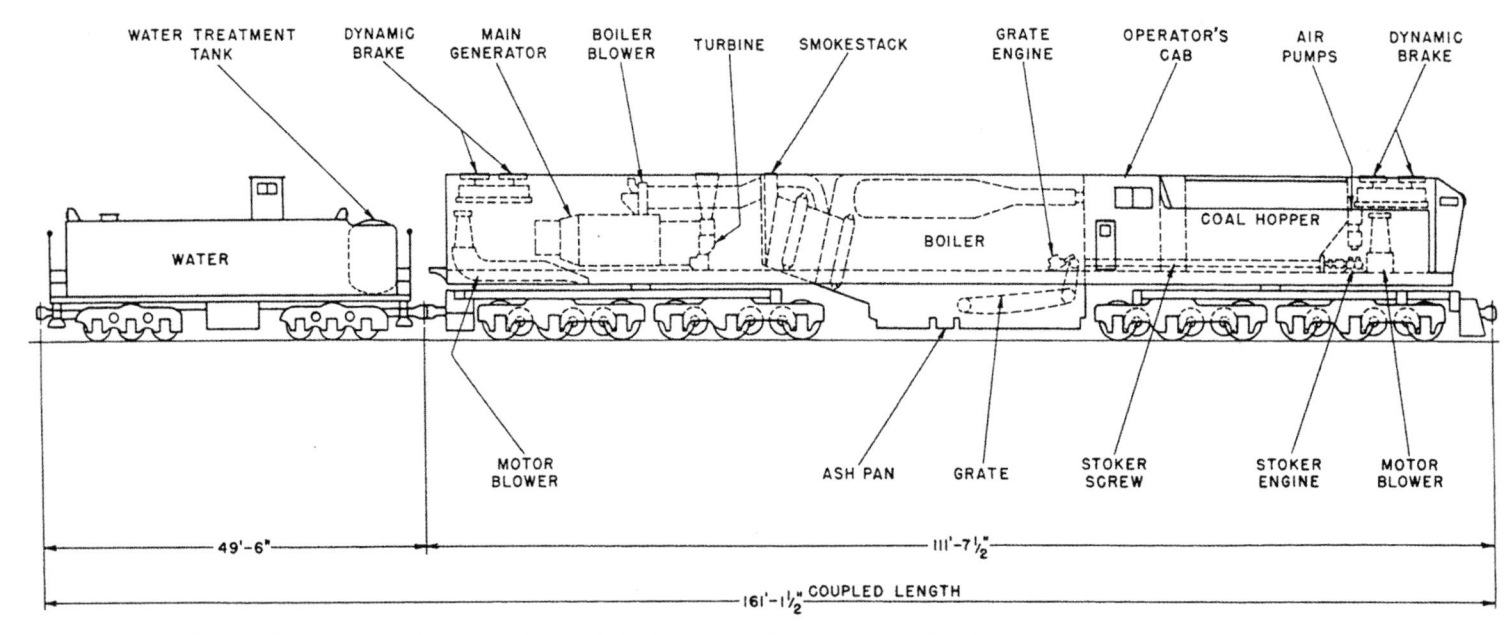

A mechanical diagram of No 2300. The coal bunker is in the nose and the driving controls in front of the water tube boiler, followed towards the rear by the turbine and electric generator. Water was carried in the separate tender coupled to the main unit. The consequential length of the complete machine was just in excess of 161 feet.

feet, and was extended by another 50 feet when working with an auxiliary water tender. The power configuration comprised an automatically controlled coal-fired water tube boiler driving a turbine that in turn generated electricity to power twelve axle-hung motors. The locomotive wheel arrangement was C+C+C+C, with the tender carried on two six-wheel bogies. The rated horsepower was 4,500 with a nominal tractive effort of 175,000lb. The total weight of the engine and tender was 409 tons.

In contrast to the C&O's high-profile and rather precipitate approach with its Class 'M-1', the NWR proceeded through scientifically controlled testing with minimal publicity. Nevertheless, the project attracted considerable interest among NWR personnel at all levels, as well as the enthusiast community. Although apparently not officially named, No 2300 was universally known as 'Jawn Henry', commemorating a legendary rock-driller named John Henry, who raced successfully against a steam drill but expired as a result of his efforts.

Road testing was conducted over more than two years, during which No 2300 was pitted against the iconic Class 'Y-6b' 2-8-8-2 compound Mallets. These formed the mainstay power for the NWR's heaviest coal trains in the closing years of steam, and in their final booster-equipped form had a 5,500hp power rating. 'Jawn Henry' matched and sometimes exceeded the best haulage efforts of the 'Y-6bs', and often at a lower rate of fuel consumption. Unfortunately, there were persistent problems with the automatic boiler control system, and a frequent recurrence of coal dust contamination in the electric motors. These factors combined to cause frequent failures during trials; the project was terminated in 1957 and No 2300 was formally withdrawn from service in January 1958.

Historically and culturally the Norfolk & Western Railway was deeply committed to the cause of steam and it is hard to imagine an organisation that would have been more determined to make a success of the steam-turbine-electric type. However, No 2300 had some challenging heights to surmount, presented by the burgeoning enthusiasm for diesel power evident elsewhere and, ironically, by conventional steam on its home system. The NWR had long built its own steam locomotives at Roanoke, Virginia, with a deep commitment to the creation and modernisation of motive power best suited to its needs. The company had matched steam fleet modernisation with a continuing investment programme in ultra-efficient service and maintenance facilities. Steam locomotives could be turned between duties almost as fast as contemporary diesel-electrics, resulting in levels of availability that almost matched those of electric locomotives.

The Class 'Y-6b' Mallets could haul trains of 13,000 tons up 1 in 333 gradients, while the equally impressive Class 'A' 2-6-6-4 simple Mallets used on fast freight work could reach 60mph on level track hauling 6,500 tons. Their operating efficiency was an integral part of the company's financial record in the mid-1950s; the all-steam NWR was, to the embarrassment of the diesel camp, the most profitable of the major American railroads.

No 2300's withdrawal confirmed that the steam-turbine-electric locomotive had no future and that the NWR, a subsidiary of Pennsylvania Railroad, must yield to the diesel-electric revolution. Steam ended on the Norfolk & Western in September 1960 with withdrawal of the last compound 2-8-8-2 Class 'Y-6b'.

CHAPTER TEN

Metamorphosis

CONCURRENT with the development of Pennsylvania Railroad 6-8-6 No 6200, a parallel strand of experimentation explored the advantages of turbine drive using alternative energy sources. While efforts in the eastern United States were influenced by the close proximity of coal deposits, oil was the preferred base energy source in the west. This led to the most prolonged application of turbine drive in rail transportation.

The Union Pacific Railroad (UP) became interested in the concept from the 1930s onwards for the next generation of motive power. Before the ascendancy of domestic airlines, the focus was on improvement of transcontinental passenger services over the important artery between Chicago and the West Coast. Extreme distances coupled with low traffic density made electrification prohibitively expensive, rendering UP a prime sales target for the diesel-electric manufacturing sector. However, the operators were unwilling to place all their eggs in that particular basket.

In assessing an alternative to diesel-electric power, UP had to consider the demands of working express services under demanding and diverse conditions. The goal was to haul trains comprising twelve passenger cars with a single high-powered locomotive capable of working unassisted through from Illinois to California. Over a route with gradients as steep as 2.2%, reaching altitudes as high as 8,000 feet, and in temperatures that varied from -40°F to +115°F, the challenges were extraordinary.

Union Pacific condensing steam-turbine-electric locomotive

In 1935/36 General Electric commenced development work on the first steam turbine locomotive design in the US, and two prototypes were delivered in 1938 for testing. They were constructed with a 2+C+C+2 wheel arrangement that carried a cab-type body, generally similar to contemporary GM E-series diesel-electric locomotives. A large condensing unit was installed towards the rear, and the whole ensemble presented a radical departure from the normal understanding of how a steam-powered locomotive should appear.

The 1939 Union Pacific steam-turbine-electric locomotive. Work had commenced on this project in 1935 and externally the locomotive looked more like a diesel engine than the steam locomotive it actually was. The vents towards the rear hide the condensing equipment.
Don Rose collection

Technical details were released in the *General Electric Review* for February 1939, and the scale of the manufacturer's expectations are best summarised by quoting verbatim from that publication:

'The operating advantages of the steam-electric locomotive include:

a. Thermal efficiency from fuel to the driving wheels more than double that of the conventional steam locomotive.
b. Electric braking resulting in savings in brake shoes and tires, not only for the locomotive but for the entire train.
c. High rates of acceleration and braking due to high adhesive weight.
d. Capacity for 500- to 700-mile performance without stops for fuel or water.

THE LMS TURBOMOTIVE

STEAM-ELECTRIC LOCOMOTIVE

Reprinted from the February, 1939 issue of the General Electric Review
Vol. 42, No. 2, Pages 87-91, Incl.

GEA-3201

The February 1939 issue of *General Electric Review* included an article on the Steam-Electric Locomotive.

The prototypical pair at work on a publicity run. *Image within the public domain*

The driving cab of the steam-turbine-electric locomotive. *The Engineer*

1-6: Traction motors
7-8: Main generators
9: Alternators
10: Exciter
11: Battery-charging set
12: Braking resistor
13: Main control contactors
14: Battery
15: Traction-motor blowers
16: Boiler
18: High-pressure main turbine
19: Low-pressure main turbine
20: Exhaust header
21: Air-cooled condensers
23: High-level condensate tank
26: 1500-lb feed-water pump
27: Feed-water heater
28: Boiler auxiliary-set turbine
29: Condenser-fan turbine
30: Compressor
31: Train-heating evaporator
33: Raw water tank
34: Boiler draft fan
35: Braking-resistor separator

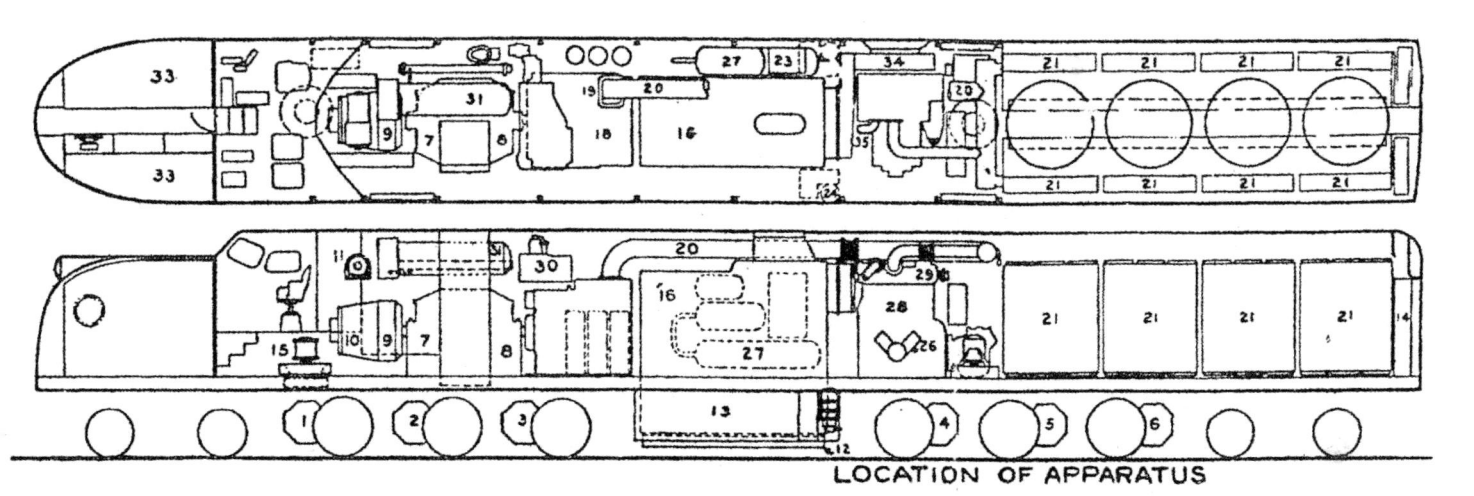

A diagram of steam-turbine-electric locomotive.

e. Elimination of corrosion and boiler scale by the use of distilled water in a closed system.
f. Elimination of unbalanced reciprocating parts which set up destructive forces in the rails, road bed and supporting structures.
g. Greater availability because of the construction of the boiler and the absence of reciprocating parts.'

The locomotive combined components almost all of which had been proven in other fields. The chassis and traction motors conformed with contemporary diesel locomotives, but it was above solebar level that the design was unusual. The driving cab, of the lightest construction possible without compromising structural strength, was immediately in front of a compartment that housed the generators and principal electrical equipment. Two main turbines were located in the rear of this section, operating in tandem on a high/low-pressure compound principle.

The automatically controlled boiler was placed immediately behind the turbines and equidistant between the two power bogies. Babcock & Wilcox built the pressure vessel in collaboration with Baily Meter Co, which supplied the control equipment. It was of the high-pressure water tube forced-circulation type, compactly built and embracing furnace, superheater, air preheater and burners for Bunker C fuel oil. The closed system minimised scaling and corrosion, and the system included an 'economizer' that used waste heat to increase the temperature of the boiler feedwater, a feature successfully used in a number of stationary boilers. Working pressure was 1,500lb per sq in at a temperature of 920°F.

As with conventional oil-burning steam locomotives, the system was not self-contained, and for lighting up it was necessary to have to a propane-gas-fired vertical fire tube boiler with a working pressure of 100lb per sq in. This auxiliary heated the fuel oil and atomised it at the burners to start the main boiler. Alternatively, steam could be applied from an outside source to activate the system. A secondary low-pressure steam circuit fed the train heating system and also pre-heated the fuel oil.

The main turbine-generator set comprised high- and low-pressure turbines that drove a two-armature direct current generator through 10:1 reduction gear. The main generator shaft was also connected to a 220V ac three-phase generator through a flexible coupling to provide power for train air-conditioning, traction motor blowers and other ancillary systems. Twin finned-type vertical tube condensers at the rear of the locomotive accepted exhaust steam through headers and the condensate drained by gravity back to a sump tank. Turbine-driven propeller-type fans for the condensers drew in air through side vents and discharged through roof vents.

The design complexity was reminiscent of the Beyer-Ljungström machine, and the preceding 'power station-on-wheels' experiments. Although considerable promotional fanfare attended delivery of the prototypes, little information was divulged on how they performed on the Union Pacific. They were provided on loan, but the railroad found them unsatisfactory, and they were returned to the manufacturer within a year. The Great Northern RR subsequently tried them briefly, then the New York Central RR. The latter reputedly found the prototypes reasonable in operation at a time of motive power shortages, but not sufficiently competent to justify continuing with the concept. The pair were apparently withdrawn and scrapped in 1943.

The Great Western Railway gas turbine project
Ostensibly, the strongly traditional GWR would have seemed an unlikely sponsor of turbine drive, even less so when linked to the adoption of the very latest technology in the primary energy source. However, there were progressive elements within the company's senior management who had been alive to the importance of providing for post-steam motive power needs as far back as the 1920s. Several factors combined to encourage experimentation with technology that in part derived from the aerospace sector.

In pre-Grouping days the GWR had enjoyed a cordial relationship with the North Eastern Railway, an early advocate of main-line electrification whose most high-profile venture had been conversion of the Shildon to Newport route (near Middlesbrough) for the transit of heavy coal tonnages. Opened in 1915, technically this investment was very successful with single electric locomotives capable of hauling 1,000-ton trains with ease. However, the fleet of ten locomotives was never fully utilised, traffic volumes progressively shrank in the 1920s, and the system was closed down in 1935. It was a cycle of visionary investment/market decline/redundancy prior to lifetime expiry that was to be repeated with the Woodhead route of the old Great Central Railway.

C. B. Collett, Chief Mechanical Engineer of the GWR, studied the NER project closely, giving rise to reservations about the viability of electrification. The concept was attractive for densely trafficked suburban routes with a captive clientele, but of the 'Big Four' the GWR had the smallest slice of the Greater London commuter market. Nevertheless, the company twice engaged independent consultants (in 1925 and 1938) to evaluate electrification of main-line routes, and in both cases it was concluded that the projected returns did not justify the investment risk. This reinforcement of Collett's concerns appeared to stimulate consideration of alternative means by which post-steam traction might be introduced with minimal infrastructural investment.

During the 1920s and early 1930s the GWR investigated diesel-electric multiple units designed by commercial manufacturers before choosing to eschew this configuration. This might in part have been due to the unsatisfactory performance of a four-car DEMU tested by the LMS in the Blackpool area in 1928/29, although this experience does not entirely validate such a key decision. Nevertheless, the adventurous styling of the well-known GWR diesel railcar fleet belied the technical simplicity of these vehicles, with their diesel-mechanical power train.

Pursuit of next-generation motive power thus far was in step with the company's conservative posture, which made the developments of early 1946 so surprising. Funds were in short supply for extensive post-war reconstruction, and entry into an entirely fresh technology seemed a high-risk enterprise at a time of significant stringency. Nevertheless, in January of that year the company entered a joint venture with Metropolitan-Vickers to produce a locomotive with electric transmission whose energy source would be a gas turbine engine derived from that used to power contemporary jet fighter aircraft.

The Great Western Railway had investigated diesel-electric multiple units in the 1920s before creating the famous diesel-mechanical railcar fleet in the 1930s. Another pioneering move was the formation in January 1946 of a joint venture with Metropolitan-Vickers to create a gas turbine express locomotive that eventually entered revenue-earning service in 1953 as British Railways No 18100. The brand-new engine is seen at the Dukinfield works of MV shortly before delivery.

The GWR's second gas turbine initiative (but the first to become operational) took the form of an order placed with Brown Boveri of Switzerland in the summer of 1946 for the supply of a second locomotive, which was delivered in 1950 as British Railways No 18000. This was smaller and less powerful than No 18100, but proved more reliable and worked until 1959. Nevertheless the failure rate with both machines rendered a level of availability well below that expected of traction that would replace steam.

The timing was significant for this all-British initiative as Sir Frank Whittle had developed the jet engine from the 1930s in circumstances of extreme secrecy, in collaboration with Metropolitan-Vickers. More or less concurrently that company was working with the LMS in the manufacture of turbine equipment for 'Pacific' No 6202. It seems possible that with similar but non-conflicting interests in turbine power, Stanier and Whittle shared their experiences. The belief that such a relationship existed is supported by Stanier's appointment as a Scientific Advisor to the UK Government during the Second World War, and by his subsequent appointment to the board of Power Jets Ltd. This company had been formed by Whittle and was later absorbed into the Turbine Division of the Royal Aircraft Establishment at Farnborough, becoming the National Gas Turbine Establishment.

If this interpretation is correct, it explains how the GWR Board and management could have moved with such alacrity between the ending of the war in August 1945 and the start of the project that eventually took shape in British Railways Co-Co Gas Turbine No 18100. Stanier had formally relinquished his position as Chief Mechanical Engineer to the LMS in 1944 and presumably was well placed to brief his former employers on the new technology, once security restrictions had been lifted.

Despite what seems to have been access to first-hand knowledge of jet engine technology, the risk was mitigated by engaging the services of a contractor to build a second gas turbine locomotive. Sir James Milne, Chairman, and F. W. Hawksworth, CME, while visiting Switzerland to attend the International Railway Congress in June 1946, called on several local manufacturers. Being a neutral country, Switzerland had survived the recent conflict in good shape and the opportunity was taken to study new manufacturing techniques, especially the use of aluminium in rolling stock construction. Also, discussions were held with Brown Boveri about the supply of a second gas turbine locomotive, and the GWR Board approved the order before the end of that month. Once again, the speed of the approval process was striking, suggesting that the decision-takers had been well briefed on intentions before the visit. The locomotive so ordered eventually became British Railways A1A+A1A No 18000.

Brown Boveri was selected by virtue of having built 1+A+Bo+A+1 Gas Turbine No Am 4/6 for service with Swiss Federal Railways in 1941. The purpose was similar to contemporary initiatives in the UK and the USA – to provide a modern source of motive power for routes where electrification lacked feasibility. After extensive testing, this locomotive had reportedly proved reasonably successful in revenue-earning service. This experience helped Brown Boveri to complete and deliver No 18000 well in advance of the GWR/Metropolitan-Vickers project. Although both were rated the equivalent of a GWR 'King' Class 4-6-0 in terms of power, there were significant differences between the pair.

No 18000 undertook extensive road testing following delivery from the manufacturer, and entered normal service in May 1950, eventually fulfilling an express role on London-Bristol and London-Plymouth duties. Completion took longer than had been anticipated, leaving a residual suspicion that construction was rather more problem-prone than Brown Boveri had sought to represent. After testing, No 18100 took up revenue-earning duties in April 1952, more than six years after the order had been placed; in this case there was little doubt that numerous difficulties had been encountered. Delays were attributed to lack of previous experience with this form of traction, shortages of materials, and ponderous administration of the joint venture.

Table 10.1: Leading dimensions of gas turbine locomotives Nos 18000 and 18100

	18000	18100
Wheel arrangement	A1A+A1A	Co-Co
Weight	115 tons 3 cwt	129 tons 10 cwt
Continuous rating	2,500 hp	3,000 hp
Maximum tractive effort	31,500 lb	60,000 lb
Maximum speed	90 mph	90 mph
Fuel type	Light, later heavy oil	Light oil
Auxiliary diesel	Yes	No
Height	13 ft 4 in	12 ft 10 in
Width	9 ft 2.5 in	9 ft
Length	63 ft 0.5 in	66 ft 9.25 in
Wheel diameter - driving	4ft 0.5 in	3ft 8 in
- carrying	3 ft 2 in	n/a
Bogie wheelbase	11 ft 9.75 in	15 ft

In service, No 18100 proved the less reliable of the pair, although it demonstrated considerable potential in load tests held in November 1952 when a seventeen-coach train (590 tons gross) was hauled unassisted from Plymouth to Newton Abbot. Towards the end of 1953 it was reported that the locomotive had suffered twenty-five major failures and had achieved a mileage of only 75,000. It was taken out of service for conversion by Metropolitan-Vickers to use heavy oil, which project suffered lengthy delays and was never completed. The venture was abandoned at the end of 1957 and the locomotive was formally withdrawn in January 1958. It had a subsequent career as an electric test locomotive.

Having entered service in 1950, No 18000 enjoyed a longer and more successful working career, although it was also plagued with teething problems and failures. After extensive testing it entered normal service in May 1950, initially on London-Swindon duties, then London-Plymouth. When working properly performance was impressive, but a review of operations between commissioning and October 1958 revealed that the locomotive had been out of service for 1,560 weekdays, which rendered an availability of less than 20%. The mileage covered in that period, at 319,000, was comparable with express steam engines, but well below the high utilisation levels expected of modern traction. A serious failure involving a flashover late in its career resulted in one traction motor being placed out of commission, and it finished its duties functioning with only 75% of its nominal power rating available. No 18000 stopped work in September 1959, was officially withdrawn in December 1960, and later returned to Switzerland for a second career as an unpowered test vehicle.

English Electric GT3

Concurrent with the two GWR initiatives, the English Electric Company also started investigation of gas turbine power in the railway context. Work started in 1946 on what was to become a locomotive designated GT3 (standing for Gas Turbine 3, following on from the earlier pair). The project was plagued with even more

METAMORPHOSIS

The third initiative with a British-based gas turbine locomotive was GT3, built by English Electric. Development of this locomotive took even longer than the preceding pair but, unlike Nos 18000/18100, it never entered revenue-earning service and had an even shorter operating life. Based around a traditional 4-6-0 wheel arrangement with the fuel carried in a tender, the machine is seen brand-new en route from the Vulcan Foundry works to Crewe. *E. N. Bellass*

1, engine—EM27L recuperative gas turbine; 2, engine-driven auxiliaries gearbox; 3, alternator; 4, fuel pump; 5, lubricating oil pressure pump; 6, lubricating oil scavenge pump; 7, starter motor; 8, transmission gearbox; 9, power turbine balance gear; 10, air intake filter; 11, exhaust chimney; 12, batteries; 13, driving cab; 14, vacuum brake ejector; 15, air-motor-driven exhauster; 16, brake cylinders; 17, electric-driven cooling pump set; 18, electric-driven pump set; 19, train-heating boiler; 20, oil cooler; 21, oil tank; 22, fuel tanks; 23, water tank; 24, oil suction filter; 25, oil pressure filter; 26, fuel filters.

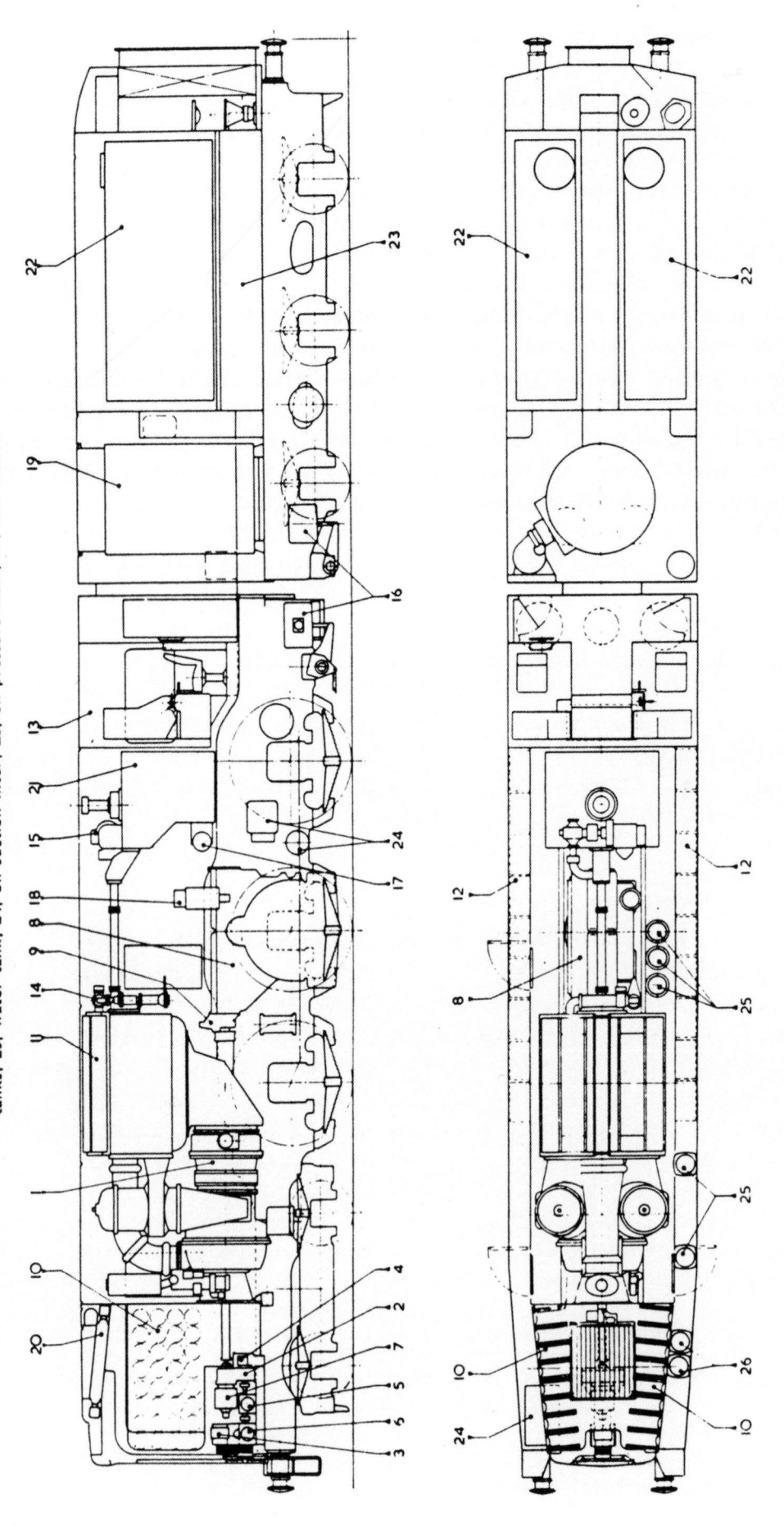

General arrangement drawing of GT3. Prior to completion an early drawing depicts the engine carrying the number 19000, with the name 'Lord of the Isles'. Starting was via a battery, a process which took 100 seconds, similar to the time taken to start the engine of an aircraft
The Oil Engine and Gas Turbine

A line drawing showing the general layout of GT3.

delay than that which had afflicted No 18100. Indicative of the elapsed project timing was the adoption of a 4-6-0 chassis, and it was even rumoured that there were proposals to base this on either a GWR 'Castle' or a BR Class '73xxx' (the latter did not appear until April 1951).

This traditional layout had the merit of a well-proven chassis configuration that avoided collateral issues such as the bogie weaknesses of No 18100. Nevertheless, delays in design and sourcing of appropriate materials meant that it was 1959 before GT3 entered service. Despite the modernistic body styling and unusual livery comprising light brown with dark green frames, the locomotive was by then unquestionably anachronistic. A single driving cab was located behind the power unit as in a steam locomotive and immediately in front of a six-wheeled fuel tender. The forward outlook from the cab was thus limited and, because of the wider tender body, almost non-existent rearwards. Rather as there had been a familial resemblance between the North British-built Reid-MacLeod steam turbine locomotive and the Modified Fairlie type, so the body style of GT3 betrayed origins in common with those of British Railways Bo-Bo Class 20 diesel-electrics.

GT3 was constructed at English Electric's Vulcan Foundry at Newton-le-Willows to the design of J. O. P. Hughes. The company's 9,000rpm, 2,750hp Type EM27 gas turbine engine was used, coupled to a mechanical transmission. This comprised a specially designed neutral, fixed-reduction and reverse gearbox linked to the centre driving axle. The gearing was suitably flexible to compensate for vertical axlebox movement, realignment of axle and gear as the locomotive rolled on its springs, and small axial movements in gear and axle.

Access to the power unit was through a doorway installed in the front of the 'smokebox', necessitating positioning of air intake louvres on either side. The tender accommodated 2,000 gallons of fuel oil together with a Spanner boiler and 1,750 gallons of water for train heating. The category of fuel oil used has not been confirmed, although it was low grade and possibly Bunker C. The traditionally located cab embraced facilities distinctly of the modern era, including lockers, toilet, washbasin and a carpeted floor. The locomotive weighed 123 tons 8 cwt and the tender 44 tons 0 cwt; the adhesive weight was 59 tons 4 cwt. The diameter of the driving wheels was 6ft 9in, the bogie wheels 3ft 0in, and the tender 3ft 3½in.

Trials were conducted in the Rugby Testing Centre over eleven months from early 1959. During this time the superstructure was incomplete and the tender had yet to be finished. It was the first non-steam locomotive to be tested at this location and achieved the equivalent of 97mph on the stationary plant. It was then given preliminary trials over roughly laid track that included a 1 in 44 gradient with a 5½-chain curve. An oil tank wagon substituted for the incomplete tender and two Stanier 8F 2-8-0s provided a test load.

On completion of these trials the locomotive was returned to English Electric for completion, and was then exhibited at Marylebone for inspection by the Institution of Locomotive Engineers. GT3 was then based at Crewe and main-line trials commenced on 9 January 1961, initially working to Whitchurch and Chester. Planned high-speed trials between Crewe and Llandudno Junction never eventuated, and it was transferred to Leicester to haul empty stock on return workings to Marylebone. The locomotive's novel appearance and livery generated considerable interest, but problems with the reverse gear soon led to workings being limited to Leicester-Woodford Halse.

A programme of dynamometer trials hauling ex-LMS empty stock was held between June and September 1961 over the GCR main line, and from October onwards between Crewe and Carlisle. Performance over the latter route was impressive, including the achievement of 44mph at Shap summit from a standing start at Tebay with a load of twelve coaches. Other trials included the successful working of sixteen-coach trains. No records have been traced of GT3 in revenue-earning service.

Despite these promising results, other factors militated against further development. The steam-locomotive-type configuration was impracticable in tender-first mode, and British Railways was intent on the elimination of turntables. The viability of gas turbine power was being eroded by technology that was finding more profitable uses for low-grade fuel. Also, British Railways had by then determined that the future lay with diesel and electric locomotives, many of which were ironically in course of development and production at Vulcan Foundry.

GT3 was returned to its makers at the end of 1962 and was progressively dismantled, the remnants finally being scrapped by commercial breakers in 1966. Gas turbine power was not to be essayed again in Britain until the Advanced Passenger Train project, which saw the introduction in 1972 of APT-E, a gas-turbine-powered four-car experimental test bed whose story lies outside the scope of this work.

Coal-fired gas turbine locomotive

There is evidence that in the mid-1940s consideration of the potential for gas turbines extended beyond the GWR's locomotives and GT3. On 23 December 1952 the Ministry of Fuel and Power placed an order jointly with North British and C. A. Parsons of Glasgow for the production of a coal-fired gas turbine locomotive that would use pulverised coal. This type of fuel had been tried as early as pre-Grouping days without any lasting success, but its use as an energy source to drive a turbine was a revolutionary concept. The idea had obviously been under consideration for some time, as references have been traced to a 'Third Report on the Proposed Coal Fired Gas Turbine' dated 1946.

The new locomotive was to have a C-C wheel arrangement, a weight of about 117 tons and a power output of 1,800hp, later reduced to 1,500hp during tests. Exhaust heat would drive a turbine coupled to mechanical transmission with a two-speed gearbox. Subsidiary gears combined with cardan shafts would have divided the load equally between the driving axles. Apparently the two-speed gearbox was stipulated to enable haulage of either freight or passenger trains.

The rated tractive effort was originally to be 30,000lb at 72mph and 45,000 at 50mph. Construction progressed only as far as the power unit, which was undergoing bench tests by 1954. The main problem was blade erosion caused by minute particles of ash from the combustion process. A press report in September 1955 expressed the hope that the unit would be ready for 'full bench tests' the following year, with road trials commencing in the summer of 1958. No other reports have been traced and, as with GT3, the project probably foundered on BR's determination that diesel fuel and electricity were the only viable bases for future motive power.

The Union Pacific gas turbine family

Following the war, jet engine technology was rapidly adopted by the US aeronautical industry, in which Westinghouse's Aviation Gas Turbine Division was a participant from 1945 onwards. This manufacturer was the first to experiment with this form of power in the railway sector with a 4,000hp B+B+B+B gas turbine locomotive, numbered 4000 to reflect its power rating. Nicknamed 'Blue Goose', it was tested by the Chicago & North Western, Missouri-Kansas-Texas, and Pennsylvania railroads. None found its performance acceptable and the project made no further progress.

More or less in parallel, the American Locomotive Company in partnership with General Electric completed a 4,500hp B+B+B+B gas turbine experimental locomotive in 1948 that was directly targeted at Union Pacific (UP) and trials started the following year. Numbered 50 in the UP fleet series and painted in the railroad's livery, this locomotive was never actually owned by the company but was extensively tested in normal service. The railroad's need was for a freight locomotive that could operate as a single unit in replacement of large steam locomotives (e.g. the 4-8-8-4 'Big Boy' Mallets) whose haulage capacity roughly equated to three or four diesel-electric engines working in multiple.

No 50 was a double-ended locomotive whose acceptable performance led to an order for ten (Nos 51-60), which were delivered in 1952, becoming UP property. The principal change with the production series was the removal of one cab to allow room for greater fuel capacity. The body styling was of the 'cab' type similar to that used with the Alco Series FA diesel-electric locomotives then in production. A further fifteen (Nos 61 to 75) entered service in 1954 with the same technical specification but a hybrid body styling. The forward cab design was retained ahead of a conventional hood-type body with the normal walkways and

The first-generation Union Pacific gas-turbine-electric locomotive (Nos 51-60) is represented here by No 51 at Cheyenne, Wyoming, in September 1957. *Image within the public domain*

This No 71 of the second generation of Union Pacific gas-turbine-electric locomotives (Nos 61-75), photographed at Ogden, Utah, in September 1962. *Image within the public domain*

The third generation of Union Pacific gas-turbine-electric locomotives (Nos 1-50) were nicknamed 'Big Blows'. *Image within the public domain*

safety fencing on either side. This feature gave rise to the 'veranda' nickname. The fuel capacity was later augmented by a tender created from a pair of redundant steam locomotive tenders, joined on the 'cut and shut' principle.

Between 1958 and 1961 Alco/GE delivered a further thirty locomotives (numbered 1 to 30) with rated power increased from 4,500 to 8,500hp. This was achieved by each locomotive being semi-permanently coupled to a B-unit companion (numbered 1B to 30B), the complete ensemble being regarded as the most powerful single-unit locomotive type to be used in the USA. With a voracious appetite, they were made even more distinctive by working with large auxiliary fuel tenders (also ex-steam engine 'cut and shut' jobs) in matching livery. The combination of powered driving unit, powered B-unit and fuel tender weighed 610 tons in working order.

The UP's fifty-five-strong fleet hauled heavy freight trains between Council Bluffs in western Iowa, through Nebraska and Wyoming to Ogden in Utah, a route that crossed the Wasatch mountain range. They were also tried between Salt Lake City and Los Angeles, but were withdrawn following objections to their use in densely populated parts of California, on account of their thunderous jet-engine-type noise. This phenomenon led to Nos 1-30 being nicknamed 'Big Blows', and to their indelible association with work in the more remote regions penetrated by the classic Union Pacific transcontinental route.

UP gas turbine locomotives operating singly inherited duties previously handled by steam super-power, but later they frequently operated in multiple with diesel-electric traction that was increasingly proving its worth on arduous duties. Gas turbines always had high fuel consumption, which was mitigated by their use of cheap heavy Bunker C oil. However, new cracking techniques improved the viability of refining into more valuable lighter grades, making Bunker C prohibitively expensive. The initial 4,500hp units (Nos 51 to 75) were out of service by 1964, and the mighty 'Big Blows' had gone by 1970.

The 'Big Blows' were the last operating examples whose lineage, however tenuous, could be traced back to the Ljungström/Stanier initiatives of the early 1930s. Nevertheless, UP's search for ultra-high power through alternative energy/fuel configurations saw one further effort. In 1963 the railroad started development of a coal-fired gas-turbine-electric locomotive with the complex wheel arrangement of A1A-A1A+2-D+D-2. Numbered 8080, this locomotive combined components existing in a number of railway and non-railway applications. In some respects it was a throwback to the 'power-station-on-wheels' idea. No 8080 worked on trials but did not show sufficient potential; it was withdrawn in 1968 after less than two years of use.

A next generation?

The potential of gas turbine traction has been explored in other exercises, although so far without lasting impact on motive power policy. A feature of this search has been the international flavour of these endeavours, as summarised in Appendix A. Constraints on the use of fossil fuels, legislation limiting carbon emissions, and scale economies enjoyed by diesel-electric manufacturers combine as disincentives to further experimentation. At present the railway industry's interest seems confined to those power station turbines that feed their energy to locomotives by means of catenary and live rail. However, with the spirit of innovation that turbine power has evoked in times past, it would be rash to assume that this chapter of railway history is completely closed.

CHAPTER 11

Concluding Assessment

OF all the British attempts during the 20th century fundamentally to redefine the pattern of steam locomotive design, only three proved sufficiently capable to be regularly entrusted with revenue-earning duties. Of this trio, the Turbomotive was the most successful measured by incidence of failures, service mileage, and career longevity.

Whether the project provided a viable alternative to the conventional reciprocating steam locomotive is best assessed in the context of the three key criteria set out in Chapter 1.

1. Capital cost compared with a comparable conventional machine

Technically the locomotive was significantly simpler than preceding steam turbines and minimal use of specialised features greatly assisted objective assessment of their effectiveness. Use of so many standardised components (chassis, driving wheels, boiler) contained initial cost but prevented substantial improvements, especially installation of separate lubrication circuits for gears and bearings, and larger reservoirs. On the other hand, at the termination of the project the standard components were re-employed in creating a conventional machine at a significant discount on cost of new construction. From the official figures, conventional 'Pacific' No 6200 cost £12,657 to build in 1933, and the Turbomotive £20,383 in 1935, a difference of £7,726, or a premium of 62%. In 1952 a new 'Britannia' cost £22,573, and the cost of converting the Turbomotive to the 'Princess Anne' type was £8,875, a difference of £13,698, or a discount of 61%. On that basis it might be argued that, allowing for inflation and amortisation over the intervening seventeen years, the net capital cost of the project was no greater than that for a production-series 'Princess Royal'.

Compared with the substantially higher first cost of other experiments, whose failure resulted in equipment with little more than scrap value, the virtuous parsimony of the Turbomotive project was a tribute to Metropolitan-Vickers and Crewe Works.

2. Operating expenses to remain in line with traditional motive power

Lengthy periods out of service, which added substantially to running costs, could be attributed to:

1. The need to manufacture replacement components in the absence of stocks of specialised parts.

2. Unsympathetic treatment by untrained personnel, especially within depot confines.

3. The impact of wartime operating conditions.

4. Caution and uncertainty induced by unique design features.

The greater weight of these factors were attributable to the unique, unprecedented nature of the machine rather than to defects in its design and construction.

3. Improved performance, measured by operating speeds, haulage capacity, or fuel consumption

The concept's technical feasibility was proven by 1939 but consistent performance gains versus the 'Princess Royals' were slight: there was a lower water consumption, and a reduced proneness to slipping.

The exercise failed to produce results that could support multiplication of the Turbomotive type, but the broad concept of the non-condensing steam turbine was definitely established. The incremental capital investment and higher running costs had resulted in a machine that provided no notable improvement upon the 'Princess Royal' Class or the later, conventional, 'Duchess' type. This contrasted with the Swedish turbine 2-8-0s, which consistently hauled heavier loads than their conventional

CONCLUDING ASSESSMENT

No 6202 is new at Crewe with its original domeless boiler. Points to note are the presence of the fitter in conventional dustcoat on the footplate and the various detail fittings on the locomotive: the sandbox fillers interspersed on the side of the casing of the forward turbine, roller bearings, and steam pipe from the header within the smokebox to the turbine. *W. H. Whitworth*

counterparts, and continued so to do with impressive reliability into the 1950s.

A prominent feature of the project was the extensive press coverage and amount of technical detail released at the time of construction. Openness about subsequent progress culminated in the informative paper presented by R. C. Bond to the Institution of Locomotive Engineers in 1946. Its first reading was in the presence of Sir William A. Stanier FRS, who had been responsible for the project from its inception. The 'warts and all' exposé speaks volumes for his broad-mindedness, and for the calibre of his relationships with erstwhile subordinates, prompting the question of how many others of his standing would have cooperated in such public dissection of their work.

As an eminent engineer and scientist in retirement, Stanier perhaps felt that there was little left to prove or protect, but the extent of disclosure set him apart. His old boss, C. B. Collett, remained secretive, aloof and isolationist to the end. It is hard to imagine that the late Sir Nigel Gresley, known as something of an egotist, would have been so forthcoming about the tribulations encountered with his most revolutionary project, 4-6-4 Class 'W1' No 10000. Most intriguing was Bulleid's absence from the presentation. The Turbomotive project was highly focussed and subject to clearly defined criteria. Sound financial husbandry governed expenditure, which was also protected by minimal deviation from original goals while revenue-earning use mitigated the expense. These elements were the antithesis of the

In this view from a similar period, note again the fitter on the footplate. (Whether the same man was employed throughout is not known, but might appear unlikely.) This sideways view shows the original boiler together with the first (small) cover for the reverse turbine. Again this view was recorded at Crewe. *W. H. Whitworth*

Now as No 46202, the locomotive is seen at Watford on 13 August 1949 in the twilight of its career as a turbine engine. Modifications since 1935 include the boiler with the separate dome/top feed, the extended casing to the reverse turbine, and the smoke deflectors. The BR livery of course also appears. Throughout its time running as a turbine no name was ever carried.
H. C. Casserley

Above: The triple-reduction gear for No 6202; as an example, this would reduce the turbine output speed of 13,500rpm when running at 90mph to a more manageable figure. (However, optimum power was achieved at 62mph when 2,600bhp was achieved at a correspondingly lower turbine rotation.) Consequently it can quickly be assessed that No 6202 was built for sustained output at moderate operating speeds rather than intending to compete on very high-speed operation. To achieve maximum efficiency the engine needed to be operated at constant speeds over long distances, a difficult if not impossible situation when attempting to fit a turbine-hauled service into a conventional operating timetable. These same issues would lead the Western Region quickly to establish the inefficiency of its own pair of gas-turbine-electric locomotives in the 1950s, while in the USA the opposite would apply with the 'Big Blow' gas-turbine-electric machines, able to work satisfactorily when engaged in heavy haulage over long uninterrupted distances.

Above: Images of the actual turbine itself used on LMS No 6202 have proved impossible to find. Possibly this was simply due to commercial sensitivity (remember that the railway companies were not scrupulously honest when it came to 'modifying' another's patent design to avoid paying royalties – the Schmidt superheater, for example). Metropolitan-Vickers would have been very wary about letting its expertise stray from its own works, so repairs to the actual turbine were undertaken at Trafford Park, while assembly and locomotive repairs were under the control of the LMS at Crewe – each conveniently close to the other. Here the final drive is seen attached to the leading driving axle.

CONCLUDING ASSESSMENT

An aerial view of the Metropolitan-Vickers factory at Trafford Park. The company was involved with heavy engineering in many spheres and for a time was one of the largest engineering facilities in the country. The site of the factory is now a shopping centre.

extravagant flamboyance that later exemplified the plan for a five-strong 'Leader' Class while the first remained unproven in any commercially realistic sense.

The degree of disclosure was also remarkable on another plane. Notwithstanding that Belpaire fireboxes, superheating, and rotary cam valve gear derived from continental European origins, engineering practice during the 'Big Four' era had settled around an uncomfortable degree of parochialism. The Turbomotive was a powerful demonstration of the opportunities available by breaking the 'not invented here' mould and exploiting what other countries and industries had to offer. This multi-dimensional and open-minded approach enhanced the project's validity in the United States, providing a rare example of British practice having influence in that country. Later, the project's technological diversity stimulated in Bond's audiences a rich harvest of creative ideas of varying practicability.

While the Turbomotive's commercial performance failed to match its technical competence, it laid a firm foundation for further development. This point was succinctly summarised by W. S. Graff-Baker, President of the Institution of Locomotive Engineers, in stating that the modifications of the preceding decade had created version No 1A. He felt that a second prototype (No 2) should be developed before No 1A ended its working life, but did not anticipate a design suitable for proliferation before Version No 3. (See Appendix F.)

The project had successfully pursued an alternative form of power transmission, but it was clear whether the additional objective of improved fuel consumption required significant boiler redesign. It is contended that with Version No 2 the following could have eventuated:

1. Retention of the Turbomotive's main mechanical features as refined by 1939. The layout of the turbines, reduction gear train, reverse gear mechanism and roller bearings on the driving and carrying wheels had all benefited from stringent fault diagnosis and/or successful modification.

2. Employment of driving wheels of a diameter of 5 feet or less (which would not have inhibited speed or riding characteristics) would permit a larger-diameter boiler, roller bearings on the gears and turbine spindles, and divided lubrication circuits, each with a larger reservoir.

3. Experience, supported by the audience consensus in the wake of the Bond paper, held that advances in performance would require a higher steam temperature and/or greater boiler pressure. Complete segregation of live steam from lubricant in the steam turbine's configuration would certainly allow stretching of conventional thermodynamic limits.

4. The Turbomotive was geared for optimal efficiency at a running speed of 50mph. Version No 2 could have been created in differing variants where all dimensions remained constant, except for the gear ratio. Thus three otherwise completely identical locomotives could be built with different optimal speeds, e.g. 40mph for fast freight duties, 50mph for normal express duties, 60mph for high-speed work. With gear ratio the only key variant, a totally new approach to standardisation would be possible, yielding substantial financial savings.

The postulated Version No 2 would also offer an alternative means of enhancing performance such as Chapelon was delivering through compounding, streamlined steam passages, etc. Views may differ on which approach offered the greater advantages, but steam turbines were conceptually simpler. Also Chapelon's work did not eliminate problems associated with weight, hammer blow and factors of adhesion. The authors feel that the Turbomotive encapsulated superior potential for steam-orientated motive power renewal.

The American dimension was also relevant to the Turbomotive saga in providing another strand to the search for modern, powerful steam locomotives. That the traditionally conservative

Pennsylvania Railroad should have espoused the duplex machines, a concept so much at odds with conventional thinking, was indeed paradoxical. Their complexity and cost left management with a commitment it might well have come to regret. Certainly this episode was an oddity in the steam story, creating a firm belief that more could have been gained technically and financially through earlier and more dedicated commitment to Baldwin's mighty 6-8-6 steam turbine. Another curiosity was the American revival of the 'power-station-on-wheels' formula. Although technological progress had been considerable in the interval, detailed appraisal of the early British failures might have warned that this idea's complexity was ill suited to operational conditions. Parochialism was perhaps not the sole preserve of British locomotive engineering.

Against these other efforts, the prospects in 1939 for non-condensing steam turbines were definitely encouraging, with more potential than that enjoyed by contemporary exercises in France and America. Therein lies an essential misfortune in the Turbomotive project, which was its timing. The LMS/LNER large locomotive comparison (Appendix C) starkly illustrates how much ground Stanier had to make up, and how far behind the LMS remained in the provision of a numerically adequate express fleet on 31 December 1947. Sir William had been a busy man in the reinvigoration of LMS motive power and the Turbomotive occupies an honourable place within so many achievements won by him under demanding circumstances.

The project's timing was unlucky in another way. The successful record of the Ljungström 2-8-0s was helped by Sweden's neutrality, which isolated that country from the turmoil suffered elsewhere in Europe. In contrast, the LMS Turbomotive, with teething troubles resolved, was on the cusp of confirming the place of the non-condensing steam turbine in the contemporary motive power spectrum. The Second World War stole that chance, making this fascinating machine yet another casualty of that conflict.

The Engine Record Card for No 6202.
National Railway Museum

Appendices

Appendix A
Motive power units using turbine drive

This summary indicates the breadth of effort undertaken by manufacturers and railway companies to exploit the potential of turbine drive. Information has been abstracted from a number of sources, but it should not be assumed as complete.

See Table next page.

Germany: The Krupp 4-6-0 experimental turbo-condensing locomotive for German State Railways. *Image within the public domain*

Germany: The interior of the cab of the Krupp locomotive. *The Railway Gazette*

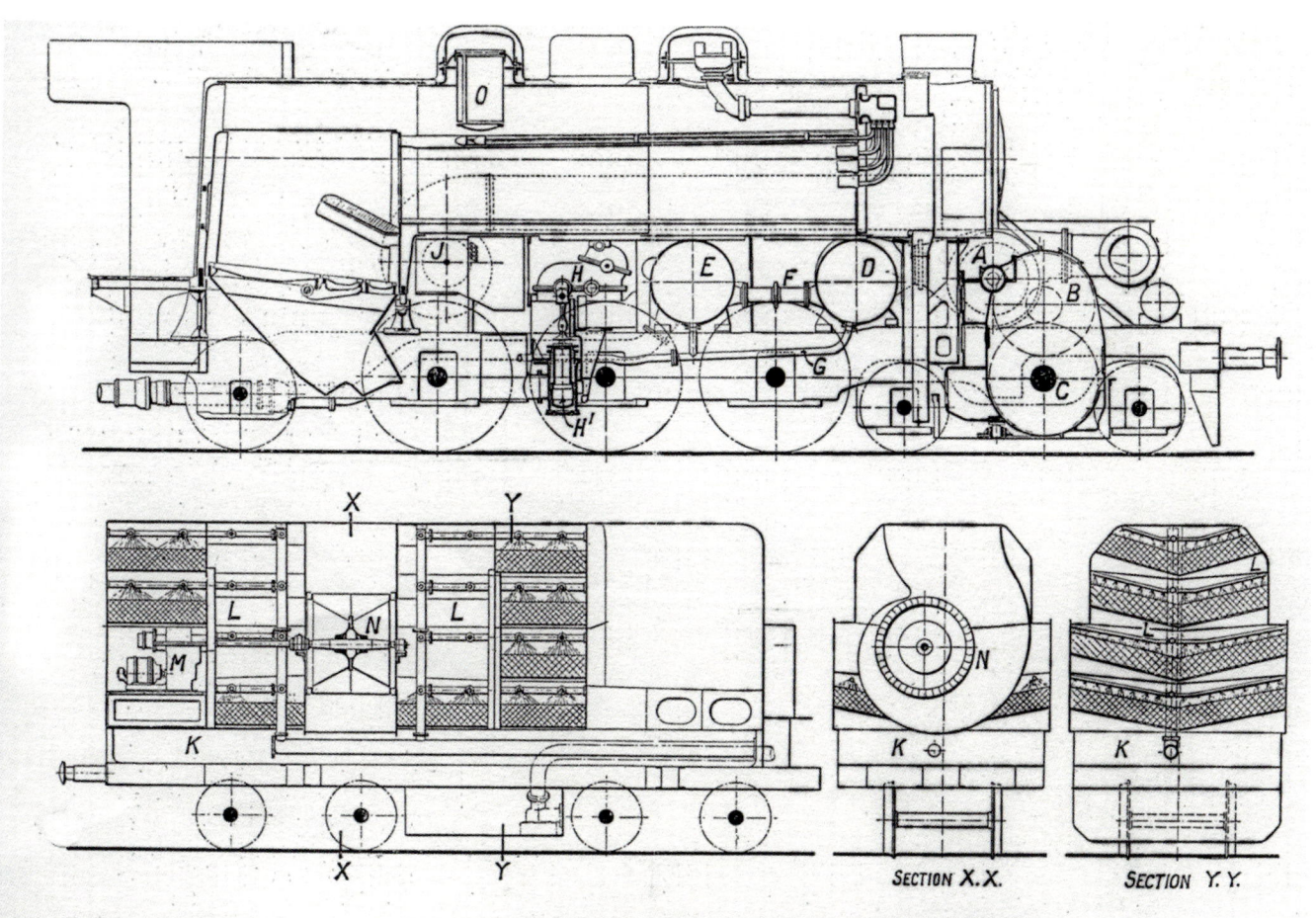

A. Main Turbines.
B. Primary Transmission Gear.
C. Jack Shaft and Gear.
D. Primary Condenser.
E. Secondary Condenser.
F. Flexible Condenser Connecting Pipe.
G. Pipes for Condensate.
H and H¹. Auxiliary Turbine and Pumps.
J. Turbine-driven Draught Fan.
K. Water Space on Tender.
L. Cooling Units.
M. Turbine Driving Cooling Fan.
N. Cooling Fan.
O. Evaporator.

General Arrangement of Details.—Krupp Condensing Turbo-Locomotive.

Germany: General arrangement details of the Krupp 4-6-0. *The Railway Gazette*

145

Country	Manufacturer/railway	Year	General description	No. built	Comments
Argentine	NOHAB Sweden		Condensing steam turbine	1	Similar to Ljungström's first design
Canada	Canadian National	1968	See USA/AMTRAK below		
Czechoslovakia	Tatra/CSD	1959/60	Gas turbine electric plus diesel helper	2	Nos TL659.001/2, C-C; first scrapped 1959; second in normal service until 1966
France	Renault/Rescara	1920s–1933	Oil-driven gas turbine		Experimental turbine drive by exhaust from piston-driven oil engine
	Nord Turbine		Non-condensing team turbine	n/a	Planned to be similar to LMS No 6202 but built as conventional compound
	SNCF	1939	Steam turbine	1	No 232Q1; war-damaged; scrapped 1946
	SNCF		Gas-turbine-electric	1	TGV 001; prototype train
Germany	Krupp-Zoelly/German State Railways	1924	Geared steam turbine*	1	Turbine by Zoelly, Switzerland; destroyed 1940
	Maffei/Krupp/German State Railways	1927	Geared steam turbine*	1	4-6-2
	Henschel	1927	Reciprocating 4-6-0 plus turbine 2-4-4	1	Rebuild of DRG Class '38' with condensing turbine tender
	Maffei/Krupp/German State Railways	1929	Geared steam turbine*	1	4-6-2; similar to Krupp-Zoelly locomotive; destroyed in air raid 1943
Italy	Giuseppe Belluzzo	?	?	?	Unsuccessful experimental engines
	Ernesto Breda/Belluzzo/FS	1931	Four-turbine/multiple expansion	1	Jackshaft drive
	Ferrovie dello Stato	1933	Rebuild of normal engine	1	2-6-2 fitted with turbines; one test run, then disappeared
Sweden	Fredrik Ljungström/Swedish State Railway	1921		1	Three driving axles under tender; cab and boiler borne by carrying wheels
	Fredrik Ljungström	1921		1	Patented quill drive for use with turbine
	Fredrik Ljungström/Nydqvist & Holm AB/ Grängesberg-Oxelösund Railway	1930-34	Non-condensing steam turbine	3	2-8-0 Nos 71–73; worked until 1950s; all preserved
	Gotaverken	?	Diesel-powered gas turbine	1	Powered by exhaust gases from five-cylinder two-stroke diesel engine
Switzerland	Zoelly	1919		1	4-6-0; dangerous design; unsuccessful
	Swiss Locomotive Works/Escher Wyss Ltd/ Swiss Federal Railway	1922	Geared steam turbine*	1	
	Brown Boveri/Swiss Federal Railway	1941	Gas turbine electric	1	No Am 4/6; 1+A+Bo+A+1: first gas-turbine-electric
United Kingdom	North British Loco Co	1910	Condensing steam turbine-electric**	1	Reid-Ramsay locomotive
	Armstrong Whitworth/Ramsay Condensing Loco Co	1922	Condensing steam turbine-electric**	1	
	North British	1924	Condensing steam turbine-electric**	1	Reid-Macleod Steam Turbine Locomotive
	Beyer Peacock/Ljungström	1926	Condensing steam turbine	1	No 6233; in partnership with Ljungström
	London Midland & Scottish Railway	1935	Non-condensing steam turbine**	1	Stanier 4-6-2 Turbomotive No 6202
	Brown Boveri/GWR/ BR	1950	Gas-turbine-electric**	1	No 18000; A1A+A1A
	Metropolitan-Vickers/GWR/BR	1952	Gas-turbine-electric**	1	No 18100
	North British Loco Co/BR	1952	Coal-fired gas turbine		Planned as C-C, later 1A1A+A1A1; not built
	English Electric	1961	Gas turbine electric	1	No GT3; 4-6-0 prototype
	British Railways	1981	Gas turbine electric	3	Advanced Passenger Train Experimental
USA	General Electric/Union Pacific RR	1938	Oil-fired steam-electric**	2	Returned as unsatisfactory; performed quite well on Great Northern RR 1939-43
	Baldwin/Pennsylvania RR	1944	Steam turbine**	1	'S2' 6-8-6; similar concept to LMS 4-6-2
	Baldwin/Westinghouse/Chesapeake & Ohio RR	1947	Coal-fired steam turbine-electric**	3	'M-1'; 2-C1+2-C1-B; scrapped 1950
	Baldwin/Norfolk & Western Railway	1954	Coal-fired steam turbine-electric**	1	'Jawn Henry'; C+C+C+C
	United Aircraft/Amtrak	1968	Direct-drive gas turbine		UAC Turbo train
	Alco-GE/on loan to Union Pacific RR	1949	Gas turbine electric	1	No 50; B+B+B+B; prototype
	Alco-GE/Union Pacific RR	1952	Gas-turbine-electric**	10	Nos 51-60; B+B+B+B; worked until 1964
	Alco-GE/Union Pacific RR	1954	Gas-turbine-electric**	15	Nos 61-75; B+B+B+B; nicknamed 'Veranda'; worked until 1964.
	Alco-GE/Union Pacific RR	1958	Gas-turbine-electric**	30	Nos 1-30; C+C+C+C; 8,500 hp; world's most powerful single-unit locomotive; nicknamed 'Big Blow'; worked until 1970; No 18 preserved in Illinois and No 26 in Utah

* Illustrated
** Illustrated in main text

APPENDICES

Germany: This was an unusual experiment, being a hybrid conversion of a Royal Saxon State Railways reciprocating 4-6-0. Built by Hartmann of Chemnitz between 1910 and 1927, 124 of this type were taken over by Deutsche Reichsbahn Gesellschaft in 1922, becoming its Class '38' (DRG had ten more built in 1927). In the latter year No 38 255 was rebuilt by Henschel in the form depicted, its number being prefixed with a 'T'. The locomotive remained largely unchanged while the tender was mounted on a chassis with a 2-4-4 wheelbase powered by a forward and reverse turbine. Exhaust steam from the locomotive powered the turbines, making the combined unit a compound, and a condenser mounted in the tender provided vacuum for the turbine exhaust. The smokebox blast-pipe was replaced with an electrically powered fan in the smokebox to substitute for the lack of draught. The locomotive reverted to normal condition in 1937 as performance of the reciprocating-turbine configuration proved disappointing.

Germany: The 4-6-2 condensing steam turbine locomotive built by J. A. Maffei of Munich and Fried. Krupp AG for German State Railways. *Modern Transport*

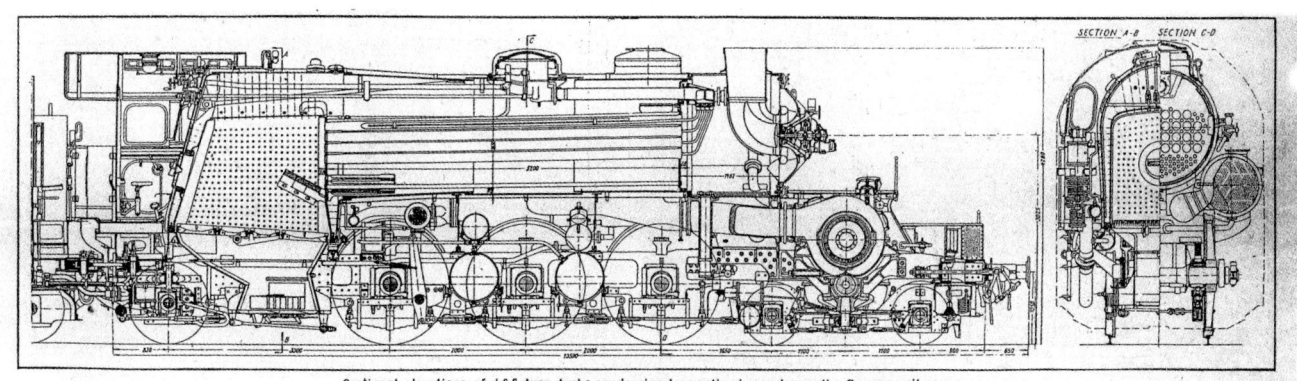

Germany: A drawing of the Maffei/Krupp 4-6-2. *Modern Transport*

147

THE LMS TURBOMOTIVE

Germany: The other 4-6-2 condensing steam turbine locomotive built by Maffei/Krupp AG for German State Railways. *Engineering*

Switzerland: This 4-6-0 condensing steam turbine engine was built in 1922 by the Swiss Locomotive Works, Winterthur and Escher, Wyss Ltd for Swiss Federal Railways. *The Locomotive*

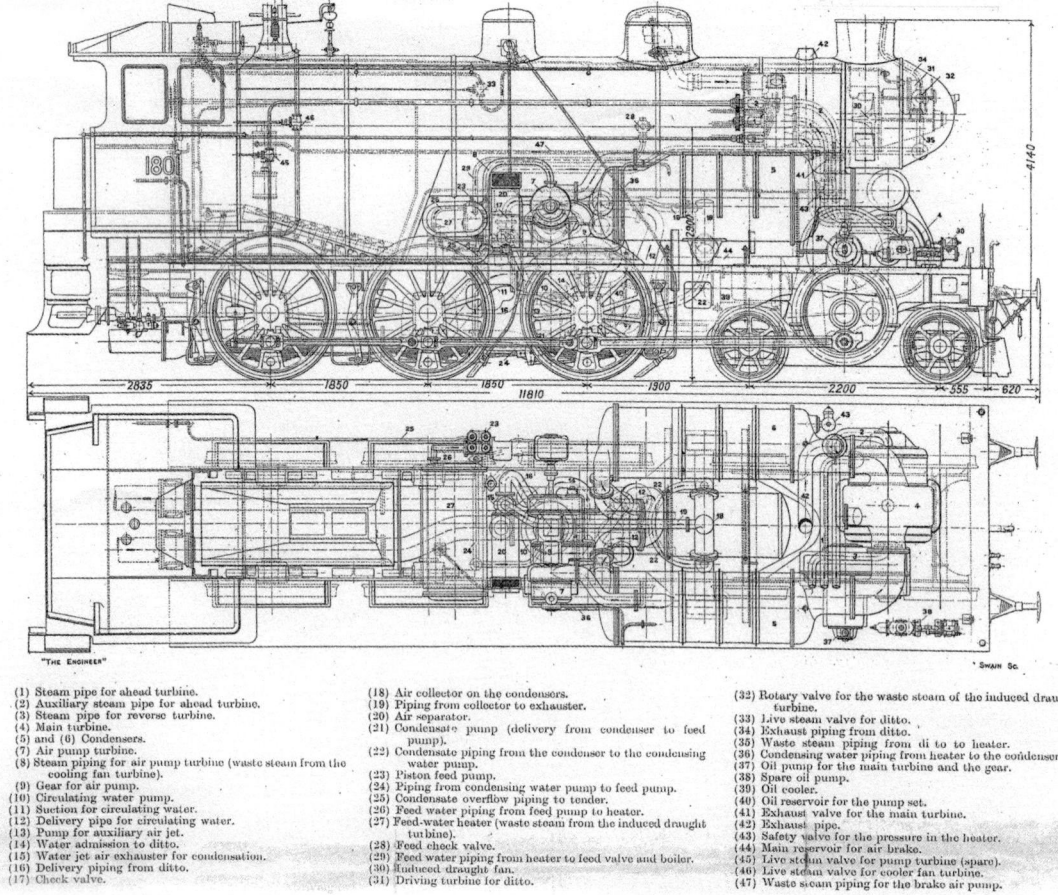

(1) Steam pipe for ahead turbine.
(2) Auxiliary steam pipe for ahead turbine.
(3) Steam pipe for reverse turbine.
(4) Main turbine.
(5) and (6) Condensers.
(7) Air pump turbine.
(8) Steam piping for air pump turbine (waste steam from the cooling fan turbine).
(9) Gear for air pump.
(10) Circulating water pump.
(11) Suction for circulating water.
(12) Delivery pipe for circulating water.
(13) Pump for auxiliary air jet.
(14) Water admission to ditto.
(15) Water jet air exhauster for condensation.
(16) Delivery piping from ditto.
(17) Check valve.
(18) Air collector on the condensers.
(19) Piping from collector to exhauster.
(20) Air separator.
(21) Condensate pump (delivery from condenser to feed pump).
(22) Condensate piping from the condenser to the condensing water pump.
(23) Piston feed pump.
(24) Piping from condensing water pump to feed pump.
(25) Condensate overflow piping to tender.
(26) Feed water piping from feed pump to heater.
(27) Feed-water heater (waste steam from the induced draught turbine).
(28) Feed check valve.
(29) Feed water piping from heater to feed valve and boiler.
(30) Induced draught fan.
(31) Driving turbine for ditto.
(32) Rotary valve for the waste steam of the induced draught turbine.
(33) Live steam valve for ditto.
(34) Exhaust piping from ditto.
(35) Waste steam piping from di to to heater.
(36) Condensing water piping from heater to the condenser.
(37) Oil pump for the main turbine and the gear.
(38) Spare oil pump.
(39) Oil cooler.
(40) Oil reservoir for the pump set.
(41) Exhaust valve for the main turbine.
(42) Exhaust pipe.
(43) Safety valve for the pressure in the heater.
(44) Main reservoir for air brake.
(45) Live steam valve for pump turbine (spare).
(46) Live steam valve for cooler fan turbine.
(47) Waste steam piping for the brake air pump.

Switzerland: General arrangement of the Swiss 4-6-0. *The Engineer*

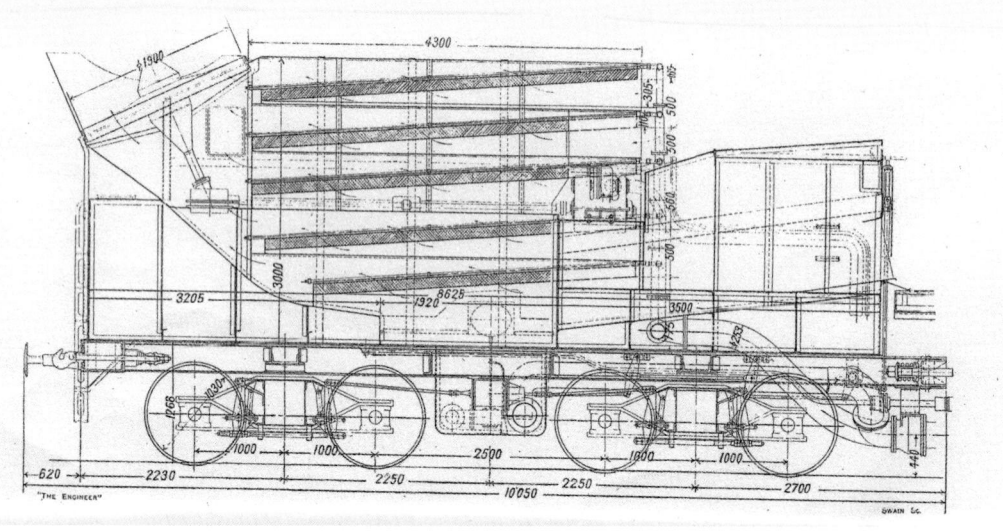

APPENDICES

Appendix B
Weight, hammer blow and factor of adhesion

Optimal weight distribution is important for the containment of wear and tear, stability at higher speeds, and minimisation of stress to the permanent way. Broadly, it is measured as overall mass, and the share of that total borne by each axle. Mass is also segregated between that which is spring-borne and that in the form of deadweight, i.e. unsuspended. In a steam locomotive, the latter can be substantial, comprising driving wheels and axles, axleboxes, coupling rods, that element of the connecting rods' weight borne by the big end, approximately 50% of the weight of the eccentric crank, that part of bogie/pony/trailer trucks that are beneath the relative bearing, and any devices installed to control lateral movement. Minimised unsprung weight improves riding quality, which is prone to deteriorate as speed increases. (This was graphically demonstrated by the intermittent lurches experienced in the early driving motor coaches of the Southern Railway's third-rail 750v dc system. The axle-hung, and thus unsprung, motors comprised a substantial proportion of the total vehicle weight.)

Calculation of load distribution assumes that sprung components are supported longitudinally by front and rear equalisation, working rearward from the leading axle. The front equalisation point is usually connected by means of levers and springs on each side of the locomotive. The resultant transverse equalisation does not contribute to lateral stability, but the longitudinal system gives static support that counteracts deflection caused by centrifugal force and rolling. This three-point suspension system thus aids stability and helps ensure a constant axle loading, which is important for balanced adhesion. It also maintains adequate loading on the leading truck/bogie to ensure that this unit fulfils its additional guidance role.

In the early days, concerns over the relationship between locomotive and track focussed on metallurgical factors, e.g. axle breakages and broken rails (the latter also due to poorly supported track). The first significant step towards larger locomotives was in 1846/47 with the GWR Broad Gauge 4-2-2s of the 'Iron Duke' Class, which weighed 35 tons 10 cwt (engine only); 12 tons 6 cwt of that weight was borne by the driving axle. These weights were substantial increases over the largest contemporary locomotives elsewhere, but the safety envelope was considerable, helped by Brunel's massively constructed baulk road, low centre of gravity, and simple driving motion. Forces exerted by reciprocating movement were thus comfortably absorbed.

Progressive increases in loads and speeds demanded larger locomotives, with overall weight and axle loadings often approaching limits imposed by the civil engineer, leading to differing views with his mechanical counterpart over prudent maxima. An example concerned the Coey/Maunsell 4-4-0 Class 'D1' No 341 of the Great Southern & Western Railway, which was so close to his prescribed limits that the civil engineer insisted that the locomotive be reweighed every six months.

When on the move, the impact of static weight is exacerbated by the effect of rotational and reciprocating parts. The movement of driving wheels and coupling rods being solely rotational, they can be completely balanced by adding balance weights to the wheels, but the horizontal reciprocating motion of pistons, piston rods, connecting rods and valve gear cannot be compensated for in this manner. Further, the impact of these forces is subject to factors such as steam pressure in the driving cylinder, effective length of the crank at which this pressure is applied, position of the valve cut-off, and locomotive speed. The result is continuously varying torque at the driving wheel.

In a two-cylinder locomotive, this unbalanced element imparts a significant fore and aft surge, which is partially redressed by adding more to the driving wheel weights, resulting in 'overbalance'. The problem is less acute with three- and four-cylinder types, as the greater number of moving parts induces an element of self-balancing within the horizontal forces, but balance weights were usually still deemed necessary.

That element of the weights' circular movement that remains unbalanced in the vertical plane has the effect of alternately increasing and relieving the static load on each driving axle. Thus as the weight moves upwards, there is a decrease in pressure upon the rail, and a matching increase on downward movement. This rapid alternation in load is known as 'hammer blow' (in the United States, 'dynamic augment'). The intensity of hammer blow is exponential, being at its most extreme with larger locomotives that typically work at higher speeds. Conventional American rigid-framed locomotives (i.e. excluding Mallet and duplex types) were almost exclusively two-cylinder machines, and large express types were particularly afflicted by the problem.

The fluctuation is approximately ± 26% in a two-cylinder locomotive with cranks at 90° to each other, and approximately ±12% with three cylinders (120° crank setting) and four cylinders (90° crank setting). Balance weights were commonly fitted to the driving wheels of two-cylinder locomotives, but were less critical with multi-cylindered machines (they were never fitted to the Southern Railway's three-cylinder 'Pacifics').

The GWR was the first British company to make successful use of four cylinders (with divided drive), and between 1907 and 1950 more than 250 4-6-0s and one 'Pacific' were built using the layout, pioneered with 'Star' Class No 4000 *North Star*. Despite the reduction in hammer blow, the rocking and twisting motion around the slide bar area could not be eliminated, and this induced stress upon the frames at their weakest point, where sections were cut away to accommodate the rear bogie wheels. This notwithstanding, the extended period of construction endorsed the efficacy of the 'Star' layout, and justified the greater construction cost. Similar balancing advantages accrue to the three-cylinder locomotive, with the added benefit of there being fewer components hidden between the frames.

Maunsell's 'Lord Nelson' Class for the Southern Railway was innovative in its approach to hammer blow, reflecting the designer's earlier experience with weight issues in Ireland. These four-cylinder engines, with four sets of Walschaerts valve gear and divided drive, were the largest type yet seen on the Southern. The civil engineer apparently accepted their 20 tons 13 cwt axle loading on the basis of the crank setting at 135°, thus giving eight beats per revolution and more even torque. Also, the use of high-tensile steel minimised the weight of the valve motion without compromising strength. These sophisticated measures contributed to the class's reputation for reliability, although at the penalty of higher construction cost.

In the later stages of the steam story, hammer blow was an issue with heavier locomotives where two-cylinder drive was preferred for reasons of economy in both construction and maintenance costs. As the need for larger mixed-traffic locomotives emerged, four British classes serve to illustrate the points of conflict: LNER 2-6-2 Class 'V2' (three cylinders) of 1936; Southern 4-6-2 'West Country' Class (three cylinders) of 1945; GWR 4-6-0 'County' Class (two cylinders) of 1945; and BR 4-6-2 'Britannia' Class (two cylinders) of 1951. The three-cylinder types could be regarded as unnecessarily complicated for the maintenance regimes of wartime and later austerity conditions, whereas the two-cylinder classes were constrained by the higher degree of hammer blow they imparted. For UK conditions it was generally accepted that a static axle loading over trunk routes should not exceed 22½ tons. However, the Turbomotive's absence of hammer blow allowed a 24-ton maximum (as was borne by two driving axles).

An under-exploited advantage of the Turbomotive concerned the 'factor of adhesion'. This was computed for conventional locomotives as the adhesive weight divided by the maximum rated tractive effort, and in UK practice the optimal factor was regarded as around 4 or slightly above. A lower factor implied excessive power in relation to weight and thus greater risk of slipping resulting from the torque variation at the driving wheel. A higher factor suggested that the locomotive might be unduly heavy in relation to its power output.

Calculation of tractive effort uses a formula based on boiler pressure and driving wheel diameter together with piston stroke and diameter. The Turbomotive's tractive effort could not be calculated in this fashion, so it was notionally allocated 40,300lb, as for the 'Princess Royals'. Experience showed this to be a reasonable estimate in view of the broadly comparable 1936 dynamometer trials results involving Nos 6202, 6210 and 6212. However, as No 6202 delivered power to the driving axle smoothly and free of torque variation, a lower adhesion factor would have been operationally feasible. This contention was borne out by the road performances of the Beyer-Ljungström turbine locomotive, whose adhesive weight was 38% of the total, compared with 45% for a 'Royal Scot'.

By 1946 the Turbomotive's technical specification concerning turbine design and power transmission had been proven, and with the modifications needed to reduce the incidence of component failure identified. It was nevertheless acknowledged that the locomotive had failed to realise the hoped-for reduction in fuel consumption. To fulfil this objective, the consensus view held that a more powerful boiler was required, with a higher working boiler pressure and higher steam temperatures. Absence of variable torque and hammer blow therefore made a significant redesign feasible using smaller driving wheels and a substantially uprated boiler.

Estimated hammer blow for two LMS locomotive types

Class	No of cylinders	Percentage balanced, outside motion	Percentage balanced, inside motion	Speed (mph)	Hammer blow at rail (tons)
'Duchess' 4-6-2	4	49.8	47.3	72	3.47
'Black 5' 4-6-0	2	50	-	64	7.59

Appendix C
Large engine fleet comparison – LMS v LNER

The LMS's need for large express types is highlighted by comparison with the LNER fleet in the 7 and 8 power classifications, as applied by British Railways in 1948. At the date of Stanier's appointment, the LMS had none, and at nationalisation there were only fifty rated 8P and fifty-four rated 7P. The LNER's large engine policy had yielded seventy-six (8P and 7P) by 1931, and 140 by nationalisation. Another sixty-three appeared to LNER designs under BR auspices, whereas the LMS camp saw only one further 8P locomotive and thirty-seven more in the 7P category – the latter all through rebuilding.

The LMS 'Pacifics' were longer than their LNER counterparts and, with the company's largest turntables being 70 feet, tenders of comparatively modest length were necessary, and were made feasible by adequate provision of water troughs.

LMS v LNER fleet profiles

LNER	1948 power rating	No at 31.12.1931	No at 31.12.1947
4-6-4			
Gresley 'W1'	8P	1	1
4-6-2			
Gresley 'A1' ('A10')	n/a	47	1
Gresley 'A3'	7P	23	77
Gresley 'A4'	8P		34
Raven 'A2'	n/a	5	
Thompson 'A1'	7P		1
Thompson 'A2'	7MT		25
Peppercorn 'A1'*	7P		
Peppercorn 'A2'**	7P		1
Total		76	140

* 49 built 1948/49
** 14 built 1948

LMS	1948 power rating	No at 31.12.1947
4-6-2		
'Princess Royal'	8P	12
Turbomotive	7P (LMS rating)	1
'Coronation'*	8P	37
4-6-0		
Rebuilt 'Royal Scot'**	7P	44
Rebuilt 'Patriot'***	7P	8
Rebuilt 'Jubilee'	7P	2
Total		104

* 1 built 1948
** 27 added by rebuilding 1948-53
*** 10 added by rebuilding 1948/49

Appendix D-1
Maintenance history

The table (*top right*), from the Turbomotive's Engine Record Card, shows the periods out of service and related equipment failures. It was normal practice for general repairs to be conducted at intervals dictated by the mileage run and the number of days in traffic. Service repairs were also scheduled, and applied on an interim basis to keep a locomotive capable of carrying out its allotted duties against deterioration in condition as mileage mounted. Casual repairs occurred when a locomotive required attention on a non-scheduled basis, usually as a result of an unexpected component failure or some other mishap. The system was flexible and repair histories varied widely. For example, all the 'Princess Royals' received their last Heavy General repairs between January 1958 and February 1960, except for No 46204, which was last so treated in May 1955. Thereafter its repair history comprised six Light Casual, three Heavy Casual, one Light Intermediate, two Heavy Intermediate and one Non-Classified.

Each repair was categorised in advance of entry into the works, based on the mileage since the last repair and assessed condition of the locomotive. A Heavy repair was so designated if the following was deemed necessary: one or more of re-boilering/boiler lift/replacement of at least four wheel tyres or two or more of replacement cylinders/replacement axles/boiler re-tube/wheel turning/axlebox refit/overhaul of motion or brakes/boiler repairs covering at least 15% of the stays.

The Turbomotive: periods out of service and related equipment failures

Out of traffic	Returned to traffic	Repair type	Reason
Jul 35	Aug 35	-	Oil leakage from turbine bearings and water in roller bearing axleboxes
24.09.1935	21.12.1935	LO	Turbine reverse mechanism failure
15.01.1936	04.02.1936	LO	Reverse turbine failure
15.05.1936	24.06.1936	LO	Reverse turbine failure
14.07.1936	31.07.1936	HO	Oil leakage from turbine bearings
28.01.1937	14.03.1937	LO	Forward turbine failure
?	11.11.1937	TRO	
29.11.1937	16.12.1937	LO	Reverse turbine failure
02.06.1938	24.10.1938	LS	Routine repairs and inspection
08.02.1939	31.07.1939	LO	Forward turbine failure
Oct 39	Jul 41		Withdrawn from traffic and stored
17.09.1941	14.07.1942	LO	Reverse turbine failure
01.08.1942	08.08.1942	LO	
21.11.1942	09.01.1943	LO	Oil leakage, both turbines
11.06.1943	22.09.1944	HG	Failure to flexible coupling between final reduction gear & driving axle
18.12.1944	18.01.1945	LO	Reverse turbine bearing failure
12.04.1945	01.06.1945	LO	Oil leakage from turbine bearings
12.07.1945	25.07.1945	LO	
09.03.1946	08.04.1947	HG	
16.08.1947	09.09.1947	NC	
23.09.1947	15.10.1947	NC	
05.12.1947	03.01.1948	LO	
16.04.1948	10.03.1949	LC	Light repair
13.06.1949	22.06.1949	LC	
27.09.1949	14.10.1949	NC	
21.12.1949	17.01.1950	NC	
18.2.1950	23.02.1950	NC	
17.03.1950	3.04.1950	NC	
06.05.1950			Withdrawn for rebuilding

Classified repairs followed the designations applied to conventional locomotives: LC = Light Casual; LS = Light Service; LO = Light Overhaul; LI = Light Intermediate; HS = Heavy Service; HO = Heavy Overhaul; HS = Heavy General; NC = Not Classified

The repair classification system might have seemed haphazard, but the repair history of the 'Princess Royals' shows that there were comparatively few occasions when two class members were undergoing Heavy General repair concurrently, and only two instances when three were in the workshop for this purpose. In a number of cases, the overlap was a matter of only a few days. This category was typically the most time-consuming, with the intention of restoring the locomotive to 'as new' condition – all the 'Princess Royals' were given their first HG repairs between December 1935 and May 1938.

A Heavy General repair typically took around two months to complete and there were comparatively few examples of periods out of service in excess of ninety days (the average elapsed time of pre-war repairs was significantly shorter), as shown in the accompanying table.

'Princess Royal' Class: periods out of service in excess of ninety days

Loco No.	Repair type	Commenced	Duration*
6200	HG	21.11.1952	116
	HI	17.01.1953	101
6201	HG	15.12.1951	111
	HG	18.02.1960	91
6203	HG	13.11.1951	105
6204	HI	15.04.1950	129
6205	HG	06.05.1952	108
6207	HG	24.11.1948	142
6208	HG	23.07.1952	91
6209	LC	04.02.1959	91
6212	HG	08.11.1948	139

* Calculated on basis of a 6-day week

150

APPENDICES

Appendix D-2
Special instructions to drivers

Set out below is a verbatim copy of procedures to be adopted by drivers.

CLASS 7, 4-6-2 TURBINE ENGINE NO. 6202
INSTRUCTIONS TO DRIVERS

Notes on Driving
The Control box in the Cab consists of:
(a)   Driving handle with valve indicator.
(b)   Safety handle.
(c)   Reversing handle with reversing indicator.

Driving Forwards
The position of the controls should be:
(a)   Driving handle shut, indicator opposite 'O'.
(b)   Safety handle in 'Running' position.
(c)   Reversing indicator in 'Forward Gear'.

To drive forward
(1)   Open main regulator.
(2)   Open turbine control valves by turning the driving handle (clockwise) till the engine moves.
(3)   Shut drain cocks.

Speed Control
Speed is increased or decreased by opening or closing a control valve by turning the handle one notch forward or back as required.
The main regulator should be fully open all the time the engine is running forwards.

During Running
(1)   Check oil pressure; should be kept at about 15-20 pounds per square inch at 60 miles per hour.
(2)   Occasionally open drain cocks.

Stopping
(1)   Shut main regulator.
(2)   Shut all turbine control valves by turning handle anti-clockwise until the indicator is opposite 'O'.
(3)   Apply brakes.
(4)   Open drain cocks.

Coupling Up Reverse Turbine (Going into reverse gear)
The engine must be stationary (brakes on).
The main regulator must be shut.
The turbine control valves must be shut and the driving handle must register on the spring slot.
The drain cocks should be open and there must be less than 10lb per sq inch pressure on steam chest.
(1)   Raise safety handle from 'Safety' to 'Locking' position.
(2)   Turn the reversing handle about five turns clockwise. The reversing indicator should move over from 'Forward Gear' to 'Reverse' Gear. If the reversing handle should stick after about one-and-a-half turns, turn it back immediately to starting position and repeat the operation.
(3)   Lower safety handle to the 'Running' position.

Driving Backwards
The position of the controls should be:
(a)   Driving handle shut. Indicator opposite 'O'.
(b)   The safety handle in the 'Running' position.
(c)   Reversing indicator in 'Reverse Gear'.

To Drive Locomotive in Reverse Gear
(1)   Open all three turbine control valves by giving driving handle two turns in an anti-clockwise direction.
(2)   Drive the engine on the main regulator.

During Running
Check the oil pressure which should rise to about 10lbs per sq inch at 30 miles per hour.

Stopping
(1)   Shut main regulator.
(2)   Shut all turbine control valves.
(3)   Apply brakes.
(4)   Open drain cocks.

Uncoupling Reverse Turbine (Returning to forward gear)
The engine must be stationary (brakes on).
The main regulator must be shut.
The turbine control valves must be shut and driving handle must register in spring slot.
The drain cocks should be open and there must be less than 10lbs per sq inch steam pressure in the steam chest.
(1)   Raise safety handle from 'Running' to 'Locking' position.
(2)   Turn the reversing handle about five turns anti-clockwise. The reversing indicator should move over from 'Reverse Gear' to 'Forward Gear'.
(3)   Lower safety handle to 'Running' position.

Slipping of Wheels
(a)   If slipping occurs in forward gear, immediately shut the control valves.
(b)   In reverse gear, if slipping occurs, immediately shut the main regulator.

Lubricating System
The Turbomotive has three oil pumps, one situated in the sump of the main gear casing, one on the left-hand side of the engine and one on the right-hand side of the engine.
The pump in the main gear casing and the one situated on the left-hand side of the engine are connected to a common oil pressure gauge, and the pump on the right-hand side of the engine is connected to another oil pressure gauge.
Both auxiliary oil pumps, that is, the one on the left and the one on the right-hand side of the engine, should be started up 15 minutes before the engine is moved, and should be kept operating whether the locomotive is running forward, backward, or standing during short-period halts.
The oil pressure in the gauge common to the left-hand pump and the main gear pump should register approximately 7lbs before the locomotive commences to move, and should rise as the speed increases, to approximately 16lbs.
The oil pressure in the gauge connected to the pump on the right-hand side of the engine should register 5 to 7lbs, whether the locomotive is standing, running forward, or in reverse.
Any exceptional variation in these pressures should be reported on a repair card.

Oil Temperatures Gauge on R.-H. Side of Cab
These gauges show the temperature of the lubricating oil circulating round the gears and bearings of the turbines, one after the oil leaves the turbine and the other after the oil has passed through the cooler.
The readings should be in the neighbourhood of, hot oil 120°-180°, cooled oil 80°-140°, the difference between the two gauges being approximately 40°.

The Driver is Held Responsible for the Following:
Filling up daily the sight feed lubricator boxes on the auxiliary pumps.
PRIOR to daily run, the following drain cocks must be opened by operating the lever on the driver's side of the engine. These cocks must be left open for sufficient time to allow condensation to be cleared, and then closed:
   Forward turbine cylinder high-pressure end.
   Forward turbine cylinder low-pressure end.
   Steam chests for forward and reverse turbine.
Open the L.-H. auxiliary oil pump front and back cylinder drain cocks, and start up the pump on the L.-H. side of engine and also the pump in the R.-H. foot frame, so they pump at about the following rates:-
   L.-H. pump 10 double strokes per minute.
   R.-H. pump 10 double strokes per minute.
After the L.-H. pump has been running for a brief period, sufficient to allow condensation to have been cleared from the cylinder, close the drain cocks. (These cocks are situated under the pump cylinder at the front and back and are opened and shut by hand).
AFTER the daily run:
   Open all the drain cocks.
   Leave auxiliary pumps running after engine is stabled. These pumps to be shut off 30 minutes after the engine is stabled.
   Open drain cocks on pumps.
   Close main regulator.
   Close all turbine control valves.

Appendix D-3
Special instructions to fitters

Set out below is a verbatim copy of procedures to the adopted by fitters.

EXAMINATION OF, AND ATTENTION TO, 4-6-2 TURBINE ENGINE NO. 6202, TO BE CARRIED OUT BY THE FITTER

Handle on top of the oil strainer to be turned daily.
After the engine has been standing, without the pumps working, for the maximum possible period, draw off all water which has separated out from the oil, by means of the cock provided at the bottom of the oil tank, **daily before the auxiliary pumps are started up**.
Inspect the oil level in the sump daily after removing all water and top up if necessary.
Leather bags on the driving axle to be drained of water daily.*

See that the following Drain Cocks are open:
    Forward turbine cylinder high-pressure end.
    Forward turbine cylinder low-pressure end.
    Steam chest for forward and reverse turbine.
    Drain sump in base of smokebox saddle casing.

To Test Oil Pumps
    Open the L.-H. auxiliary oil pump drain cocks and start up the pumps at a rate of about:
    L.-H. pump 20 double strokes per minute.
    R.-H. pump 10 double strokes per minute.
The pressure on the oil gauges, which should be registered while the engine is standing and the auxiliary pump working, is about 7lbs per sq inch.
When all the water has been cleared from the pipes and cylinder, partially close the pump drain cocks of L.-H. auxiliary pump.

Attention to Turbines, Gear, Auxiliary Pumps, etc., after daily run
    Open all drain cocks.
    Shut down auxiliary oil pumps after engine has been standing about half an hour.
    Open drain cocks on pumps.
    Check forward turbine thrust bearing indicator.

Examination at Wash Out and Firebox Examination with Boiler Full
    Oil strainer and magnets to be removed and cleaned.
    Oil ways in steam chest cam housing to be oiled with cylinder oil.
    Nipples on control rod bracket bearings and control rod bevel gear boxes to be greased.
    Nipples on control rods between driver's cab and turbine to be oiled.

Examinations at 6,000 Miles
    Oil in sump to be drained off and oil system cleaned and refilled with clean oil, every 6,000 miles.
    Feedwater heater tubes to be cleaned.
    Inspection plates over reverse turbine rotor bearing and cover plate on reverse turbine exhaust casting to be taken off to inspect turbine bearings and blades. 'Timken' roller bearings to be checked for oil and refilled where necessary.

* The purpose of the leather bags is not clear, but perhaps they acted as catchments for condensate leaked through the main turbine bearings.

Appendix D-4
Commentary on the slow-speed gear flexible drive failure

A serious failure was sustained in July 1943 at Camden shed, following arrival from Liverpool. The coupled wheels locked without warning during shunting operations, necessitating special arrangements to move the locomotive to Crewe. The following extract from R. C. Bond's paper to the Institution of Locomotive Engineers in January 1948 describes the causes:

'The examination at Crewe showed conclusively that the trouble leading to this failure had originated in the flexible drive between the slow-speed gear wheel and the driving axle. As a result of wear which had taken place, in the normal course, at the driving pins and bushes connecting the gear wheel to the floating link and the driving axle, clearance between the nuts securing the driving pins and the access hole in the gear wheel centre discs had become reduced sufficiently to cause contact. The effect of wear in the driving pins and bushes is cumulative and is a maximum for two pins (Nos 2 and 5). The knock set up caused the locking device to be damaged and the nuts became unscrewed. Excessive slackness in the drive caused by the loss of these nuts resulted in the transmission of heavy shocks, particularly when changing direction from forward to reverse. These shocks were sufficient ultimately to fracture one end of pin No 2 and the teeth of the high-speed pinion, ten of which were found to be broken, all on the left hand helix. Other damage to the flexible drive was rather extensive. The fractured end of No 2 pin was heavily bruised, and the nut and washers at the opposite end were damaged by hammering against the clearance hole in the gear wheel disc. Similar damage had occurred to pin No 5. The crank arm of the driving axle, to which the broken pin had been attached, was scored very heavily to a depth of ¼ inch, the solid keys locating the washer behind the missing nut being completely worn away. The sides and end of the driving arm were deeply marked by the broken end of the pin.

Broken plates were found in twelve of the sixteen leaf springs in the left-hand side of the slow-speed wheel but, in the right-hand side, three springs only contained broken plates. Of the total of 256 spring plates, 68 were found to be broken. The remaining 188 plates were subject to a crack detection test and were found to be in good condition.

The left-hand helix of the second reduction pinion was slack on its centre to the extent of 3/16 inch circumferentially, but the bedding of the gear teeth on this, as on all other gears throughout the transmission, was excellent.

Repairs were carried out satisfactorily to the slow-speed gear wheel and flexible drive, during the course of which the pockets in the gear wheel discs containing the leaf springs were re-machined to remove wear and slight surface roughness. An additional plate was added to each of the springs to correspond, but in view of the removal by opening out the slots, it was not found possible to increase the clearance between the driving pins and the holes in the gear discs. This failure, serious and expensive though it was, did not denote any unsoundness in the principles of design, but should properly be regarded as part of the price to be paid for new experience.'

Appendix E
Assessment of GWR design features imported by Stanier to the LMS

As summarised by H. A. V. Bulleid in *Master Builders of Steam*.

	Feature	Typical LMS comment, 1934	Ultimate fate
1	Churchward firebox	Excellent	Became standard
2	Taper barrel	'Is it really necessary?'	Became standard
3	Top feed	Good	Became standard
4	Smokebox regulator and elimination of dome	Inferior to LMS	Discontinued
5	Jumper blast-pipe	Often stuck, or bolted down	Discontinued
6	Parallel fusible plugs	Probably better	Became standard
7	Low-degree superheat	Classic error	Corrected
8	Reduction in heating surface of small tubes	Intended to facilitate repairs	Successive boiler batches had greater heating spaces
9	Deflector plates in smokebox	Reduced spark throwing but affected steaming	Discontinued
10	Coupling and connecting rod lubrication	Very good, except brass weakened by elongated pads	Further improved
11	Phosphor bronze replacement of case-hardened steel valve bushes and die blocks	Wear increased but occasional seizure eliminated	Became standard
12	Steel axleboxes with press-in brasses	Great improvement on LMS bosses	Became standard
13	Little-end lubrication of connecting rod	Admirable arrangement	Became standard
14	Bogie and pony trucks with side bolsters	Good ('Churchward, de Glehn')	Became standard
15	Mechanical trickle sanding gear	Unsatisfactory	Reverted to steam sanding
16	28-inch stroke	No trouble	Became standard

APPENDICES

Appendix F
Digest of views expressed by other engineers

The paper presented by R. C. Bond on 30 January 1946 to the Institution of Locomotive Engineers generated a number of responses. Bond responded directly to the President's remarks and in writing to other matters raised. The following is a précis of significant views aired and replies on aspects not otherwise covered in the main body of this work.

M. A. Crane (Member): Noted the reverse turbine power rating of Pennsylvania 6-8-6 No 6200 was 65,000lb compared with 70,000 in forward mode, whereas the Turbomotive's reverse power rating was undisclosed.

H. Holcroft (Member): Stated that the Turbomotive was undoubtedly successful within its limited field but the trend was to build general-purpose engines, e.g. the Southern's practice of using 'Pacifics' between Salisbury and Exeter – passenger one way, returning on a freight working. Doubted whether a turbine locomotive could cope under such conditions, noting the need for specially trained crews. Wondered if fully softened water was used and what would be the effect on the turbine blades of using partially softened water.

Absence of hammer blow allowed an axle loading of 24 tons but there was no need for reciprocating weights in a three- or four-cylinder engine, as demonstrated with the Southern's three-cylinder 'Pacifics'. Bridge stress diagrams had shown these locomotives to run more smoothly than electric stock, indicating that a 24-ton axle loading was feasible with multi-cylinder engines. This was one more case where the theoretically desirable refinement of a variable blast-pipe had proven unsuccessful.

Economy due to superheat was limited by exhausting at only 5 to 10lb above atmosphere and by the maximum possible boiler pressure. A revision in boiler design would be needed for working pressure above 300lb per sq in.

R. C. Bond (in reply): The locomotive used fully softened water with a continuous blowdown valve. In earlier years it had used unsoftened water for lengthy periods without this affecting the turbine blades. Internal turbine parts and steam passages had remained remarkably corrosion-free. Partly agreed on balancing in multi-cylinder locomotives but drew attention to two papers dated 1941: 'Balancing of Locomotive Reciprocating Parts' by E. S. Cox for the Institution, and a paper by Sir H. Colam and Major Watson to the Institution of Civil Engineers.

J. E. Spear (Member): Believed the rotation of the bearings' outer races on the leading coupled wheels was caused by a machining error in the boxes; re-machining had solved that problem. Normal practice was to make the outer races of roller bearings in which the shaft rotates of such a fit in the housing as to prevent their movement. To prevent localised loading it is necessary to rotate these races about 120 degrees at 200,000-miles intervals or during shopping. Starting resistance would be about 4lb per ton with roller bearings compared with 16-18lb per ton with plain bearings.

R. C. Bond (in reply): Acknowledged this amplification regarding roller bearings, but noted that their lower starting resistance had little ultimate effect (i.e. in long-distance non-stop running).

Lt Col K. Cantlie (Member): Noted with pleasure the Turbomotive's technical success but queried its commercial viability. Such a new design needed extended testing and resultant modification to maximise efficiency but, notwithstanding the hiatus of the war, the experiment had continued for a long time. Noted plans to increase temperature and pressure to increase efficiency, and hoped that this would happen.

Commented on the suspicious number of experimental fittings to locomotives that were worth neither perpetuation nor removal, and trusted the Turbomotive would not be so burdened. If improved economy and efficiency with the modified engine outweighed the greater maintenance and capital expense, then the exercise could be regarded a success.

Col C. R. L. Rice (Associate Member): Sought the author's views on the comparative merits of electrical and mechanical transmission. Noted the possible weak spot in the reversing mechanism and risk of costly damage with misuse or failure of the interlocking gear. Based on experience with electric transmission in diesel and electric locomotives, there appeared potential in the steam-electric turbine combination.

T. Henry Turner (Member): Queried how serious was Holcroft's view that new locomotives must be general-purpose types. Cited special locomotives used for services such as the 'Silver Jubilee' and 'Coronation', and opined that if such duties were not to return then there was no case for the turbine engine. However, passengers would prefer smooth turbine haulage to the intermittent jerks imparted by reciprocating engines.

W. S. Graff-Baker (President): Use of two turbines was like cutting a big hole for the cat and a little one for the kitten. If recourse were taken to a reverse clutch (power- or hand-operated), it seemed preferable to have a clutch and reverse gear for the main turbine. Queried why roller bearings were not fitted to gear train and turbines, as such equipment should help avoid some of the very few problems encountered.

Did not entirely agree with Mr Cantlie, as viability could not be solely assessed financially. Greater passenger comfort and reduced track wear could not be measured in monetary terms. Noted the national fuel crisis and the importance of saving fuel however possible, which must be considered in any expenditure plans.

Thought the Turbomotive as had been modified to be No 1A in the turbine project. A second prototype (No 2) should be developed well before No 1A reached the end of its working life but did not anticipate a design capable of standardisation (i.e. multiplication) before Version No 3.

R. C. Bond (in reply): Personally felt it had been correct to fit two turbines. Early control box modifications and removal of steam reversing cylinder had eliminated the reversing problems. Believed a mechanism to change direction of the whole gear train would have been more troublesome.

Had often been queried about roller bearings for turbines and gears. In future, such features would be used, subject to available space. Believed that Dr Guy (of Metropolitan-Vickers) would confirm that there was inadequate room within the existing locomotive.

Major J. R. Gould (Visitor, in correspondence): Considered the linkage of turbine and gearing to the leading driving axle with secondary transmission by coupling rods to be a weakness. It was generally thought that crank action was only 40% efficient compared with 100% through turbine drive and gear action. Also, side rods were inefficient at high speeds due to their weight describing fantastic figures and setting up gyroscopic and centrifugal strains that trend towards misplaced energy. Suggested either to extend gearing to the driving axles or to use three separate, smaller turbines for each driving axle independently; thought this would gain a 25% efficiency improvement.

Alternatively advocated that turbine be placed longitudinally between the frames, linked by worm gear to driving axle, yielding less gearing and more efficiency. The usual splined shaft drive would take up the wheel springing, making for a convenient layout although a mechanism would be needed to disengage worm on the over-run or for movements while out of steam. Smaller driving wheels could be used.

Noted that 8lb of water evaporated for every lb of coal was very low, as with most locomotives. The cause was undersized boilers that had to be forced with heavy draught, leading to high smokebox temperatures and loss of up to 25% of fuel passing straight through the tubes. Loss in smokebox temperature (?) will also be about 25%. These factors combined with other losses reduced boiler efficiency to less than 50%. Thus a boiler of at least twice the heating surface is required to raise efficiency to 75-80%, which would be more in keeping with marine practice.

R. C. Bond (in reply): Noted comments with interest but could not accept contention that efficiency of crank and coupling rod transmission is no greater than 40%. This could only mean that horsepower measured at the wheel tread of a conventional locomotive would not exceed 40% of IHP. Results of dynamometer tests and on stationary plants clearly disprove this conclusion. Felt that the transmission and final drive in use was simpler and more reliable than any of the suggested alternatives.

In the dynamometer tests, the average firing rate of approximately 50lb per sq ft of grate per hour using coal of 14,000 BTU per lb with an evaporation rate of 8lb of water per lb of coal yielded a 76% efficiency factor. Loss rate of 25% unburnt fuel is unusual in British practice and LMS locomotives would not approach this level. Although heating surface is important, the vital factors in achieving reasonable efficiency levels are adequacy of the grate area and a moderate rate of combustion. Combustion efficiency declines rapidly with higher firing rates but the effectiveness of heat absorption remains practically constant over the whole range of operation.

J. Dearden (Derby, in correspondence): Concluded from dynamometer comparisons between the turbine and reciprocating engines showed that neither type operated close to respective thermal efficiency maxima. Average horsepower delivered throughout each journey was the key determinant in water and fuel consumption levels. Attributed the Turbomotive's slightly superior results to heavier trains and greater tractive resistance.

R. C. Bond (in reply): Agreed with the contention that overall efficiency measured by coal and water consumption is influenced by average DBHP-hour developed. When running light, engine's DBHP-hour is nil whereas indicated thermal efficiency will be high. Overall efficiency rises rapidly in step with rise in DBHP-hour up to a limiting point beyond which it commences to decrease, albeit at a lower pace.

THE LMS TURBOMOTIVE

This is due to the effect that later valve cut-off, necessary at higher power outputs, has on thermal efficiency and so also on DBHP efficiency. Declining boiler efficiency at higher firing rates influences final shape of the coal consumption rate curve against DBHP. He drew attention to a lucid review of this topic published in *The Railway Gazette* of 19 May 1939, based on experience with the 'Duchess' Class.

W. Paterson (Member, in correspondence): Noted that Bond intended to improve sensitivity of the controls and pleaded for assurance that they be made simpler. Footplate men, despite assumptions to the contrary, were not opposed to innovation if it led to economy or improved availability but were positively and inflexibly opposed to decrease in either, or to loss of control simplicity. Hoped for elimination of any unnecessary or inconvenient movement in controls, as there was no room for such in modern high-speed locomotives.

R. C. Bond (in reply): Acknowledged the importance of these remarks in the context of Paterson's wide operating experience and knowledge. Confidently expected that the Turbomotive would meet the maintenance and availability improvements sought. Noted that the general layout of controls closely conformed with Stanier's other classes, which had given general satisfaction. Improvement was possible in the operational sequence to engage reverse gear, with reference to Cox's notes on the Pennsylvania locomotive in this regard.

Lt Cdr D. R. Carling (Associate Member, in correspondence): Remarked on progress in Russia and Germany with condenser-equipped reciprocating locomotives. These worked at atmospheric pressure, occupied less space and required less maintenance than such equipment on earlier turbine locomotives. Fewer washouts and lower boiler repairs offset extra cost. Reportedly, crews preferred these locomotives to non-condensing versions. Comments offered as future possibilities rather than to suggest that LMS engine be condenser-equipped. Noted that the author might have mentioned that success with the original Swedish Ljungström engine had led to a repeat order for three [sic] more. A problem with these engines was their being too long for standard turntables, requiring use of shorter four-wheel tenders.

As troublesome reverse gear was only needed for light duties, wondered whether a small reversible reciprocating engine should substituted, which could also act as a low-speed booster for forward starting, thereby possibly replacing two of the six steam valves. Considered performance very encouraging but regretted that Rugby plant had not been completed. Stationary testing might confirm need to revise the blast-pipe; steam temperature was about 100° below hoped-for maximum. With adequate feedwater heating, reduced evaporative space in favour of more superheating area should avoid shortness of steam. These views apart, considered the project most praiseworthy. A subsidiary point – what happens to the steam bled from the turbine to supply the feedwater heater?

R. C. Bond (in reply): While concurring with the comments on condenser reciprocating engines, doubted their prospects for lasting success in British conditions but performance information would be welcome. Despite the reverse turbine problems having been overcome, the idea of installing a geared reciprocating engine was interesting. However, the reverse turbine's tractive effort is significant and there would be problems in finding room for a reciprocating engine capable of delivering commensurate power. Making such a unit reversible would complicate the control gear. While reduction in steam consumption at lower speeds would be achieved, this was insignificant for an express locomotive and would erode the advantages of design simplicity. Subsidiary point – condensate from feedwater heater passes by pipes and non-return valves to the tender tank.

E. C. Poultney (Member, in correspondence): Drew performance comparisons with contemporary North American designs [see Chapter 9]. Noted that indicated horsepower compared closely with that for four-cylinder reciprocating type but wanted to know whether IHP was measured at the rail or turbine shaft. Interested in comparative starting pulls and whether accelerative capacity matched the reciprocating engines.

R. C. Bond (in reply): No direct measurements of indicated or shaft HP have been taken. The DBHP under various conditions was accurately determined in dynamometer tests and from measuring internal resistance while coasting. Relative evaporation rates were deduced approximately from the dynamometer tests. No specific tests were conducted but little difference is discernible in acceleration rates.

* * *

The paper was re-read on 18 February 1946 at a general meeting of the Institution's Birmingham Branch, held at the Midland Hotel, Derby. The following is again a précis of the subsequent discussions.

E. S. Cox: All should agree this was a model of how best to conduct a large-scale experiment, and of how to address teething troubles through careful diagnosis and implementation of means to prevent recurrence.

D. W. Sandford: Author had shown that the Turbomotive offered no appreciable efficiency advantage over conventional engines but the turbine system could work at higher pressures without resorting to compound expansion, while higher temperatures were possible without lubrication problems. Exploitation of these features might lead to appreciable economy. Considered that 300lb per sq in boiler pressure would be possible but superheater temperature would have to be at least 800°F to maintain suitably dry steam at the exhaust end. If turbine shaft could run in roller bearings away from the steam casing, lubrication should be simpler with risk of frothing oil avoided.

Locomotive was intended for express duties; did author think it would be suitable for general utility work (i.e. passenger and freight)? Asked whether consideration had been given to using a fan instead of the ordinary blast-pipe. Suggested that the kinetic energy in the steam jet was about 4½ times the energy necessary if gases were expelled by means of a fan without being mixed by the steam.

With a conventional locomotive, there is a definite limit to the degree to which backpressure could be reduced. Regardless of blast-pipe size, friction remained in the ports while a very free exhaust might cause power loss. With a turbine it was possible to expand steam down to atmospheric pressure although steam exhausted at no velocity would cause visibility problems for the crew. However, with a turbine locomotive there might be a case for a fan to produce draught.

R. C. Bond (in reply): Until quite recently, 250lb per sq in had been regarded as the highest practical pressure to be borne by stayed surfaces although 300lb per sq in was being applied in the USA and 280lb per sq in by the GWR and Southern. Was reluctant to nominate a limit for future development as so much depended upon water conditions, design, and workshop practices for boiler maintenance. Nevertheless experience probably confirmed the desirability of alternative construction methods permitting 350lb per sq in or higher.

Sandford on previous occasions had drawn attention to possible advantages in boilers where all tubes would be flue tubes – he concurred with this view. American Type 'E' superheater had gone some way towards this objective but the idea had still to be tried in the UK.

Use of an exhaust fan instead of the blast-pipe would reduce expenditure of an undue amount of energy but existing arrangement had the merit of simplicity and automatic adjustment of work done to the steam demand from the boiler. While an experiment with a fan might be instructive, felt it had been wise to avoid this extra departure from convention at time of construction. Had space permitted, there was little doubt that roller bearings would have been fitted to the turbine spindles; lubrication would have been simpler and aeration of oil avoided.

Sandford's comparisons of actual steam consumption against that theoretically available were valuable additions to points raised, gave an indication of possible extent of further improvement, and confirmed the turbine efficiency measured while on test at the makers. About 8% of steam fed to the turbine is bled to the feedwater heater.

F. H. Sutherland: Noted that the amount of information provided was unusually complete, and very valuable. Considered all problems capable of resolution by modern engineering standards, thus rendering a reliable machine capable of providing mechanical and thermo-dynamic advantages.

Pending opening of the Rugby test plant, comparative calculations based on dynamometer results had used water consumption over specific distances to estimate weight of steam per IHP hour. The minimum value for 'Duchess' 4-6-2 was 14.5lb (175 BTUs per lb) whereas that for the Turbomotive was 13lb (196 BTUs per lb) at a turbine speed of 7,950rpm (54mph). The entropy diagram for steam at 250lb per sq in superheated to 682°F yielded turbine efficiency of 81%. Noted that under similar conditions the 6-8-6 Pennsylvania locomotive yielded a turbine efficiency of 84%.

These calculations showed that the gap between the actual weight of steam used and that theoretically required which, if only partly bridged, would add marked economy to the non-condensing turbine engine. From his studies it seemed that boiler pressures not much higher than 250-300lb per sq in would be needed to achieve these advances although an increase in superheater temperature would be needed.

Enquired if author could advise percentage weight per lb of entering steam that is bled from the feedwater heater, and state whether this steam drains away completely from the heater as condensate. Information concerning the heater was very interesting as a feed temperature of 275°F would assist the boiler considerably as, with steam at 250lbs per sq in superheated to 682°F, only 1,100 BTUs per lb would be required.

154

APPENDICES

H. I. Andrews: Enquired about the turbine's performance consistency over a wide speed range as relevant information had not been disclosed, with regard to what compromises had been reached in shaping the blades and to the optimum speed for which they had been designed.

Also, it was difficult to understand exactly what happened within the turbine when exerting tractive effort at standstill, i.e. on starting. It seemed that steam passed initially through a double impulse blading from which it emerged in an unusual direction while in subsequent stages no energy would be extracted from the steam. Thus turbine absorbed a large amount of power, evidently without it overheating, and it was not clear what was the condition of the steam at the exhaust.

Author's conclusions regarding condensing seemed to be based on comparison with two earlier experimental engines that had too many novel features. Cited Bulleid's recent view that condensers on reciprocating engines showed promise in operating advantages and reduced boiler maintenance – as had been endorsed by recent practice in Germany and Russia. Enquired whether author would not find the combination of a satisfactory turbine locomotive and a condensing tender the basis for a promising experiment.

R. C. Bond (in reply): Acknowledged assistance of R. A. Struthers of Metropolitan-Vickers in response to questions related to turbine design. It was intended to maintain high efficiency over a wide speed range, with efficiency characteristics proven by testing at the maker's works. Efficiency characteristics for change of speed are flatter than is customary in turbines intended to operate at constant speed, achieved by:

 a. Blading shape was chosen for high efficiency over the wide range of steam inlet angles of a variable speed turbine.
 b. Turbine comprises a two-row velocity compounded stage, one impulse stage and a number of reaction stages. Each type of stage has a different characteristic with change of speed, the total expansion being suitably apportioned between the different stages.
 c. Provision of six nozzle control valves reduces throttling losses.

Tests by the makers show that the optimal speed for the complete unit is about 50mph; the tractive effort of the locomotive at rest is about 40,000lb. Steam flow conditions on starting differ considerably from a reciprocating engine where steam consumption, being dependent upon steam chest pressure, cut-off, and number of strokes per minute varies with the speed of the locomotive. Demand upon the Turbomotive's boiler is dependent only upon the steam chest pressure and the nozzle area open. When four valves are open for starting the rate of steam consumption would be about 6½lb per second; if five valves were required, the rate would rise to 7½lb per second.

When steam is admitted to the turbine and until the force exerted on the blading is sufficient to start the locomotive, steam expands through the various stages and will be exhausted without having done any useful work. The exhaust steam temperature tends to rise and the turbine to become heated but, as soon as the locomotive moves, work will be developed in each stage of the turbine. As speed rises, normal working temperature is rapidly attained with exhaust steam falling to about 275°F. Time interval between steam admission and locomotive movement is small and there is no prolonged heating.

F. A. Harper: Noted that Timken roller bearings did not allow for end play in the axles and asked if this had caused any trouble; also asked if there had been any misalignment of gears caused by one bearing suffering more wear than another.

R. C. Bond (in reply): Harper, together with other speakers, had referred to roller bearings on the axles. They had proved most satisfactory in practice and in author's opinion their use would extend. Could not advise costs in comparison with the ordinary variety but noted roller bearings were being fitted to new locomotives in many countries as a matter of course.

R. C. S. Low: Found roller bearing axleboxes very interesting as they offered potential in reciprocating engines although extra weight might be problematic. Enquired whether author could provide estimated cost comparisons between roller bearing boxes and standard axleboxes, wheels and journals.

D. W. Peacock: Noted two cylindrical chokes above the variable steam nozzles and enquired whether these should not be relocated as they appeared to impede the flow of gases towards the exhaust steam jets, by restricting entrainment area.

Regarding the six steam valves, enquired about feasibility of Vernier-type control making one of the nozzles adjustable so that power was not released in a series of jerks. Pointed out that on test the locomotive had run faster over heavy sections than was necessary to keep to schedule, which eroded economy. With a reciprocating engine working at constant power, the engine had to be notched back from say 50% at slow speed to 15% at high speed. On the turbine engine, the number of steam valves open determined the power output almost independently of the speed.

R. C. Bond (in reply): Intended to move the cylindrical chokes above the blast-pipe caps and to simplify the blast-pipe design in line with the double blast-pipe that gives good service with the standard 'Pacific' type. Regarding the perceived lack of control sensitivity compared with fine regulator and cut-off adjustments possible with a reciprocating locomotive, this is of little practical significance and not sufficient to warrant complexity of Vernier equipment.

W. R. Carslake: Added to H. I. Andrews's remarks favouring condenser by noting that German locomotives so fitted had worked well under wartime conditions, essentially because they operated at atmospheric pressure. Use of such a condenser with a turbine engine offered advantages in improved quality feedwater; in Germany engines worked up to four weeks between washouts and boiler scale deposits were slight. Also, higher ratio of expansion would be possible, as advocated by D. W. Sandford, without attendant difficulties associated with low exhaust pressure.

J. C. Loach: Noted the author's statement that mechanical efficiency was superior to that of an ordinary engine of similar weight, and that internal resistance was lower when coasting. Asked how much of this was due to the prime mover and how much to the roller bearings. Had an attempt been made to measure the roller bearing resistance? This could be measured by disconnecting the turbine and towing the engine behind the dynamometer car. Recalled disappointing roller bearing tests made years previously with coaches so fitted, the resistance being similar to that with plain bearings. Presumed therefore that roller bearings were used on the Turbomotive for their ability to work long periods without attention rather than for any frictional advantage.

Assuming that improved mechanical efficiency rested with the prime mover (i.e. turbine and gears) and noting the author's statement that fuel consumption was similar to that of a reciprocating 4-6-2, could it be concluded that the prime mover was thermally less efficient, thus nullifying improved mechanical efficiency?

R. C. Bond (general response): Although aware of developments with condenser reciprocating locomotives in Germany and Russia, little meaningful performance information was available and proof of success or failure depended upon their operating record in large numbers under peace-time conditions. Doubted whether their complexity was suited to UK usage. Not possible to give a detailed reply to Loach's points regarding locomotive's resistance as a vehicle. Further, based on the information in the paper, it would be incorrect to assume that the Turbomotive as a prime mover was less thermally efficient than a comparable reciprocating engine.

* * *

The paper was given a third reading on 2 May 1946 at the Annual General Meeting of the Institution's Manchester Centre, held at the Reynolds Hall, College of Technology. A précis of the subsequent discussions follows.

H. H. Saunders (Chairman): Noted that permanent way engineers had permitted a heavier axle load – did this apply also to fully balanced reciprocating locomotives and would this also apply to diesel locomotives? Secondly, issue of frothing oil had been encountered in military transport (specifically tanks) at the beginning of the war and motorcar designers had been consulted. Solution had been to increase reservoir capacity and to install weirs in the circuit to allow oil to settle.

A third point was that of unqualified, inexperienced shed crews handling the Turbomotive with faulty handling causing some failures. Finally, was aware of Indian locomotives fitted with roller bearings achieving similar high mileages. Examination had shown that on one occasion water had penetrated the bearing due to washing down with high-pressure water. To examine the bearings, wheels had been pulled off the axles and then replaced without any alteration whatever. Understood similar procedure had been done by the LMS.

R. C. Bond (in reply): Could not give a definitive answer whether a heavier axle loading would be appropriate to diesel locomotives, but the heavy unsprung weight with electric engines would be influential in the matter, requiring each case to be determined on its merits. The measures to combat oil frothing in tanks were interesting as they were similar to changes proposed for the Turbomotive. Confirmed that examination of roller bearings and final drive axle assembly was achieved by forcing the wheel off the axle, then pressing back into place without any problems.

Mr Power (visitor): Asked whether performance data was available for the first reduction pinion compared with its replacement.

155

R. C. Bond (in reply): The broken high-speed pinion teeth following the flexible drive failure were the result, not the cause, of the trouble. Replacement pinion had performed well, and general gear performance and teeth condition had proved most satisfactory.

J. Hadfield (Member): Stated many attempts had been made to recover energy lost in the toe of the Rankine Cycle [which closely describes the process by which steam-operated heat engines used in thermal power generation plants produce power] and the Turbomotive offered many possibilities.

Design had been simplified by discarding the condenser but a steam locomotive's availability was largely determined by boiler condition as affected by water contamination. Use of an air-cooled condenser improves thermal efficiency and reduces water consumption to about 5% of that used in a conventional locomotive. Savings in total operating costs were obviously more important than improvement in thermal efficiency as washouts and associated repairs caused by contaminated water could render a locomotive out of service for one-eighth of its service life. Beyer-Ljungström locomotive had shown 95% water savings compared with normal locomotives.

Author had frankly admitted that between the same limits of pressure and temperature, the non-condensing turbine locomotive showed no significant economy compared with a similarly sized conventional locomotive. Thus significant thermal improvement could only be achieved with pressure and steam maxima well above those practicable with a reciprocating machine. In this respect boiler design would be limited by what was possible with an orthodox Stephenson-type vessel. In considering future development, enquired whether author had considered potential competition from the emerging gas turbine.

R. C. Bond (in reply): Agreed that boiler performance was key to a steam locomotive's availability. While water economy in condensing engines was important in tropical regions, this was less a factor in Britain where softening processes had overcome many problems. Pros and cons of condensing turbine locomotives could be argued at length but fact remained that experience with such types had not been encouraging. Progress might be made later with condensing equipment but his opinion was based on experience to date.

Regarding maximum steam temperatures, wished to see a boiler where all the tubes were superheater flues, as was being explored in the USA. Given correct proportions, believed such a boiler could steam well with substantial savings in fuel and water. Believed aim should be to achieve highest temperatures permitted by lubrication and metallurgical limitations.

Mr Struthers (visitor): Frank analysis of operating troubles, causes and cures was no less important than assessment of a new engineering development's benefits; author's candour added weight to the conclusions he had drawn.

Operating troubles – it was pertinent to ask whether these are inherent in a gear-driven turbine locomotive, whether their cause had been clearly established, and whether they had been successfully overcome. Author's analysis had convincingly answered these questions in showing that the forward turbine and gear train in over 300,000 miles had proven as mechanically reliable as a conventional locomotive.

1. Reduced coal consumption – dynamometer trials had shown:
   a. Tests at 30,000 miles and again at 100,000 had revealed that turbine efficiency was unaffected by mileage.
   b. Turbomotive's efficiency should thus be compared with a reciprocating engine in average condition, as was No 6212 during the tests.
   c. On this basis, Turbomotive's coal consumption was 8% less and water consumption was 11% less than that for No 6212.

Author states that moderate fuel economy alone is not enough to justify the greater operating charges; what fuel economy target would justify a study of how it might be realised?

Ways of improving turbine efficiency might include:

   d. Adjustment of the gear ratio to maximise efficiency at the projected average cruising speed. Turbine was set for optimal efficiency at 50mph whereas the average speed in the tests had been 65mph.
   e. Research and development over preceding 10 years especially with smaller turbines added to belief that substantial improvements might be possible with the Turbomotive.
   f. Variable blast-pipe induced greater backpressure at higher loads (i.e. using 3 to 6 steam valves). This equipment is correct in principle and better proportioning might improve matters with reduced backpressure.

2. Increased availability and lower repair costs:
   g. Author had provided information that suggested a longer boiler life might be achieved than with a conventional locomotive, due apparently to the steady blast. Previously mentioned variable blast-pipe modifications might reduce backpressure and consequential boiler wear, thereby adding to working life.
   h. Dynamometer tests having shown an 11% advantage in raw water consumption, it should be possible to extend periods between washouts, thus adding to availability.

3. Greater power to weight capacity:
   Additional power available from the turbine with a standard boiler is a function of greater fuel economy and reduced internal resistance with appreciable results at high speeds. This conclusion is supported by dynamometer trials where turbine bhp was taken from readings during a routine test rather than a special test to obtain maximum sustained bhp at high speeds.

R. C. Bond (in reply): These remarks were a valuable contribution to the debate, coming from someone closely connected with design and construction of turbines and transmission. Struthers had been most helpful in resolving faults encountered with the locomotive. Their accurate diagnosis and effective correction had greatly aided the project's success.

H. Fowler (Member): Financial advantage of a new type should be considered in light of effect on departments other than the CME's. Absence of hammer blow should be credited to the turbine locomotive against its reciprocating counterpart. Noted that it had just received its first replacement firebox and wondered how this compared with fireboxes of near contemporaries, 'Pacifics' Nos 6200/6201. Allowing for the boiler change, had constant blast caused less wear?

Mr Patrick (Member): Noted the unusual feature of surface feedwater heater fitted in line with exhaust injector, and enquired whether heater functioned properly without need for frequent cleaning to remove scale deposits, and whether provision was made for bypassing. Noted also large of amount of lubrication equipment compared with an orthodox locomotive, and which seemed a major source of problems. On the other hand did total enclosure of the lubrication system mean that oil consumption was lower?

R. C. Bond (in reply): No problems occurred in keeping feedwater tubes clear; periodically cleaned with wire brushes to remove light scaling.

Mr McPherson (Member): Noted that speedometer had been fitted giving the impression that slipping was more prevalent. Had information on tyre wear shown this to be so? Was there a control to prevent too many steam valves being opened when starting under load?

R. C. Bond (in reply): Locomotive was less prone to slipping than reciprocating engines but it was hard to detect. Measures applied to the Pennsylvania duplex [as mentioned by Rigby below] were necessary for particular operating conditions and characteristic of that type but were an unjustifiable complication for the Turbomotive.

G. Rigby (Member, in correspondence): Author mentioned that with continuous blast and absence of disturbing forces in the motion, it was difficult to detect slipping from the cab, making speed indicator important. Noted anti-slip device installed in Pennsylvania duplex 4-4-6-4 Class 'Q-2' [see Chapter 9] and enquired if there was a case for something similar with Turbomotive.

R. C. Bond (in reply): See MacPherson above.

Mr Topham (Member, in correspondence): Noted statement that whether blast is pulsating or continuous has no significant effect on draught and asked for elaboration as it seemed that an even draught was beneficial to combustion, especially in starting. Queried statement that effect of blast on fire at starting leads to fall in pressure more rapidly than with a reciprocating locomotive. Did this occur in practice as continuous blast should improve draught so as to balance steam consumption?

Noted also that comparative tests had been between the Turbomotive (40-element superheater) and reciprocating engines with 32 elements. As many of the latter now had 40 elements, new tests would be more truly comparative, showing Turbomotive to be at less of an advantage.

R. C. Bond (in reply): Professor Goss of Purdue University had conducted elaborate tests on scale models that showed beyond doubt that capacity of an exhaust steam jet to move the products of combustion through boiler tubes and eject them to the atmosphere is dependent solely upon the weight of steam discharged in a given time, and its pressure. Whether steam was exhausted continuously or in a series of puffs had no effect upon the results. In practice, though, it had been found that the heavy beat of a two- or four-cylinder locomotive gave better steaming than the larger number of softer exhausts per revolution that obtained with a three-cylinder engine.

Did not agree with Topham's views and referred him to Sandford's remarks earlier and to the 1938 paper by Messrs Loubser and Cox to the Institution – 'Locomotive Boiler Design: Theory and Practice'. To produce equally free steaming, turbine locomotive's continuous non-pulsating draught might require a smaller blast cap than on a similar reciprocating engine. Turbomotive's differing exhaust arrangements were recognised but tests had not been possible to clarify matter. Suggestion for comparative tests between Turbomotive and a 40-element reciprocating 'Pacific' was reasonable.

Appendix G
Executive connections

Despite the Great Western Railway's reputation for conservatism in mechanical engineering and other matters in the post-Churchward period, three of the company's senior executives who held progressive views were destined to play significant roles in the application of turbine power for locomotives. Felix Pole, William A. Stanier and F. W. Hawksworth (the first two were later knighted) had commenced their working careers as employees with the company. Stanier and Hawksworth were engineering apprentices, while Pole started in 1891 at the age of 14 years as a junior telegraph clerk.

The key points of their careers as relevant to turbines are as follows:

June 1921	Felix Pole appointed General Manager of GWR
June 1921	Stanier appointed Principal Assistant to Chief Mechanical Engineer, GWR
April 1925	F. W. Hawksworth appointed Chief Draughtsman, GWR (a close ally of Stanier)
1925	Dawson Review of potential for electrification by GWR
1926	Beardmore Engineering unsuccessfully promoted sales of diesel-electric multiple units to GWR; this, coupled with the Dawson Review, probably raised Pole's profile within electricity manufacturing sector
1927	Sir Guy Granet resigned as Chairman of LMS; succeeded by Sir Josiah Stamp, who was later influential in recruitment of Stanier as CME
From late 1928	Granet and others courted Pole to lead newly formed Associated Electrical Industries (AEI)
June 1929	Pole resigned from GWR to become Executive Chairman of AEI, and director of AEI's subsidiary companies including Metropolitan-Vickers and British Thomson-Houston
June 1929	James Milne (later Sir James) replaced Pole as General Manager of GWR (Milne and Stanier were brothers-in-law)
January 1932	Stanier became Chief Mechanical Engineer of LMS
1932	Dr Guy of Metropolitan-Vickers approached Stanier re steam turbine locomotive; both visited Sweden to inspect Ljungström turbine locomotive
February 1933	Approval given for third Stanier 'Pacific' to be built as non-condensing steam turbine
May 1935	Turbomotive entered ordinary service
January 1936	Power Jets Ltd, created by Frank Whittle, commenced partnership with British Thomson-Houston to build prototype jet aircraft engine
July 1941	Hawksworth appointed CME of GWR
1942	Stanier seconded by LMS to UK Government as Scientific Advisor; later became director of Power Jets
1944	Stanier formally resigned as CME of LMS
Early 1945	Pole retired as Chairman of AEI (by then aged 68 years and totally blind)
January 1946	Joint venture commenced between GWR and Metropolitan-Vickers to build gas-turbine-electric locomotive that became BR No 18100 (entered normal service in April 1952)
June 1946	Milne and Hawksworth visited Brown Boveri, Switzerland; contract signed by GWR for supply of gas-turbine-electric locomotive that became BR No 18000 (entered normal service in May 1950)
November 1947	Milne resigned as General Manager of GWR
December 1949	Hawksworth retired

Index

Appointments
Assistant General Manager 45
Australian Prime Minister 37
Chairman 37
Chairman 45
Chief Mechanical Engineer 45, 53
Chief Officer 45
Chief Running Superintendent 46
Deputy Chairman 45
Deputy CME 51
Enquiring Officer 116
General Manager 45
GWR Board 45, 134
Harrow signalman 115
Locomotive Superintendent 45
Mechanical Engineer, Crewe 53
Midland Board 45
Principal Assistant to the CME 51
Scientific Advisor to UK Government 63, 134
Vice President 51

Boiler
Dimensions 71-75
Superheater dimensions 71-73

Design components
Belpaire firebox 7, 16
Blastpipe jumper 107
Caprotti 43, 116
Condenser 16 to 30, 33 to 37
Control system 80, 81
Cooling 78, 79
Double blast pipe and chimney 72-75
Duplex drive 14
Four cylinders 7
Gas turbine 13, 14
Hammer Blow 43
Impulse & reaction turbine 39
Lentz 43
Livery 81
Ljungström radial turbine 31
Lubrication 78, 79, 91
Newton's Second Law 76
Newton's Third Law 76
Non-condensing turbine 13
Poppet Valve 43
Pre-heater 33
Roller bearings 78, 79
Rotary cam valve 11, 12
Sand Gun 107, 108
Schmidt-Henschel boiler 64
Smoke deflectors 93
Speedometer 37, 95
Steam feed 75
Stephenson's Link 38, 43
Still engines 9, 10
Swedish Loading Gauge 39
Traitment Integral Armand (TIA) 11
Transmission system 76-78
Valve actuation 11, 12
Walschaerts 38, 43, 86
Water tube boiler 64
Westinghouse brake 107
Worthington pump 78, 79, 107, 122

Design concepts
Gas producer combustion systems 16
Power station on wheels 16

Events
1923 Grouping 7
1924 British Empire Exhibition 20, 21, 25
Diamond Jubilee Review 12
Dynanometer trials 83, 95-99, 111
First World War 13, 16, 51, 109
General Strike 53
Great Depression 53
Great Smog of 1952 114
International Railway Congress 134
Second World War 63, 118, 134, 144

Fuel
Bunker C fuel oil 129, 139
Heavy oil 134

Failures
Forward turbine 91, 92
Lubrication system 91
Oil leakages forward and reverse turbines 93
Post-1946 91
Reverse turbine 91
Slow speed flexible drive 92, 93

Impressions
From footplate 105-108
From lineside 108

Livery
BR Black 109
GWR style Brunswick Green 111
LMS livery (final) 109
Quasi-LNWR 109

Locations
BR, 222 Marylebone Road 109
Harrow & Wealdstone 114
Rugby Test House 137

Locations (foreign)
Adelaide 121
Allegheny Mountains 127
California 129
Cape Town 30
Chalottesville, Virginia 126
Chesapeake Bay 127
Chicago 119, 121, 129
Clifton Forge 126
Council Bluffs, Iowa 139
Crestline, Ohio 121, 122
Detroit 121
Eskilstuna 40
Fort Wayne 123
France 144
Grängesberg 40, 42
Grängesbergbanornas Järnvägsmuseum 40, 42
Harrisburg 119
Illinois 129
Los Angeles 139
Nebraska 139
New York 119
Norfolk, Virginia 127
Nullarbor Plain 37
Ogden 139
Oxelösund 40
Philadelphia 118
Plymouth, Indiana 123
Roanoke 127
Salt Lake City 139
South Africa 25
Stockholm 33
Sweden 14, 31, 37
Swedish National Railway Museum 42
Switzerland 13, 134
The Great Karoo 30
Toledo 121
Union Pacific transcontinental route 129
United States 16, 144
Washington DC 119
West Coast, USA 129
West Virginia 127
Wyoming 138, 139

Locomotives - experimental
6399 Fury 4-6-0 60, 64, 94
Armstrong-Whitworth Turbine Electric 30
Baltimore & Ohio N-1 119
Beyer-Ljungström 12, 14, 32 to 37, 98, 132
Cape Government Railway No 800 18
Chesapeake & Ohio M1 8, 125, 126, 128
Coal-fired gas turbine locomotive 137, 138
English Electric GT3 134, 137
Gas Turbine No. Am 4/6 134
Kitson-Meyer/ Meyer 18
Kitson-Still 94
Ljungström 2-8-0 37 to 43, 144
Ljungström non-condensing turbine 37
Ljungström Turbine 5
Ljungström turbine-driven locomotive 31
Metropolitan-Vickers-Lysholm-Turbomotive 64
Norfolk & Western No 2300 127, 128
Pennsylvania 6-8-6 Turbine 122-125, 129, 144
Ramsay Turbo-Electric Condensing Loco 26 to 30
Reid-McLeod Steam Turbine 19 to 26
Reid-Ramsay Steam-Turbine Electric 16, 17, 19, 20
Southern Class N No A816 10, 51
SR Leader Class 94, 109, 141
Steam-turbine-electric 129
Turbine Condenser locomotive 31

Locomotives - individual
42389 2-6-4T 114
45637 Windward Islands 115
46202 Princess Anne 74, 75, 111, 114-116
46242 City of Glasgow 114
46257 City of Salford 115
6100 Royal Scot 64
6200 Princess Royal 71
6201 Princess Elizabeth 75
6205 Princess Victoria 86
6208 Princess Helena Victoria 75
6210 Lady Patricia 95, 98, 99
6212 Duchess of Kent 73-75, 95, 98, 99
6229 Duchess of Hamilton 108
BR 4-6-2 No 71000 116
GWR No 111 The Great Bear 62, 63
GWR No 5000 Launceston Castle 62

Locomotive types - LMS Group
Beames 0-8-4T 51
Bill Bailey 4-6-0 51
Black 5 4-6-0 51, 91
Claughton 4-6-0 51, 59, 60
Crab (Hughes 2-6-0) 6, 37
Diesel-electric Nos 10000, 10001 14
Duchess 6, 11, 95, 111
Fowler 2-6-4T 51
Fowler 4F 4-6-0 51
Hughes 2-6-0 (Crab) 51, 59
Jubilee 4-6-0 51
LMS 7F 0-8-0 51
LMS Garratt 51
LNWR 0-8-0/ 2-8-0 51, 91
LNWR 17' Coal Engine 7
LNWR Class Dx 7
Mickey Mouse 2-6-2T 55
Patriot 4-6-0 60
Prince of Wales 4-6-0 59, 60
Princess Anne Type 111, 140
Princess Royal 4-6-2 6, 60, 62, 64, 71, 86, 91, 95, 99, 111
Royal Scot 4-6-0 34, 46, 59, 62, 64, 81, 83, 91, 111
Stanier 3P 2-6-2T 55
Stanier 4P 2-6-4T (2-/ 3-cylinder) 54
Stanier 5P5F 2-6-0 53
Stanier 8F 2-8-0 54, 111

Locomotive classes - other
BR Britannia 11, 140
BR Class 9F 2-10-0 44
Garratt types 31, 51, 109, 111
Great Central 2-8-0 7
GS&WR Class 400 86
GWR 4-6-0 types 11, 46, 62, 86, 134
GWR Broad Gauge locomotives 13
GWR De Glehn compound 64
GWR Gas turbine locomotives 132-134
GWR Hurricane & Thunderer 127
GWR Proposed Compound Castle 64
GWR Small & Tank Locomotives 7, 55
GWR/ BR Nos 18000/ 18100 132-134
Lancashire & Yorkshire locomoitves 30
LNER 2-8-0 Class O2 44
LNER Class W1 4-6-4 64, 94, 111, 141
LNER Classes A1 4-6-2/ P2 2-8-2 62
LSWR M7 109
NER Class 4.6.2 (LNER Class A2)/ Class Z 62
New York Central Hudson 119

INDEX

Norfolk & Western Class Y-6 2-8-8-2 128
Pennsylvania I1s/ N1s/ N2sa/ J1 121
Pennsylvania K4s 118, 125
Pennsylvania S1/ S2/ Q1/ Q2/ T1 119, 121, 125
SAR Classes 25/ GA/ GM/ GMA/ GMAM 18, 25, 30
SAR Modified Fairlie Class FC 25, 26
South Australian 520 121
Southern Classes Q/ Q1 7, 109
Southern Pacifics 11, 109
TGOJ 0-8-0 37, 43
Union Pacific Big Blow/Big Boy/ Veranda 138, 139

Locomotive types
4-car DEMU 132
Advanced Passenger Train APT-E 137
Alco FA Series Diesel Electric 138
B-Unit 138, 139
Duplex 118-122, 143
Garratt 111
GM E-series diesel-electric 129
Mallet 25, 119, 121
Meyer 109
Modified Fairlie 25, 26
Union Garratt 26
Union Pacific Challenger 119
Vauclain Compound 118

Manufacturers
Aktiebolaget Ljungström Angturbin 31
ALCO/ GE 139
Alfol Insulation Co Ltd 81
Allmänna Svenska Elektriska Aktiebolaget (ASEA) 31
American Locomotive Company 25, 138
Armstrong-Whitworth 26
Babcock & Wilcox 127, 132
Baily Meter Company 132
Baldwin 5, 14, 25, 118, 127
Baldwin-Lima-Hamilton 127
Beyer Peacock 10, 25, 26, 31, 32, 37, 51, 109, 118
British Timken Ltd 81
Brown Boveri 13, 134
CA Parsons 137
Colvilles Ltd 81
Davies & Metcalfe Ltd 81
Dübs & Co 16
English Electric Co 134, 137
General Electric 129
Geo.Turton,Platts & Co Ltd 81
Gresham & Craven Ltd 81
Henery Wiggin Ltd 81
Henschel 30
Kitson & Co 9. 10
Krupp 20
Maffei 20
Metropolitan-Vickers 13, 62, 77, 81, 86, 134, 140
National Gas Turbine Establishment 134
Neilson, Reid & Co 16
North British Locomotive Co 13, 14, 16, 17, 26, 30, 51, 64, 137
Nydqvist & Holm AB (NOHAB) 31, 39
Power Jets Ltd 134
R & W Hawthorn 12, 13
Royal Aircraft Establishment 134
Sharp, Stewart & Co 16
The Superheater Company Ltd 64
Vulcan Foundry 137
Westinghouse Gas Turbine Division 138
Westinghouse Electric 127
Worthington-Simpson Ltd 81
Yarrow & Co 64
Zoelly 20

Motorcycles
British Rotary and 2-cylinder 12

Named trains
Merseyside 100, 101
Royal Scot 95, 99
Chessie 8, 126

Nicknames
Big Blow 139
Big Boy 138
Blue Goose 138
Crab 6
Lizzie 6
Semi 6
Veranda 139

Organisations
Admiralty 12
Anglo-German Fellowship 46
Assoc. of Railway Locomotive Engineers 51
British Empire 32
British Pathé News 25
Institution of Locomotive Engineers 141
LMS Research Dept 46
Locomotive Committee 60
London School of Economics 46
National Railway Museum 5
Railway Companies Association 45
Railway Students Association 46
Royal Navy 12
Stephenson Locomotive Society 5
Still patentees 10

Performance
Haulage capacity 101, 104

Personalities
Anderson, APH 10, 11
Anderson, JE 46, 53, 62
Beames, HPM 53
Bond RC 141, 143
Bond, RC 71, 91, 94
Brunel 11, 12
Bulleid, HAV 55
Bulleid, OVS 11, 51, 55, 109
Caprotti, Arturo 11, 12
Chapelon, A 143
Chapelon, André 5, 11
Churchward, GJ 7, 45, 51
Clark, Edward Kitson 10
Collett, CB 51, 64, 132
Collett, CB 141
Cox ES 94, 123
de Laval, Gustaf 11
Deeley, RM 45
Fay, Sir Sam 37
Follows, JH 51, 62
Fowler, Henry 46, 51, 53, 62
Garratt, HW 10
Gracie Fields 6
Graff-Baker, WS 143
Granet, Sir Guy 45
Gresley 7, 45, 62, 64, 94, 141
Guy, Dr 62
Hawkworth, FW 64, 134
Henry, John 128
Hughes 6, 53, 62
Ivatt, HG 14
Jackson, Samuel 33
Johnson, Ralph P 118
Lemon, EJ 46, 51, 53
Lentz, Dr Hugo 12
Link, O Winston 127
Livesay, EH 105
Ljungstrom brothers 76, 77
Ljungström, Birger 31
Ljungström, Fredrik 31
Lowey, Raymond 122
MacLeod, James 19
Maunsell 10, 51
Milne, Sir James 134
Paget, Cecil 45
Parsons, Charles 12
Porta, LD 11
Ramsay, DM 16, 26
Reid, Hugh (Sir) 16, 19
Riddles 109, 116
Stamp, Sir Josiah (Lord) 45, 46, 94
Stanier 5, 6, 14, 40, 51, 53 to 60, 62, 64, 71, 94, 141
Thompson, Edward 51, 62
Vauclain, Samuel M 118
Webb, William 64
Wedgwood, Sir Raplh 45
Whittle, Frank 134

Publications
Beyer-Peacock Quarterly Review 31
General Electric Review 129, 132
The Engineer 105

Railways/ railroads
Atchison, Topeka and Santa Fe 118
Baltimore & Ohio 119
Big Four 109
British Railways 109, 137
Chesapeake & Ohio 125, 128
Chicago & North Western 138
Great Central 118, 132, 137
Great Northern RR 132
Great Southern & Western 86
Great Western Railway 109, 132
Liverpool & Manchester 9
LNER 7 to 9. 45, 51, 62, 109
London & North Western 7, 45
London Midland & Scottish 5, 8, 14, 37, 51, 62
Midland 45, 46, 111
Missouri-Kansas-Texas 138
New York Central 118, 132
Norfolk & Western 127, 128
North British 19
North Eastern 132
Pennsylvania 5, 118, 128, 138, 143
São Paulo 51
SNCF 5
South African 18
South Eastern & Chatham 51
Southern 6, 51, 109
Swedish State 31, 32, 37
Swiss Federal 134
Union Pacific 14, 118, 129, 132, 139
US Class 1 128

Repairs
Categories 83
Days under repair 86
History 87
Routine maintenance 94

Routes
Anglo-Scottish expresses 99, 111
Edinburgh-Aberdeen 62
Edinburgh-Dundee 62
Euston-Glasgow 62, 99
Euston-Liverpool 99, 100
London-Edinburgh 62
London-Liverpool 62, 111
Tring-Euston 111
West Coast Main Line 11, 111

Safety systems
BR Automatic Warning System 116
GWR Automatic Train Control 116

Statistics
Annual mileages 86, 99, 100
Engine History Cards 71, 83, 86, 92, 94
Locomotive repairs 54, 59
Motive power fleet totals 54
Reliability assessment 94
Ticket sales 53, 54
Transport market trends 53, 54

Tender
Comparative dimensions 81
Corridor tender 62
Tender No 9003 81, 116

Vessels
HMS Dreadnought 12
Steam yacht Turbinia 12

Wheel arrangement
1+Bo+A+Bo+1 134
A1A-A1A+2-+-D-2 139
A1A+A1A 134
Co-Co 134
B+B+B+B 138

159

Other titles from Crécy Publishing

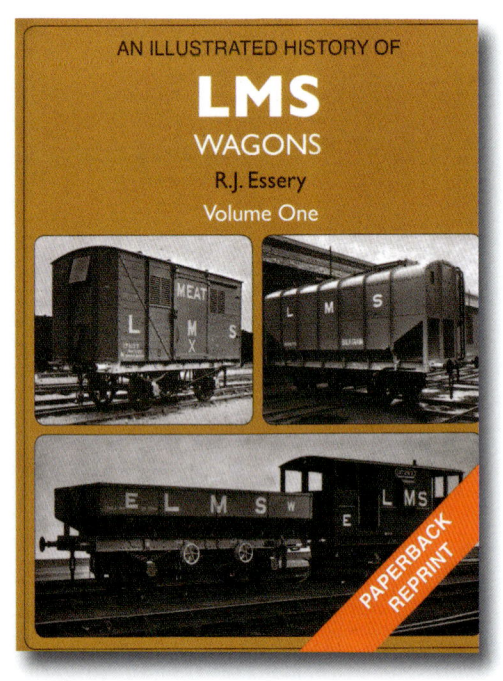

An Illustrated History of LMS Wagons
R J Essery
Highly regarded as the standard work on the subject
180 pages, paperback. 275mm x 215mm
9781906419332
£19.95

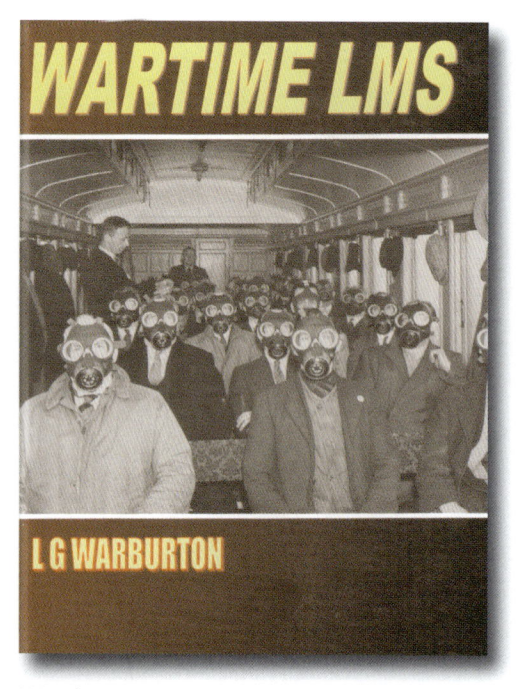

Wartime LMS
L G Warburton
Behind the scenes at the LMS as they prepared for and dealt with war.
184 pages, hardback. 275mm x 215mm
9781906419550
£30

Order online at www.crecy.co.uk
Telephone 0161 499 0024